Encounter with Erik Routley

dedicated to Erik

"There was, of course, the sheer fertility and industry of his mind and pen as author and composer. There was the warmth of his response to almost any new work in hymnody. There was a readiness to help and encourage those who sought his advice and received so much more than they expected...."

John Wilson, as quoted in *The Hymn*, January, 1983

The editorial staff of *Ecumenical Praise*: left to right: Dr. Carlton Young, Dr. Alec Wyton, Dr. Austin C. Lovelace, Dr. Erik Routley, with George Shorney of Hope Publishing Company. Picture Courtesy of Hope Publishing Co., Carol Stream, Illinois 60188.

Encounter

with

[signature: Erik Routley]

Erik Routley

B.D., M.A., D. Phil, F.R.S.C.M., F.W.C.C., F.H.S.A.

by Adrienne Tindall, M.M.

DARCEY PRESS

P.O. Box 5018 · Vernon Hills, IL 60061

On the cover
Photo by John Simpson
Dr. Erik Routley in Princeton University Chapel at
Westminster Choir College Commencement, May, 1976.
Picture with the approval of Westminster Choir College, courtesy of Hope Publishing Co., Carol Stream, IL 60188
Signature enlarged from 9 December 1981 letter

ISBN 1-889079-17-0

Library of Congress Catalog Card Number: 97-67961

CONTENTS

Many thanks are due --

to Margaret Routley, for approval, for reading the early manuscript, for encouragement and ideas such as including Erik's signatures on the letters through the book, and including his holograph (pp. 139-140);

to Dr. Austin C. Lovelace, for initial enthusiasm, for 19 tunes to set the texts, particularly the unusual meter texts, for gentle but persistent prodding, and for almost daily advice and ideas during the assembling of the book;

to Jack Goode, for three tunes;

to George Shorney for interest, encouragement, for reading the manuscript, and of course for the many copyright permissions on examples included;

to the Reverend Caryl Micklem, Dr. Morgan Simmons, and Dr. Carlton Young for reading the early manuscript, and giving advice and evaluations;

to George Rohrer, of commercial artistic experience, who visited at precisely the moment of pasting up the manuscript, and who pitched in and did all the pasting (except the signatures, which I did...);

to Jackie Tindall Moser for help with cover design;

to the family, who lovingly endured when a two month project stretched out to eleven;

to Erik ....

PRELUDE

Sometime before I even noticed the event ... I "noticed" hymns. Although the details are lost to memory, I know that at some point I became aware of a growing conviction that no art form can have more significance -- more potential for blessing all humankind -- than a well-thought-out, well written, theologically valid, uplifting, memorable, vitally communicating hymn text, married to a heart-felt, compelling hymn tune with a satisfying harmonization, thereby made available to be sung by people expressing their praise and gratitude to God. Whether sung individually or by a congregation, hymns are the language of the soul, made more eloquent by the talents of poets and composers.

After I recognized this conviction, I took courses at two local seminaries, studying their denominational hymnals, and laying the groundwork for one of the great loves of my life. Too broad a statement? No, I don't think so.... If I, like Philipp Nicolai, could write one or two hymn text/tune combinations as wonderful as "Wachet auf, ruft uns die Stimme" and "Wie schön leuchtet der Morgenstern".... well, I don't think I'd ask much more....

It was after those two courses that I became aware of "Erik Routley." I think the first time I noticed his name was when George Shorney gave all the attendees at a conference a copy of *Ecumenical Praise*, a small hymnal supplement pulled together by Erik, Austin Lovelace, Alec Wyton, and Carlton Young, published by Hope Publishing Co. in 1977. Erik's credentials, which I never thought about specifically except to know he must be very busy, undoubtedly exceed what I find in an April 14, 1979 letter in my file:

> Erik Routley is a minister of the United Reformed Church of England, which in 1972 was formed out of the Congregational and Presbyterian Churches in England, and was ordained in 1943 in the Congregational Church and later served as President of that Church in 1970-71. He has pastored four churches in Britain including Edinburgh and Newcastle upon Tyne and has served as lecturer in Church History at Mansfield College, Oxford.
>
> Dr. Routley is presently Professor of Church Music and Director of the Chapel at Westminster Choir College, Princeton and was visiting Director of Music at Princeton Theological Seminary in 1975. He is the author of 32 books [at that time]....
>
> Professor Routley holds a B.D., M.A., and a Doctorate of Philosophy from Oxford University. He is a Fellow of the Royal School of Church Music and a Fellow of Westminster Choir College [and later a Fellow of the Hymn Society of America]...
>
> (4-14-79 letter from Tom Richardson, Flossmoor [Illinois] Community Church)

Early in 1979 my friend (Dr.) Don Spies (who later introduced the subject of protocol [P. 227] by referring to "Mr. Routley") sent me a flyer announcing that Erik would give a series of talks at Lawrence College in May (p. 325). Appleton (Wisconsin) was close enough to Don's home in Ripon that it was feasible to stay with his family and to lure him into attending the talks with me. While there, I learned that Erik was going to teach a summer session course on hymns at Garrett Evangelical Seminary (in Evanston, IL) that very summer, a two week continuing education course in my next-to-home town. It was easy to decide to be there also! That two week course at Garrett "sets the stage" for the correspondence which makes up the bulk of this book.

The first few of my letters had "valid" reasons for writing Erik -- corrections to the text/tune from the Garrett class, finding a misprint in a hymn text of his, asking him to look at the text done at the HSA convocation the next year. But it didn't take long for me to realize that, in an ordinary day's mail, *his* letters were a joy to receive! Somewhere around Psalm 34, I realized I might have a fabulous opportunity at hand... to versify psalms and ask him for comments and corrections. I didn't "confess" my decision to him. For this one-to-one workshop the modest retainers I sent were surely inadequate, but he went along with it, and I *loved* it! Erik's letters were always kind; I think the fact that I wrote as student to teacher evoked from him consistently generous and helpful evaluations, with unpainful correctings.

I kept all the letters to and from Erik (logical, considering the tutoring that I was getting). And because of a lack of ability to clean out my files, jammed full even after items have been held for far longer than a "reasonable" period of time, Erik's and my letters and my psalm versions (at all stages of editing) remained in my files from 1979 until 1996, through two household moves. Most have been recoverable, even after 16 years.

In late 1982, shortly after Erik's death, I photocopied his letters to me and sent them to his friend in England, John Wilson, asking whether anyone was going to publish Erik's letters; the letters I had received indicated to me that his total correspondence would be informative, insightful, amusing, amazing reading, and I thought some of the letters I had received should be included. Wilson's reply was interesting: ". . . I have not heard of any plan to publish a collection. . . . Was it perhaps because of the fact that you were consulting him professionally that he wrote in such a full and careful way about such topics as the Trinity? . . . Perhaps there would be some way in which your correspondence from him, with notes of what questions you had asked, could be made available as a booklet. . . ." [letter, May 6, 1983]. I think Erik answered as fully as he did because he was taking into consideration my non-doctrinal, non-liturgical background. As a superlative teacher, he was responding the needs of an individual pupil....

In 1996, 14 years after Erik died, I read an article in *The Hymn* which discussed Erik's thoughts on sexist language in hymns. I recalled that Erik and I had touched on that subject many times. And when I reread Erik's letters, I decided they *should* be published.... now.

I have some 43 letters from him, many of which delve in depth into broad subjects of general interest (including sexist language and revising to mitigate it). I have included my letters and the items which were under discussion. There is a certain amount of brazenness involved in this step, as my own credentials are very modest (AB Vassar College; MM American Conservatory of Music, Chicago; AAGO; some published poems by that time...). I acknowledge the brazenness, but still feel that the teacher - learner framework makes it desirable to have both halves of the correspondence, for it gives the fullest context for Erik's comments. Although this involves putting in early, uncorrected, versions (a bit painful), I am being philosophical about it: it was a long time ago.... I invite you to read as selectively as you wish; Erik's letters alone are well worth the reading.

There is also an awareness that a one-to-one correspondence is a "personal" thing (for lack of a better word). But there is really nothing of a personal / private nature. I asked Margaret Routley to read through the manuscript, to be sure everything here is fine. I invite you to read the letters in order to share with you a singular view of this remarkable man. And this permits me to share a small treasure-trove of his ideas, verbalized in his own unique way.

I recommend to your special attention the ideas relating to "words only" versions of hymnals. The blessing available through reading hymns as poems is one I have known all my life, and one I recommend to American hymnal publishers. Erik was impressively eloquent in their support. English publishers all offer them.

At the time I was writing Erik, I had not yet learned word processing, and my unedited letters are occasionally almost incomprehensible (it impresses me that he never once complained when I took forever to make a point). I have done (unacknowledged) minor editing of my own letters, sparing readers of some of the convoluteness but not affecting the context. I know I was trying to make my letters interesting, "enjoyable," and reasonably relaxed in style, so that Erik would not dread opening them; some of the convoluteness probably came from efforts to be amusing and/or clever. I think that often my letters embodied almost a stream of consciousness; I used to sit down at the typewriter and type at (great) length about things, without a lot of advance planning....

I have held to only two presentations of individual texts. This creates certain problems; in some cases, if Erik mentions a correction which already is included in the "Revised Version," it's because of this limit. Another problem: in some cases he answers a question which must have been a hand-written addition to the typed copy of the text; the question is not on my carbon copy. Some texts have their "final" revisions only in Appendix C. Most of the texts have tunes, and appear in Appendix C, interlined . Special thanks to Austin Lovelace for providing many of these. The most recent tunes, simply titled "LOVELACE XX," are particularly reassuring, as they set unusual meter texts, and prove their singability.

In some cases, Erik's music corrections are on an original manuscript copy I had sent to him, which is the version here. Look for his additions.

Some photocopied material is reduced to fit the pages. Erik's signatures are genuine; each is matched to its specific letter. (In a few cases, where he typed on onion skin paper and turned the page over to finish the letter, you'll see the typing from the other side around his signature.) Only about 20% of my signatures are "genuine" -- as they appear on the carbon copies of my letters to him. The others I have signed as I probably signed them then (there may have been more smile faces; I 've included only carboned ones). I have included his letterheads (often address stickers, once upside down); he must have been a fantastic customer for the local stationery store! Once he mentioned that he had 52 letters to answer when he came home from a trip! I include one letterhead of mine because he found "Lac du Flambeau" so fascinating (hence the name of his hymn tune for my Psalm 147).

I apologize for making the editorial decision to eliminate almost all Erik's typographical errors, because I loved them! It made me feel comfortable to know that while I might go through multiple bottles of white correcting fluid, Erik did not take the time to worry about typos. Readers will enjoy Erik's humorous "one liners" which he interspersed with spontaneous abandon, even though I have denied them the smiles I got from such typos as "conflunded anti-sexist withhunters", "14 Narch 80", analysis of a stanza with rhyming "souplets", a discussion of "Christian dictrine," seeing "wnat hot" for "what not." I did leave in one typo. I mentioned typos once, thinking a jazzy typewriter like mine might be a help to him; he said it wouldn't help; "My typewriter is a shocking speller!" It *was* fun, to chuckle at "his typewriter"!

A word about extender lines in Appendix C. Accepted usage seems to be changing. You may prefer Austin's "clean" look, with almost no extender lines. Or, like George Shorney, you may think that approach looks like "something is missing." I decided not to decide, and have been inconsistent. The musical intention is clear either way....

I think that if Erik's and my correspondence had continued for a few more months, I would have waxed eloquent on the subject of wedding hymns, speaking out in favor of texts appropriate for the congregation to sing *about* and in support of the wedding / bride and groom; my eldest daughter was married October 2, 1982, and I watched first-hand how the wedding party really is not able to sing a hymn (unless they have it memorized), whereas members of the congregation can have a copy of the words in hand. I never got Erik's comments about my own wedding hymn (recast in Appendix C: see p. 328); that letter from him was lost in the mail.

Some time after the Garrett sessions I heard of and ordered Erik's audiobook, six hours of audiocassettes entitled *Christian Hymns: An Introduction to their Story*. I discuss it a bit in the letters, and heartily recommend it to anyone as marvelously enjoyable educational listening; I still have my set, and still love it! The ISBN 0-911-009-11-6 listing should find it through regular bookstores.

How uniquely delightful it was to correspond about this favorite subject with Erik! I invite you to encounter him, this knowledgeable, kind, feisty, incredible man, through the correspondence. Be ready to appreciate his insights and to smile at the inevitable moments of humor. And note how awe-ing is the generosity of his sharing --- with a mere student in a one of his two week summer courses! Quoting "A Tribute by John Wilson" in the January, 1983 issue of *The Hymn* (p. 18) :

> ... There was, of course, the sheer fertility and industry of his mind and pen as author and composer. There was the warmth of his response to almost any new work in hymnody. There was a readiness to help and encourage those who sought his advice and received so much more than they expected. . . .

Well! If ever a statement was *proved*, this book proves *that* one! *I had no idea*, until organizing all the letters, how much I had asked of him, and how phenomenally generous he was in his response....

THE CLASS

My files surrendered letters, rough drafts, manuscripts, programs, multiple versions of psalms, and class handouts, but the notebook from the June 1979 Garrett Continuing Education sessions on Hymnody, taught by Dr. Erik Routley was separated from this correspondence, to be discovered at the proverbial eleventh hour....

So I include (in Appendix B) some of the handouts from the classes, and some excerpts from my class notes, and I recount in this chapter the things I remember from the class sessions.

I lived about 10 minutes from Garrett Evangelical Seminary, and knew that I would want to be in Dr. Routley's class even though I planned to take no other classes in that two week sequence. This meant two or three trips to the campus daily, as the classes met mid-morning and mid-afternoon, with a few at night. My four daughters were old enough that minimal arrangements were required -- the youngest was 13 -- and I don't recall any difficulty in seeing that home needs were met while I was attending class.

I had met Erik at his Lawrence College workshops the month before (see flyer on page 325), at which time I had told him I was going to try to be at Garrett. The Garrett class included 13 of us -- enough people to be interesting, not so large as to be a limiter on individual participation and communication. I recall that Erik recognized me. Of course I was a bit of an "odd man out" (pardon the sexist jargon) because I was the only one not sharing the other students' classwork in the other classes. This feeling was minimal, though, perhaps existing only in my own thought....

I remember that Erik had a small wooden lectern set on the desk, from which he spoke. I can remember he walked a curving path about 12 feet long, between the desk and the blackboard behind it, extending from east of the desk to west of it, and intermittently he would walk back and forth, vigorously, as he spoke. Behind him was a full size blackboard, which he used frequently. To his right in the classroom was a "functional" upright piano, its keyboard angled and in view of the class. The windows, overlooking Lake Michigan, were on that same east side of the room.

Erik's classroom style was friendly and informal, with good give-and-take between professor and students; he spoke with authority, depth, expansiveness, a great knowledgability, humor, spontaneity, interest. The teaching was thoroughly enjoyable.

I remember getting the bibliography he handed out first (pp. 310-312), which was very interesting to me! I mentally patted myself on the back as I skimmed down it and saw that I already possessed and used many of the books; at the same time I determined to look into all of the others, in order to purchase them.

I remember getting the handout about Amen being sung at the end of hymns (p. 316). The topic was not particularly startling one way or the other to me, as my own church (and its hymnal) had never used Amen at the ends of hymns. The handout may have evolved (I think it did) because of some discussion in class as to whether hymns should have Amen sung at the end of them or not. Some evaluating had been going on in the hymnic world, questioning the practice, and I think Erik summarized his own views, passing out photocopies of his "position paper" the next day.

The outline of the course material is given in the handout on page 309; Erik stuck to the outline efficiently and painlessly. And he warned us about a big homework assignment, which was to be finished by about Wednesday of the second week.

Erik gave class members a choice for that assignment:
    1. Plan a hymn festival, choosing the hymns and readings to be used.
    2. Write a hymn (*i.e.*, text).
    3. Write a hymn tune.
    4. Write out a particular Order of Service (see p. 319).

In preparation for this assignment (the only one for the two weeks), Erik shared several hymn festivals he had planned (pp. 321, 322), and together the class wrote a hymn tune for an existing text. EVANSTON NEW (p. 323) was done phrase by phrase, with careful consideration of the setting of the words. I remember the purposeful choices made for the notes setting the first word - "Jesus", with a short/accented note followed by a long/unaccented note.... The melody was composed first, everyone entering into the discussion as we went along. The bass line was done next, with Erik (with some suggestions from the students) pulling it together, and then Erik filled in the inner voices in about a half minute.

8

Although the whole class participated in writing the hymn tune, Erik pointed out that the tune needed to be copyrighted, mainly so that someone would be able to give permission for its use if requests were made. Sam Chizmar volunteered to take on that responsibility, and that's why his name and address are on the page. I recall that the first phrase, including the rhythm for setting the word "Jesus", were Sam's, and I remember Erik commenting on how very well that rhythm fit the word. As this is so distinctive an element in the tune, Erik thought that Sam should hold the copyright.

My decision as to what to do to fulfill the assignment crept into my thought silently and persistently (and secretly, I might add), and I embarked on it. I have mentioned my dream of writing something like "How brightly shines the Morning Star" or "Sleepers, wake!" both text and tune. Here was a great opportunity! I decided that I would take on double duty, as it were, by writing both a text and the tune for it. This meant that the text could have an unusual meter, which seemed like it would be interesting to do. And strategically it sounded desirable, as no existing tune would fit, so my own would have to be the best possibility.... Doubling the assignment would require double work / evaluation by Erik, but really, it was irresistible, to take advantage of the opportunity in this way....

I got away with it, too.... I recall that most of the students did hymn festivals and orders of worship, modeled after the ones Erik planned out and shared with us at the beginning of the second week. I think there were a few other texts written, which Erik read aloud, and then the class commented on. I don't remember any one else's texts or tunes, perhaps because I was feeling so intrepid about my own "double" assignment / demand on his attention.... Actually, I recall giving it to him in two separate parts -- when asked for it, I gave Erik the text, which he read out loud (that in itself was a thrill, to hear my text read with his understanding; I can still "hear" his reading of, "The Father's love is proved". . .).

He pointed out in a kindly way that the meter was unusual and that finding a tune for it.... at which point I confessed that I had also attempted a tune.

I remember him sitting at that upright piano playing the tune. It took rereading our correspondence later, to bring to mind that when he was halfway through the tune he turned and asked whether I had a Welsh grandmother.... My reply was, no....

He wanted to know how I had maintained the unusual meter through the stanzas in a way that all stanzas fit the tune accents so well. I showed him my paper (p. 324) and how I had laid out the syllables in accented / unaccented columns. I know he commented to the class later, in a way that was fun and a bit teasing, that this "tool" had given me an "advantage", but I don't recall the actual comment.

Several class members said they would like a copy of the hymn. I was delighted to promise to send copies to them, but not until some problem spots were corrected. I know there was a theological problem in one of the later verses, and I think it was Thursday that I stayed at the school for lunch, sitting with Erik and I think discussing the correct theological use of the word "angel," although that reference is not in my text....

The morning class sessions were followed immediately by a chapel service. It was during the second week that Erik and the class led the service. It was held in the Howes Chapel, just outside the main Garrett building in which our class met. I did not participate because the "choir" rehearsed at times when I wasn't at the school. But I remember choir and congregation sang EVANSTON NEW at that service.

One of my strongest recollections, complete with intonation and impact, has remained in my conscious memory, and comes from that service.

Erik read from John 9, the healing of the man blind from birth (I can remember sitting there in the chapel, hearing it). This is a passage I knew extremely well. I don't know what translation Erik was reading; the "feel" of the text was very like the King James Version. I sat there listening to his reading of Scripture, which, with his English diction and his understanding, was beautifully inspiring.

Have you ever had a moment when you continue to sit calmly, but inside, in your thought, you have suddenly been made to sit up and come to 1,000% alertness? That's what happened next. The passage progressed through all the things which I knew, and I was again thinking about how John had described the blind man's increased seeing -- both the physical healing, and the awakening in his thought to what he could "see" about Christ Jesus, who had healed him. And I was again seeing how "blind" the Pharisees were, in not recognizing the Messiah through the works. And then, when the healed man tells the Pharisees, "If this man were not of God, he could do nothing" (v. 33), the KJV verse 34 says, "They answered and said unto him, Thou wast altogether born in sin, and dost thou teach us? And they cast him out."

But Erik didn't say that. Instead, it was: "They answered and said, "Thou bastard! ....." And Erik said it with emphasis.... he wasn't portraying mild-mannered erudite theologians gently saying remember now, son, you've not studied the law like we have, so you are not the one to hold and voice such an opinion, you know....

Of course I realized, even as I heard it, that "altogether born in sin" says pretty much the same thing as "bastard" does, but my goodness how breathtaking to hear it spoken like that! I wish I knew what translation Erik was reading! That word, and the vocalization of it, had great impact on my thinking about the Pharisees, and stimulated my increased "questioning" of their sense of righteous living....

I invited Erik to come home with me, for a home-cooked dinner, during that second week, and he accepted. There was an organ recital scheduled one evening, and so to take him home with me after the afternoon class, and take him back to campus in time to attend the concert, was easy. I remember having him sit down and try my little practice (pipe) organ while I abandoned him, in order to get dinner on the table. I remember that I felt rushed, but he was an "easy" guest. Charcoal broiled steaks, and very simple side dishes, and he and my husband and I ate together on our breezeway porch. And then I took him back down to Garrett.

The last day of class I can still visualize. On that last morning, Erik turned to the blackboard and wrote his name and address on it, "singing" his zip code (thereby illustrating the way he remembered zip codes...). He invited class members to write if they wished, about anything they might have a question about. How very approachable and kind he was! It was a fully credible invitation, and I took it at face value....

THE LETTERS

July 7, 1979

Dr. Erik Routley
929 Rte. 518 RD 1
Skillman, New Jersey 98558

Dear Dr. Routley:

Enclosed is the text and tune from the two weeks at Garrett. There are some changes in it (I'd certainly be interested in anything you would have to say about them!), but it seems as "finished " as it will get for the present. Among the many things I don't know how to do at this point is how to head the page (should the hymn be titled?), how to get a good tune name ("God's Love and Power" sounds a little too much like - well like some of the names in the Baptist hymnal I have, and the tune doesn't sound that way. "Omnipotence" sounds presumptuous, and the Welsh flavor would be nice to portray - but I don't know any Welsh....), so I've just guessed, hence the heading.

Also, trying to get text and tune on one page precluded listing even one stanza in its poetic format. But then, I'm not at all sure the format is correct anyway - should the last line match the indenting of the second and fourth because of the rhyme scheme?

My thought at this moment is to send this to the couple of members of the class who asked for it, at about the end of July. So one reason for sending it to you early is that if there are flaws which should be corrected (mainly theological) you could perhaps let me know before I send them out. I wouldn't want to cause problems with that, if the hymn were used. But I know you are completely busy, and wish not to encumber you in any way with unnecessary bother. Any nagging questions I can check with Austin, as he has agreed to a kind of consultant-aide response to questions I have musically (and now hymnically), for which I pay him a modest retainer. But I would prefer your help with the text, in this case. And if any further very sporadic requests for help would be interesting to you, as I have worked it out with Austin, would you say so?

Needless to say, the sessions at Garrett were thoroughly inspiring and solid groundwork for my endeavors of the next few years, when I plan to dig in to hymns and how they're used. I can't tell you how grateful I am to have had the lectures at Garrett at this point. And I am enthusiastically investing in your Panorama, hoping you get past the first thousand quickly... I also continue to pursue Watts' text on the commandments.

Sincerely,

These are specific questions, if you had the time. . . .

Text:
  1. . . . Does it seem to have enough focus? Is there too much use of the word "power" for instance, for good hymn text writing? I've kept it on different spots in the stress pattern.
  2. The last stanza "Christliness" includes the "ness" on a strong beat, which it shouldn't have, but I decided it was not bad enough to avoid. Was I right? Is "ever-wise" okay?

  When you asked if I wrote the text or tune first, of course the text was "first," but by now so much of the revising has taken the tune and its stress patterns, its modulation, etc. into consideration, that I think I must say they were written simultaneously. The text was reasonably complete and the tune was written, and then the text was revised and shaped to fit the tune.

```
        From the depths of rolling oceans
            To the heights of outer space,
        I will witness God's all-power
            Holding strong its steady pace.
                No might but His sustains,
                His law forever reigns.
No other force, no mortal power usurps His place.


        Taking wings of brilliant mornings,
            Finding farthest shores of seas, --
        Even vales of dealthy shadows
            Will not hide His love from me!
                His everpresent care
                Is with me everywhere,
A steadfast power to help mankind eternally.


        In the love of our Redeemer
            And the healing proofs he gave,
        In his ministry's instruction
            And redemption from the grave, --
                The Father's love is proved,
                The sting of death removed.
The power of God is law to heal and bless and save.


        In the Christliness of mercy,
            In the noblest deeds of man,
        In each act of lovingkindness
            I can feel God's holy plan.
                His ever-wise control
                Stands fast while ages roll.
The heavenly kingdom is secure within His span.
```

Rev. p. 20; App. C p. 370
ER comment p. 17

God's Power and Love

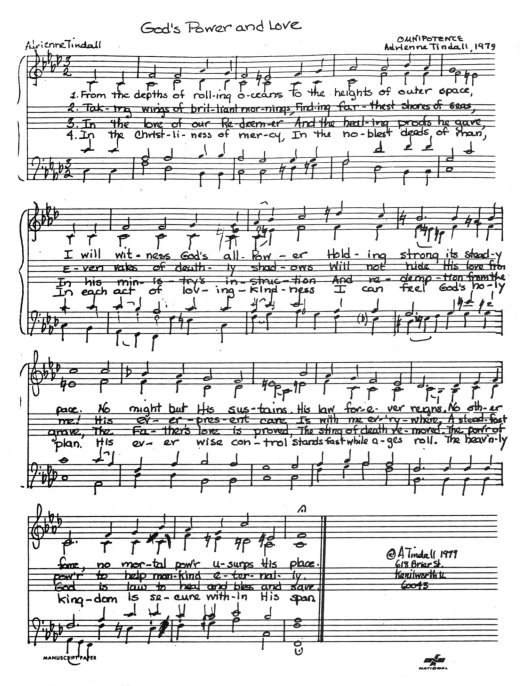

© A Tindall 1979
618 Briar St.
Kenilworth IL
60045

Rev. p. 20; App C. p. 370
ER comment p. 17

Erik Routley
929 Route 518, R. D. 1, Skillman, N. J. 08558
9 July 79

Dear Mrs. Tindall -

Thank you for sending me the revised version of your hymn.

I think the text is now good, The indentation in your written-out version is exactly right: when a very long line is associated with shorter ones, length takes precedence over rhyme in indentation. I think it will all do very well.

The tune is most captivating, as we all thought. I would suggest only these tiny modifications:

System 2 measure 0-1: I should recommend having the bass an octave higher on 'I will witness'; and in measures 1-2 I believe you emphasize the tenor seventh just a little too much; if the tenor went C-C-C-B-A on 'God's all-power', and the alto were modified to correspond (like my red ink marks if they are intelligible) I think you would get through that passage more smoothly.

System 2, last measure: personally my ear wants all those E's flattened, and the natural E to be kept until the first chord of system 3. There's bound to be a false-relation somewhere, but there are nice ones & nasty ones, and I think this one is very powerful.

In system 4 I've made a mess on your paper, but what I think is that you'd get stronger harmony if your tenor sang C-G-A-B-C on 'mortal pow'r usurps'.

You might consider those points: but otherwise I think it is a good piece and am glad people are asking for it. Do please include me in the mailing list.

The way to give names to tunes is to call them by some place name that has special associations for you. That way you are most likely to keep out of the way of names used before. I would suggest KENILWORTH, for example - but there's an existing one with that name. Where's your summer home? Where were you born? If the name is euphonious enough it would do. But that's the procedure I follow - I'm lucky, maybe, in having lived where there are so many places with nice names. New Jersey is liable to land one with names like Blawenburg or Netcong - or Union City! (Don't by the way, choose a name that people are likely to mispronounce! If they can, they will).

17

Thank you so very much for my very pleasant short stay in your home. Greetings to you all!

Yours ever,

(unsigned)

August 1, 1979

Dear Dr. Routley:

I still don't really think this is the "finished" version, but perhaps I would revise eternally, given the chance.

We're going up to Jingwak (Chippewa for "Pine Tree") near Minocqua, in the Lac du Flambeau mailing area. And seeing as I was born in Evanston, you can see that nothing particular suggested itself as a tune name... I just couldn't see putting an obviously Indian word as it didn't seem to fit.

The tune name is just an idea - Mead being my maiden name, it's more or less named for my Dad. "Eugene" would work too, if I could just pretend to being born in Oregon.

There are some changes in the harmonization of the tune, but none too overwhelming -- mainly a few passing tones and the like to keep the movement going. The text has two changes that I think are all right - although after I'd finished the copies, I wondered if calling God a benign power would seem incorrect to anyone? To me it's inconceivable that He would be anything but benign.... Also, the last verse is changed to avoid the "sexist" reference - just because people seem so uptight at this point in time. And I preferred leaving the last word "hand" rather than "span," hoping that the meaning was not really changed. But in each case I've been thinking of having the last line a strong statement to leave in the singer's thought, and "span" seemed to need thought that distracted from what was being said by the line. It's so uncommon a word in everyday usage.

18

I've also enclosed the Xeroxes of Watts' ten commandments - not a hymn, obviously. When I reread the reference to it, I could see I'd not read very accurately the first time, and it was my own fault that I'd misunderstood. A copy of <u>Divine and Moral Songs</u> was right there at Garrett, back in some tin building which houses books from another library, brought to Garrett when that school joined ranks and added the "Evangelical" to the name of the school. And I've enclosed an envelope is just in case you're stirred to say "No no no" to the text changes, or something. We're leaving Friday (8/3) and will return September 1. Thank you again for your help, as well as everything else in the course.

Sincerely,

Adrienne Tindall

DIVINE AND MORAL SONGS.   67

THE TEN COMMANDMENTS.

Out of the Old Testament, put into short rhyme for Children.—Exodus XX.

THOU shalt have no more Gods but me.

2. Before no idol bow thy knee.

3. Take not the name of God in vain.

4. Nor dare the sabbath day profane.

5. Give both thy parents honour due.

6. Take heed that thou no murder do.

7. Abstain from words and deeds unclean.

8. Nor steal, tho' thou art poor and mean.

9. Nor make a wilful lie, nor love it.

10. What is thy neighbour's dare not covet.

GOD'S POWER AND LOVE

Adrienne Tindall

MEAD'S BRIER
Adrienne Tindall, 1979

1. From the depths of roll-ing o-ceans, To the heights of out-er space,
2. Tak-ing wings of bril-liant morn-ings,— Find-ing far-thest shores of seas,—
3. In the love of our Re-deem-er And the heal-ing proofs He gave,
4. In the Christ-li-ness of mer-cy,— In a life that's no-bly grand,—

I will wit-ness God's all-pow-er Hold-ing strong its stead-y
E-ven vales of death-ly shad-ows Will not hide His love from
In His min-is-try's in-struc-tion And re-demp-tion from the
In each act of lov-ing-kind-ness I can see what God has

pace. No might but His sus-tains. His law for-ev-er reigns.
me! His ev-er-pres-ent care Is with me ev-'ry-where.
grave, The Fath-er's love is proved, The sting of death re-moved.
planned. His ev-er-wise con-trol A-bides while a-ges roll,—

No oth-er force, no mor-tal pow'r can take His place.
His pow-er stead-fast and be-nign a-ter-nal-ly.
The law of God is pow'r to heal and bless and save.
The heav'n-ly king-dom held se-cure-ly in His hand.

© A. Tindall
618 Brier St.
Kenilworth
IL 60043
8/1/79

App. C. p. 370
ER p. 21

20

4 August 79

ERIK ROUTLEY
Route 518, R. D. 1
SKILLMAN, N. J. 08558
(609) 921-7806

Dear Mrs. Tindall -

Many thanks indeed. I think the hymn is now in excellent shape and shouldn't be tinkered with any further. It is admirable.

Thank you also for the xx of Watts's Commandments. I had entirely overlooked this! I have a copy of the <u>Divine & Moral Songs</u> - a copy with magnificently hideous Victorian illustrations! - and of course it's in that. I had forgotten about it. But age is in various ways making itself only too apparent to me, and I am forgetting everything of importance.

Lac du Flambeau sounds romantic & mysterious: the Lake of Flame! What a place it must be! (Perhaps it suggests something out of the book of Revelation, but I hope it is pleasanter than that. I am bound to say that New Jersey just now is very Revelation-like: yesterday humidity and temperature coincided at 94).

I expect you are wise to sidestep these confounded antisexist witch-hunters. You are, anyhow, prepared to call God 'him' and that's something. How vexatious it all is!

I shan't be at Evanston next summer. I am being asked to take further duties in our Summer Session here, which include a daily service four days a week for seven weeks: and I would rather do that than take a plane in the summer. Experiences this summer have decided me in favour of doing less travelling. Oregon, where I was in mid-July, was at 107°, and no air conditioning. That's enough! I took a week to recover. But I hope our paths will cross some time.

Yours ever -

21

JINGWAK

ROUTE 1   LAC DU FLAMBEAU, WISCONSIN 54538

August 26th, 1979

Dear Dr. Routley:

By now it is way too late to warn you ahead of time that a token surprise / thank you is arriving by mail... but time gets away from one in the North Woods.... But I do appreciate your kind patience with the pestering I've done.

I'm enclosing a postcard of Lac du Flambeau - I wonder if there's country like this in England? It's been colder than usual this month, but the lake is really beautiful. And one can't tell that from town - one has to be right near (and in) the lakes themselves. If you get to this part of the country in your sojourns . . . I surely do wish it were when we were here, and could let you stay in a log cabin for a night or two ("you" being in the broad sense of you and your family members), . . . When we first started coming up about ten years ago, I got re-acquainted with the Milky Way, which is no longer evident around Chicago. And now we enjoy stargazing every clear night, counting shooting stars and satellites, and sometimes (quite often in August) seeing the Northern Lights.

Enough travelogue - as I wanted to mention an old book I found in an antique store in town (the kind where all the things are piled on each other and still need refinishing). Too bad the subject isn't perhaps more erudite - it's <u>Moody and Sankey in Great Britain and America</u>, copyright 1876. I thought of you because it combines with theology through the author - Rev. E. J. Goodspeed. Didn't he translate the Bible and his version is quoted often?

One other thing I wondered about - at least I think you'd possibly see what I mean. That translation to the kingdom of God being within - among you - I decided that it seems to me they would have to be hand in hand in any case. I think that is more or less what Jesus was telling the Pharisees wasn't enough. And it seems to me that the Sermon on the Mount kind of describes that the "within you" Kingdom of Heaven would be the irresistible producer or cause of

22

the "among you" evidence of it - the walking two miles instead of the required one. I'm not a theologian, but that did give me sort of an "answer of peace" about the translating, and a feeling that Jesus' meaning hadn't been lost or obscured, for me.

I can't tell you how timely it was to be able to have the two weeks' overviewing of hymnody this past June, with your understanding doing the overviewing. And I must acknowledge that the next Hymn Society Convocation being in Princeton whenever it's scheduled looks rather interesting - we haven't been back there since my husband graduated form Princeton (although I was there often enough the four years preceding!). And so even though I don't feel free to pester you, perhaps the paths will cross sometime. I certainly have been blessed by their crossing up to now!

Thank you, + best wishes!

Adrienne T.

1 September 79   **ERIK ROUTLEY**

Dear Adrienne -

     Yes, indeed a most toothsome and succulent surprise! Which will do my figure plenty of no good. (Nothing of that sort ever has any effect on my wife's). We English barbarians have found some difficulty in finding American candy that we can eat (which in my case is just as well); but this is magnificent. I now realize what it means about Wisconsin being the dairy state and so on.

     So thank you very much indeed. Our Labor Day week-end is apt to be more self-indulgent than usual because of this. Since the weather is unusually lousy at this end of the country that will cheer us up.

     Your book on Moody & Sankey in England will be interesting. I can never decide whether they come out of history as having done more good or more damage on balance. I tend to think they started something which went wrong & has now produced a dynasty of religious gangsters. Oh yes, Goodspeed wrote a Bible [translation] - he was one of the first modern US translators and is reputed to have made a million or so on the job - and there are worse ways of doing that. I was told by a reliable American scholar that the publisher was unwilling to take the translation in the first place & offered him 5% on the first 5,000 and 10% thereafter, to which he replied; 'No. 0% on the first 10,000 and thereafter 25%.' I don't see the Panorama doing quite that! And indeed I didn't have the courage to suggest quite that sort of contract.

I am sure you are basically right about the Kingdom within. Undoubtedly the Greek does put 'you' in the plural but that can be taken either way. Both ways must be right; the thing is neither exclusively private nor exclusively public.

I will look out for you at the Princeton convocation of the Hymn Society. Good luck with your continuing researches: and again, from both of us, thank you very much indeed for the delightful present!

Yours ever,

November 12, 1979

Dear Dr., Routley:

I'm ambling through my project to study which tunes get matched up with which texts - a card catalog arrangement - and I ran into your text "All who love and serve your city"!

First of all, it was exciting to know the author! And then it was exciting to study the ideas, the relevance, etc.

But the two versions I found - the Canadian <u>Hymn Book</u> (1971) and the <u>Lutheran Book of Worship</u> (1978) had a little word difference with a big meaning difference. I couldn't resist asking you about it, presumptuous though it may be. And if you don't have time please don't bother, but I'm really interested.

Stanza 4 line 4 of the Canadian has "offering peace and Calvary's hill." Lutheran Book of Worship has "offering peace from Calvary's hill."

Several possibilities - possibly one is a misprint? Or perhaps one requested to change the original to the version they preferred? It doesn't seem possible that such a "minor" change is permissible if you didn't like it.

My becoming acquainted with what the Lutheran 1978 hymnal has done in revising . . . seems to me that the usual flavor of Lutheran texts would not have had them make that particular change on purpose. So perhaps that's the original form?

It was exciting to hear Dr. Wyton last Tuesday night, as he spoke about the Episcopal revision of their hymnal [1940]. I loved it when he took out a thick sheaf of papers and offered to tell anyone what was scheduled to happen to any hymn in the present book. And the changes he quoted (just a couple were mentioned) certainly seemed to be in excellent taste. (I will probably never like the line, "Good Christian <u>friends</u>, rejoice..." It just doesn't have it for me. Much preferable to leave the Latin). Glad they will leave the "thee" and "thy" type of address as it was originally written, too. It would feel very peculiar to think of God in a "Hey, you" kind of vernacular, and yet it always feels that way when I read God / "You" in a text. I'm just used to the other, I think.

How precisely must a hymn text (or tune) be re-presented when it's under copyright protection such as laws now permit?

Sincerely,

Adrienne M. Tindall

P. S. If you'd like any more super candy I know where to get it!

ERIK ROUTLEY
929 ROUTE 518, R. D. 1
SKILLMAN, NEW JERSEY 08558

21 November 79

Dear Mrs Tindall -

Your letter has laid for 2 days on my desk - so sorry the pre-Thanksgiving rush has gotten to me.

The Canadian hymnal does indeed misprint 'All who love & serve' - and I had never noticed it! The true reading is 'offer peace from Calvary's hill'. The other makes no sense. I must have that corrected.

The Lutherans did want to make a lot of changes in that text - nearly all of these I rejected, but I did allow them to say 'drawing near his friends who spurn him....' to by-pass what they thought a sexist offense: but it's not really what I meant. . . . Some textual changes . . . have provoked as much indignation as the 'sexist' originals would have done.

When you write a hymn text out which is controlled by copyright you are required to make no alterations without getting permission at the time when you get copyright permission. Sometimes there is no problem but it is against the law to make alterations without asking whether you may. The same applies to a tune; but here there's an awkward complication when a melody is public domain but its harmonization is copyright. That can favour you, of course, if you take a PD [public domain] tune and reharmonize it, but it can catch you if you reprint as given a tune whose harmony is copyright. American hymnals now often give exact details on the same page as the hymn, which is helpful: older books & English books always make you hunt about in the index of acknowledgments. Boring but, I am afraid, necessary.

Yes, we absolutely loved the candy. Would you be prepared to part with the address of the maker so that we could order some?

Happy Thanksgiving!

yours ever,

26

December 10th, 1979

Dear Dr. Routley:

In the words of current jokes, I have some good news and some bad news....
The good news (I hope!!!) is that if you'd just look at the enclosed and make
any helpful comments that seem right, you will be the recipient of some
fabulous English Toffee, sent direct from the North Woods upon having been
ordered on Monday, December 24. (I have to admit that it will be sent in any
case...) The bad news is that the store from which one orders it closes from
January 1 to May 30th. So I hope your addiction is still under control...

The French carol is sent merely to honor the season, and because I fell in love
with the tune when I found it a couple of years ago. Last Christmas I asked my
mother-in-law to do an interlinear exact translation, which I then versified (if
that's what it's called) in the form enclosed. At the time I just removed all the
slurs, ignoring the regular meter of the melody with the slurs, and did a syllabic
type length of line which fit the notes. I'm not sure how the meter should be
indicated, or whether the verse form is accurate.... The original French (at least
the one I started with) is in the Oxford Book of Carols. I sent it to Austin, to
see what he thought of the translation, and he has set sts. 1, 2, 3, 5 as an
anthem. Although I asked him about whether it was plagiarism to start with his
harmonization and revise it, in order to come up with my harmonization (I use
that "my" advisedly therefore, although there are several changes) -- that's what
I did.... But he seemed to toss it off, assuring me I had not erred.... My eldest
did the art work. Anything you'd like to say would be very interesting; I've
had this printed up for a couple of carol sings we have here at the house.

The other - "Let your light so shine for men" (boy will that get the women's lib
up-tighters!) would you say anything helpful please? (delicious toffee...)
There are a couple of other verses, but I think perhaps the four are enough? Or

too short? Is there any difficulty with the capital on "Love" (v4)? In Christian Science such capitalization would make the word a synonym for "God," but that might not make good sense elsewhere? The tune is quite straightforward -- too boring? When I hear some of the things coming out (like that little HSA set of 3 hymns which just arrived) I recognize myself as *very* conservative! Part of that is because a CS church has no choir, and only a soloist to help the congregation with hymn singing.

Well, I pester Austin like this (for a fee, or I wouldn't feel free) and recognize my hymnic efforts as so new I the need assurance. Is there anything theologically problematical in either text? And I won't bother you again unless the addiction is severe (or you'd tolerate a fee...). Have a lovely Christmas. And thanks so much....

Sincerely,

LET YOUR LIGHT SO SHINE FOR MEN

GLENCAYNIG 76.86.
A Tindall, 1979

1. Let your light so shine for men
    That they who see its glow
Will glorify the God of love
    For proofs your works will show.

2. Towering cities are not hid
    But shine forth through the night.
A candle on a candlestick
    Will fill the house with light.

3. Listen to the Christ's commands!
    His teachings light the way.
To follow in obedience
    Will lead to endless day.

4. Through a life of Love's good works,
    Impelled by selfless prayer,
We each can let our light show forth
    God's glory everywhere.

A Tindall, 1979

Revision in App. C p. 366
ER p. 33

30

What Is This Lovely Fragrance?

French Carol Melody

WHAT IS THIS LOVELY FRAGRANCE?

1. What is this lovely fragrance, shepherds, which
        gently enfolds our hearts this night?
   Sweeter than all the flow'rs of springtime,
        as they exhale unique delight!
   What is this lovely fragrance, shepherds, which
        gently enfolds our hearts this night?

2. What bursting light has come through darkness, to
        dazzle our eyes with living hues?
   Even the day-star's radiant orbit
        has not a radiance so profuse!
   What bursting light has come through darkness, to
        dazzle our eyes with living hues?

3. Fear nothing, faithful people! Open your hearts to
        the angel of the Lord.
   He tells us all the news of blessing:
        Goodness for all fulfills God's Word.
   Fear nothing, faithful people! Open your hearts to
        the angel of the Lord.

4. Savior of God, your birth in Bethlehem's
        manger exalts this holy night.
   Nothing shall hinder our adoring,
        witnessing our Redeemer's light.
   Savior of God, your birth in Bethlehem's
        manger exalts this holy night.

5. God of all-pow'r, may you be glorified!
        Hearts overflow with thanks and praise.
   Let endless peace embrace all people.
        Let grace abound in all life's ways.
   God of all-pow'r, may you be glorified!
        Hearts overflow with thanks and praise.

App. C p. 365
ER p. 33

French Carol
(tr. A.M.Tindall)

[missing letter from AT, probably sent in the same envelope, accompanying commandments text]

from Exodus 20 (First Version)

When God demanded Israel's flight
from Pharaoh's land of pain and night,
He shielded them upon their way
and gave them laws they should obey.
The listening ear of Moses heard
instruction in God's holy Word.

"You shall have no more gods than me,
before no idol bow your knee.
Take not the name of God in vain,
nor dare the Sabbath day profane.
Give to your parents honor due
so that long life will come to you.

"When you obey this holy pact
you will not do a murderous act.
You will abstain from sensual deed,
nor steal, though you may be in need.
Give true reports of happenings,
and covet not your neighbor's things."

Obedience to these ten commands
still fosters peace in earthly lands.
Fidelity to God above,
and actions proving kindly love,
will bless the human family
and witness heaven's harmony.

> A M Tindall, 1979
> sts. 2 & 3 Isaac Watts, 1715, revised
> taken from <u>Divine and Moral Songs for Children</u>

88.88.88.

[original tune lost]

Rev p. 48, App. C p.328
ER p. 33

ERIK ROUTLEY
929 ROUTE 518, R. D. 1
SKILLMAN, NEW JERSEY 08558

15 December 79

Dear Adrienne -

Thank you for both your letters and the various enclosures. In these three pieces there is a good deal that I like very much. I will take them one by one.

What is this lovely fragrance? [p. 31] - a very agreeable translation. The only word I am dubious about is 'profuse' which I think a little mannered, and it doesn't rhyme with hues'. But all the rest is very easy to sing and pick up. I think you have arranged the tune pleasantly. I only ask whether you expect this and the others to be sung in four parts. If you do, you shouldn't write the bass below F for singers: not many choirs have a bass who can hit E flat. But the descending scale is very effective, and you should keep it for the player or for a singer who can manage it, adding only alternative cue-size notes for those who can't reach the low note. I'd suggest cue-size quarters an octave higher doubling A-G-F-E flat, the E flat being a half note. But that's only a detail. If you write in 4 parts but require unison singing it's best to give a unison direction. The final bass chord suggests that you want unison, so just mark the tune so.

'Let your light so shine' [p. 30] makes a good point. Most of it runs very well. I have a little doubt about a city shining (st. 2); I don't think it can. Couldn't you say 'their lights shine through the night'? And is 'obedience' four syllables in modern speech? I think not myself - the line needs an extra syllable somewhere. The tune is a very pleasant melody but it raises the same point as the previous one: if you wish it to be sung in unison, the third phrase lacks sonority in the harmony; on the other hand, if you want it in harmony then I think all those high notes in the bass might produce an effect you don't want; and I should myself hesitate to write a high f# for tenors on a weak beat. You tend to write repeated notes in the bass which have a slightly obstinate effect and I wonder whether in measure 3 the second bass note mightn't sound better as a D. But I think this works well.

The Commandments hymn [p. 32] is a sensible text. Myself I don't quite see what one would do with a hymn paraphrasing the Commandments - but they had one in Calvin's Geneva! (I doubt if

33

Watts intended his to be sung: I expect he wrote it simply to be learnt by heart). However, you have summed it up very skilfully. (By the way - you use 'obedience' as a three syllable word in st. 4, and you ought to be consistent - refer back to 'Let your light....'). When writing a text out, let the indentation represent the rhyme-scheme when possible. In this text all lines should be to the margin because the rhymes are in couplets.

About the tune I have many doubts. I am afraid I think the ending of the tune, whose tonality is F minor, on its dominant is not really useful: it is a defiance of what our ear expects, and in hymnody one shouldn't do that as blatantly as this one does. If you are in F minor, then that's where you should finish. (A final F major chord is perfectly proper - that doesn't affect the tonality). You can begin out of key if you want to & are clever: but in that case it should become clear at an early stage that you are in C minor. I think you really are in C minor, but the first long phrase plainly isn't until it reaches its final chord (dominant of Cm). I'm sorry: I don't think this works. I would also object rather heavily to all those repeated bass notes. I expect you wanted to represent the tramping of the Israelites through the wilderness, but in a hymn tune that's the sort of pictorial effect that shouldn't be attempted in the harmony: anything of that kind you want to produce should attempt the effect through the texture of the melody. (Do you compose hymn tunes at the piano? I suspect perhaps you do. Cease to do so! Compose the melody first & then take it to the keyboard to see if it works). I think this would be a good tune if its last few notes led back to F minor, and if the bass were more contrapuntal and chorale-like.

In answer to your specific questions, I don't violently object to 'bow the knee' - it's in the AV Philippians 2.12 after all: but perhaps 'bend' is a bit less mannered. I think Israel genuinely did believe that God was commanding them to get out of Egypt and find the Promised Land, so I don't have any problem with the opening.

I have one general point to make. I think you are capable of writing both a good tune and a good text; but I would advise that you don't always feel that when you have written a text you must write your own tune. You must be aware, with your knowledge of history, how rarely this happens in hymnody. Luther is one of the very few examples and he didn't always bring it off. The difficulty is to maintain the same level of inspiration in both. Hymnody is an activity conducted by a community to which writers and composers contribute, and the mating of texts and tunes is (as you will remember) a process usually conducted by people who neither compose nor write. I think when one writes texts one leaves them with no more than a suggestion of what well known tune would fit them, remembering that a text stands much more chance of being widely sung if it can be introduced with a tune that people already know. When one writes a tune one should have a text in mind but it doesn't have to be one's own text. I think it's putting too heavy a strain on one's creative powers to attempt to write both tune and text: but by the same token I am impressed by the success with which you often do it yourself. All I ask is that you consider sometimes writing one without the other, because if you do you're acknowledging the conversation that's already going on. Don't forget, what I am sure I told you at some time, that the text and tune of 'Our God, our help in ages past' met when the text was 142 years old and the tune 153 and both had had other partners before. It sounds all very immoral but that's the way it goes!

It was very kind of you to enclose a check. Feel free, on whatever terms, to write when you want to: I shall likewise feel free to answer your questions as put. I hope you will have a delightful Christmas and many blessings in 1980. Thank you again for sending me these good things.

Yours ever -

[Note: The Reverend Caryl Micklem, Erik's lifelong friend, says, "In praise of God meet duty and delight", tune SHERIDAN, both written 1976. Margaret Routley says there is also "The earth is the Lord's and its fulness", tune NEW HOPE, both 1977. *Our Lives be Praise* lists also, "Christ, the Church's Lord, you know us" (unpublished), set to PADUCAH.]

35

December 12th

Dear Dr. Routley:

I sent off that "double" letter to you this morning, and as I thought back over it realized something about the "Let your light so shine" text.

Capitalizing "love" in stanza 4 is probably wrong, and a small "l" makes more sense. I was thinking about a verse that is omitted in the version I sent you, where I think a capital would be accurate; insofar as my understanding of Christian Science is concerned [where a capital "L" signifies "Love" as a synonym for "God"]:

> Let my motives, steps, and goals
>   be Love's own way, defined.
> And let me see with eyes that look
>   with love on all mankind.

If that makes no sense to you don't worry about it - but I think stanza 4 of that text should have a small "l" in any case.

Many thanks.

ERIK ROUTLEY
929 Route 518, R. D. 1 :: Skillman, N. J. 08558

In reply to your most recent letter - I am in favor of omitting capitals whenever possible & would omit them in both the cases under review. I can't think of a case where 'love ' should have one; the only possibility is if the word is being used as a synonym for (not a description of) one of the persons of the Trinity: and that is a thing I myself wouldn't do. 'God is love' - not 'God is Love': because one might end up by saying 'Love is God' - which perhaps is tolerable once in Christopher Smart but not normally.

Best wishes -

12 19 79

36

December 26, 1979

Dear Dr. Routley:

Thanks for the letter with all the suggestions! . . .

The bad news is first ... and that is that the fudge store ran out of toffee a couple of days before we got here . . . .

The "fragrance" setting was a hit at both our carol parties. My youngest daughter really loved it, and I got lots of practice before the parties, as she wanted to sing it "a few times". . . .

I see what you mean about a city shining, and agree. . . . Ranges have again been a weakness, eh? Would you just indicate what good ones would be? I suppose ranges in a hymn book would be "conservative" because specifically aimed at people in the pew who sing once a week and then only in "early" morning, right....

Repeated notes in the bass and other supporting parts are because I thought if one were expecting the basses to sing the syllables they needed a note to indicate the pulse of the text syllables. With unison singing, I can see that one needn't notate each beat that way, though. . . .

Your comment about the ten commandments text interests me a lot, although I can see that you're undoubtedly right. I've not understood why there are no hymn texts on the 10 commandments, and why one wouldn't be highly desirable and useful. The one in Tate and Brady is very long - about 48 lines if I recall correctly. I Xeroxed it at home, because I thought even that would be an interesting possibility. Why do you suppose there aren't even Sunday School hymns using the ten commandments? If nothing else, the music / versification would help memorization, and what better material to have young and mature people be able to recall to thought without any other prop than memory?

As to the tune - I expected the non-enthusiasm, and even more as I "lived" with the tune for a few more days. My husband and I go swimming a couple of times each week, and I "sang" the hymn to myself as I swam laps. Distressing in a "live and learn" sense was the realization that I, the composer, couldn't sing it! And of course that's because I was relying on the harmonies so much that I didn't feel the shiftiness of the tune itself. What a sad coupling! to set the commandments to a non-solid basis of tonality! . . .

The repeated bass notes were just because I thought they had to be there in order to permit the men to say the text. The tramping of the Israelites is a valid picture, but I think I'd probably prefer not having that dogged and slogging sense of struggle connected to the commandments, as it implies obedience being unnatural, difficult, toilsome, etc. I like better a solid sense of on-the-right-track, but something that acknowledges that man feels most comfortable and at home and secure when living in accord with Micah 6:8 (my favorite summation).

One specific question I would like a yea or nay on if you would - that fifth commandment couplet. The original I had was "Give to your parents honor due / So that long life will come to you." I didn't like the second line much. I think the interpretation of the Exodus verse is long life though, isn't it? Or is the emphasis really on "in the land which the Lord thy God giveth thee?" Do you see what I mean about that "honored praise" being rather too close to potential hypocrisy? Or am I straining at a gnat?

Re writing texts and tunes. I really feel comfortable in acknowledging that one needn't write both. I'd love to do something like Philipp Nicolai, though - a couple of hymn texts with tunes that are magnificent. More recently as I've explored some of the humbler (musically and textually) hymnals that are around, I can see a rather less interesting (to me) type of hymn that comes typically from that background [one individual writing both text and tune] . . . . The "fragrance" text of course started from the French melody and text. The others that you've seen have all been in meters which don't have many representatives around, so far as I know. The one for Garrett I did deliberately, realizing that if I were writing an original text I didn't really have to limit myself in meter, as I was planning to do the tune for it anyway (taking advantage of the assignment and your patience and expertise...). The "Let your light" combining trochaic and iambic again seemed less likely to have easily found tunes, and I wanted to write tunes anyway. And the ten commandments I did look for briefly, but an 88.88.88. indexing I'd done suggested about three, none of which grabbed me much. More like that contest the Hymn Society is sponsoring, where they invite texts, and recognize that one can or needn't send a suggestion for a tune with it. I wouldn't be offended or uptight about one or the other being uninteresting for use; it just seems like fun to use a text as a chance to write a tune.

I do hope sending a check with things for you to look at won't seem undesirable - I wish I could think of the right word for what I'm trying to say. There's no way that I even know what your time is "worth" and I certainly think you could invest it in better things than writing long letters to yours truly! But if you don't mind my writing now and again with things, I would feel much more comfortable even with so token a gesture as that is. I couldn't even put a price tag on what it's worth to me, because it's worth more than the checks, let me assure you! And I'll try not to do write too often...

I'm really sorry about the toffee (we didn't even get any, and I'm sorry about that too!). . . .

How's your Book Three of the Panorama set coming? I used the first two books in a research project I did, and they were extremely helpful and informative. I was particularly pleased to have Lowell's poem complete, from which they took "Once to every man and nation." Is the actual hymn ghastly that resulted from that adaptation? Is it bad because of the way it was done, the theology of the result, or what? . . . But so many people really are enthusiastic about that hymn! And of course it may be largely because of the greatness of the tune?

Thanks again, and best wishes,

ERIK ROUTLEY
929 ROUTE 518. R. D. 1
SKILLMAN. NEW JERSEY 08558
29 December 79

Dear Adrienne -
    Many thanks for your last letter.
    Commandments. The difficulty is, I think, that hymns are usually something we say to God: and the commandments are something which Israel thought God said to them. But that depends really on one's view of what hymns are for. The Genevan Commandments-hymns are like the Psalms - which are essentially the Bible read to music. Calvin didn't believe anything else was permissible in church, and therefore his notion of what a hymn was is entirely different from ours (or from Luther's). So singing the

39

Commandments is like singing the Psalms (without antiphons) - a reading of the Bible: if they're communally sung it's like a communal, or what people call a 'unison' reading of the Bible; like the Psalms, the Commandments are equally suitable for being sung by a soloist or choir <u>to</u> the congregation - just as most of the Bible is. I think I should expect to find a metrical setting of the Commandments in churches where the Calvin-view of hymn singing remains - the Old Free Kirk of Scotland or the Dutch Reformed Church. But in the sort of church I am used to I shouldn't use such a setting because I think of hymns as being sung to God.

<u>Once to every man and nation</u> - oddly enough my criticism of the congregational use of this stands, I think, on the same ground. I don't think it's a <u>hymn</u>. The original is an eloquent poem - though perhaps rather over-written: the adaptation is still eloquent as a poem, but it's a bit of a sermon - rather argumentative. As for its popularity, that is, as you say, based on the extraordinary vitality and expressiveness of the tune: and if some proper hymn had been set to it, they'd have enjoyed that just as much. There is no fathoming the depth of congregational insensitiveness in these matters: one can't do anything about it by argument: one can only set a proper example! I do indeed enjoy hymns in which there is fine poetry and I find this in many of the pre-Watts 17th century poets whose work has got into hymnals: but I do want them to be <u>hymns</u>, not sermons or exhortations. That's why I can't abide 'Rise up, O men of God' and things of that nature. Who's speaking to whom?

Well, as to the line you are in doubt about in the Commandments hymn - in the thought of the original hearers of the Commandments undoubtedly 'the land that the Lord thy God giveth thee' was important: but I don't see how you are to get all that sort of thing into a manageable hymn, and there's an abridged version in Leviticus, I think which leaves out a good deal of the comment in the Exodus version: so I should leave that as it is. Theologically, of course, there are all sorts of questions to be asked about the Commandments considered as a rule of life for Christians. Our Lord's own comments on them seem to add up to: 'Of course you will follow them, and don't dare to think you can manage without them: but that won't get you the whole way'.

I thought the tramping of the Israelites was probably in your mind and generated those repeated notes. But musically the image doesn't really fit. What you want is a relentless scale, not a repeated note - which suggests they weren't getting anywhere at all.

Some time, have a look at a hymn beginning 'Through the night of doubt and sorrow' - a rather good hymn about pilgrimage with touches of Exodus about it. The 'old' tune to that was by Dykes (though he didn't write it for it) and it had a repeated D throughout the first line: it is called ST. OSWALD (Hymns A & M 292: English Hymnal Appendix 61); compare it, as an image of marching, with the later tune by Martin Shaw, called MARCHING, for the same words (English Hymnal 503: Hymns A & M 182) and you'll see an illustration of what I've just said. A strongly moving bass, not a static bass, suggests pilgrimage.

I have nothing yet to report on my third hymnology book. The Press has it but hasn't yet sent a contract for it. I shall soon be asking them whether they want to send it back and let me place it elsewhere if I can.

How kind of you to send those goodies on their way. I shall have to trust my wife to keep some of them in the icebox because I shall be out of the country January 4 - 20. But I shall certainly enjoy them: we both will!

A very good new year to you -

yours ever,

ERIK ROUTLEY
929 Route 518, R. D. 1 :: Skillman, N. J. 08558

Thank you so much for the goodies from Wisconsin: they arrived while I was away in Britain and we are now enjoying them immensely! Most kind of you.

Warmest greetings,

1.24.80

41

January 29, 1980

Dear Dr. Routley:

I'm working still on the ten commandments text - I have an idea about it that might be worthwhile, but wanted to dash off a letter about something without waiting....

Because I read your article in the HYMN about sexist language - much interested in it - and your discussion of your city hymn particularly stirred thought. Having been one of those to suggest using the word "those" [in a missing letter?], I of course followed your reasonings in that area with concentrated attention.

Now don't bother to answer this letter if there's no point - but I was thinking about that troublesome line. It seems to me that there's no significant difference in the implications of "Drawing near to men who spurn him" and "Drawing near to those who spurn him." When you'd pointed out that it implied perhaps only drawing near to the spurners, and not drawing near to the non-spurners, I could see immediately what you meant, but still kind of felt that both versions (and the one using "friends" also) could imply that.

So it kind of percolated on the back burner a bit, and it occurred to me later that if you could incorporate the word "even" in that line it would clarify that the non-spurners are included in the referring. Non-scansion version "Drawing near even to those who spurn him." And as I thought of it away from the text (and the rest of the stanza) I thought "Loving even those who spurn him" would fit nicely. . . .

Your drawing near has that beautiful sense of Jesus doing the action - of his reaching out to those, and letting his circle of love include those, who have counted him out in their lives. I couldn't really come up with another verb to do that in two syllables, and saw no point in pursuing it as I felt there were things in the rest of the stanza that would relate to exactly which word did the job best. "Calling" of course doesn't include that reaching out and embracing, but rather relies on the action being taken by the one who is spurning at this point.... "Loving" could be taken as a non-active sense of including them...

When I consider all this, it seems impossible that editors would find the courage and self-assurance to do extensive revising of texts . . . and when you mentioned revising whole lines in order to avoid a "thee" use - I ran across one of those in the Lutheran Book of Worship, where the "thee" form was the rhyming word, and (gee I should look it up) the whole stanza virtually, was changed, and much much worse, the sense of the meaning was so altered as to not only offend me, but also to seem a questionable meaning, remote from the author's original intention. I was <u>mad</u> about that one!

Enough. The other thing I wanted to tell you is for fun - and I really couldn't wait....

If you recall the sessions at Garrett last summer, and the assigned hymn texts and tunes, and yourself sitting at the piano trying out my hymn tune, and asking if perhaps I had a Welsh grandmother? Well, I mentioned the incident to Mother last Sunday, when I told her that I have become interested in writing hymns - texts and tunes as well, and recounted that because it's rather picturesque and fun...

You can guess why it's amusing in total - because she said, "Well, yes, actually you do - my grandmother's mother was Welsh...." Now family trees have never much interested me, and although I knew the Mead family (my maiden name) had a big fat book about it, only knew that Mother's mom was English and her dad was Swedish. But I think the whole thing is marvelous fun, and am delighted because it seems to me some of my favorite hymn tunes come from that sector. Seems to me one of the other articles in that issue of <u>The Hymn</u> described Welshmen singing hymns before a sports event while they waited for it to begin - what a neat sense of song!

I hope I've not been brazenly offensive about your text...?

Sincerely,

[signature]

WESTMINSTER CHOIR COLLEGE

PRINCETON, NEW JERSEY 08540

4 February 80

Dear Adrienne -

That's a very intelligent suggestion of yours about the offending line in my hymn, and I assure you I shall take it seriously. Thank you for offering it.

I am delighted to hear that you are anyhow one sixteenth Welsh! I am not in the least surprised, and it looks as if it stays in the blood somehow.

It is certainly true that Welshmen sing CWM RHONDDA at football matches. It is also normally true that they are drunk while singing it. I am afraid that the real genius has gone out of Welsh hymn singing - it is a little like the situation in the Black churches where spirituals have given place to degenerate white 19th century music. But in the remoter parts of Wales one can still hear the authentic sound.

Greetings!

yours ever -

March 11, 1980

Dear Dr. Routley:

I hope you won't mind my asking again about this [Commandments] text, and also your ideas about the 88.88.88. tune which could fit with it .... but first the text.

I can see what you mean about a hymn being what one addressed back to God. This really is a rather peculiar vehicle in that sense, I suppose. But I am quite interested in it nonetheless, and do you think the added fourth verse incorporates an idea that helps? My own church has no choir, and a hymn which focuses so clearly on the commandments might well be used in Sunday School as well as for Wednesday night meetings, which focus on such a subject as "law" or "commandments" or something like that. I suppose practically speaking, one could regard the congregation as acting in the place of the choir, singing a Bible text to each other, rather than it being presented by the choir to the congregation....

I feel very much as I think you intimated in your letter about this text, that obedience to the commandments is not the ultimate, but that Christ Jesus expected and required much more. For me that is more or less summed up in the Sermon on the Mount, and its feel (I think) of love so complete and holy, that a disciple (then or now) just overflows with love to everyone everywhere, all the time, no matter what the conditions or background. The ten commandments just don't epitomize that, but rather spell out (I think) the bare essentials of minimum behavior between people, in order for a community to function, and maintain its awareness of God as the Sustainer of every individual, and to keep being God-centered. I don't explain these things very well - but it's just that a text such as this, which I think is potentially good, must still be modest in its scope, because the really wide scope must come, and fulfillment of the Kingdom of Heaven, etc., through the Christ.

The lines that I've struggled with most are the last of the 4th stanza - does it seem to say something logical? I'm just trying to say I couldn't hope to come anywhere near success without "Christly grace," and that obedience to the commandments relies on that too, even in seeing just how they best govern one's living.

Well in any case, even bearing in mind that the text is really more a singing of scripture than a hymn, I am toying with sending it in to the HSA search - and so I'm hoping if you have any insights that would improve its clarity or appropriateness, you could let me know. That's kind of tacky, to give you not much notice, as the deadline is March 31st. But if you don't have time just don't worry, and if you do I'd be pleased. You seem to have a very helpful and good promptness about answering letters (I guess they really take less time that way, don't they?), and your past kindnesses in letter writing have indicated that there is good hope for this one.....

Tunes: The meter of this isn't so hard, and I've found a couple that would work. VATER UNSER is possible, although I really am more inclined toward the school of leaving a recognized tune with the recognized text it sets. The problems with this text seem to me to be that there should be no marked and single climax, but rather a steadiness, beginning to end, with non-simplistic harmonies. Probably minor because of the Hebrew background, but really the important thing is that the feel of the harmonization be non-eighteenth century English (I think that's what I mean - do you get what I'm trying to say from it?).

So I grabbed the British Baptist hymnal which seems to me to have nice balance in warmth of music and excellence of qualities (Geer and Harvard are rather erudite; I don't have the hymnal you helped with - where could I get one?). And as I went down the 88.88.88. tunes came across CREDO which seems okay, and then later found one called WYCH CROSS which I just adore. It's just as well I didn't know your hymn tunes before last June - all the ones I've seen are so neat to me that I doubt I could have heard what you were saying, for the personal awe I would've had because of them. Do you think WYCH CROSS fits okay? Is it troublesome as a potential marriage? . . .

The other day I was looking through 100 Hymns for Today and found my absolute favorite text as a basis for a hymn - Micah 6:8 (I guess I'd better not exclude a number of other texts, all of which are also absolute favorites). And when I played the tune - fabulous!!! Then..... I noticed the composer's name.... Well those are all the ones of yours I've run across so far, but I suspect I can see the writing on the wall......

So it makes me even more self-conscious about asking you to look over my measly efforts, and even more determined to ride roughshod over the self-consciousness and hope that you will indeed do so, because the potential blessing is even greater....

46

Speaking of Micah 6:8 it is, of course, the basis for the new stanza in the enclosed [commandments] text. Does it come across as perhaps too impossibly perfect a standard for an individual to espouse to - what do you think? That of course is why the fifth line must come next..... But even though I think the Micah verse is a fine OT summation of the law, does it seem like an "extraneous" or "too much" situation to include reference here in the midst of the ten commandments?

One other question, this a general one to clarify something I think I understand, but I think a friend of mine doesn't..... the word "hymn" really refers to the text independent of the tune, doesn't it? Although it is a text to be sung to the glory of God, isn't it still complete without the identity of a tune taken into consideration? In common usage in this country anyway, and especially for the layman, a hymn is a combination of text with tune. The HSA searches make things clear by avoiding the use of "hymn" without "text" or "tune" in direct conjunction. The definition in the Harvard Dictionary of Music really doesn't say unequivocally that the "Hymn" is the words, even though I think the implication is there.

And last but for me not at all least, a friend has called and we have agreed to rooming together for the HSA Convocation in June. It really sounds grand (she says "all the big brass"). I think I shall stay through the week for the classes too.....

Thanks again and again for your patience.

Sincerely,

From Exodus 20 (final Version)

When God demanded Israel's flight
from Pharaoh's land of pain and night,
He shielded them upon their way
and gave them laws they should obey.
The listening ear of Moses heard
instruction in God's holy Word.

"You shall have no more gods than me,
before no idol bow your knee.
Take not the name of God in vain,
nor dare the Sabbath day profane.
Give to your parents honor due
so that long life will come to you.

"When you obey this holy pact
you will not do a murderous act.
You will abstain from sensual deed,
nor steal, though you may be in need.
Give true reports of happenings,
and covet not your neighbor's things."

Lord, I would live a righteous life
with inner peace through outward strife.
I would be just, and humble too,
with mercy guiding all I do.
I must rely on Christly grace
to give Your laws their proper place.

Obedience to these ten commands
still fosters peace in earthly lands.
Fidelity to God above,
and actions proving kindly love,
will bless the human family
and witness heaven's harmony.

> A M Tindall, 1979
> sts. 2 & 3 Isaac Watts, revised
> (from <u>Divine and Moral Songs for Children</u>, 1715)

88.88.88.

App. C. p. 328
ER p. 49

48

ERIK ROUTLEY
929 ROUTE 518, R. D. 1
SKILLMAN, NEW JERSEY 08558
14 March 80

Dear Adrienne -

Thank you for your latest letter (and the graceful enclosure).

(1) I think the last two lines of stanza 4 certainly give distinction to the whole, and don't at all want them altered.

(2) Do by all means send it to the HSA. . . . I hope they will see the very real merits of this.

(3) Do not be too much put off by my thoughts on a hymn sung by the congregation to each other; as a general rule I think that modern hymnody doesn't really admit of this sort of text - but I would make an exception of yours because there certainly is a very respectable precedent in the Genevan Psalters. As I may have said before - the idea of a 'Commandments Hymn' came out of the kind of worship in which if the congregation didn't sing a psalm they did nothing whatever: that is, a tradition much less liturgically flexible than we now allow ourselves to be. But all the same, I think there is enough good thinking in this text of yours to get clear past that generalization.

(4) WYCH CROSS: well, that is an agreeable idea, of course. The British Baptists altered it because they didn't set it to the text it was written for. Originally the last note of phrase 5 was a whole note and the first of the succeeding phrase another whole, because the stanzas of the hymn I wrote it for, ('Lord Jesus in the days of old': Congregational Praise 628) demanded that. But yours requires the alteration, so let that stand. I am very glad you like it. (You might need to say 'copyright E.R.' if you decided to send it in: the composition date was 1947). I am also much delighted that you like the Micah tune. That of course is the only available tune in the metre of that text, so it is getting the occasional showing over here because the text is so good (More Hymns & Spiritual Songs has it, and so does the new United Church of Christ hymnal).

(5) You are right. If one speaks of a hymn, one means words: its tune must be called a hymn tune. It is the very thing that has suffocated hymnody in the USA, that people have tended to think of texts and tunes as wedded together indissolubly. That has come from the Gospel Song tradition, and is one of the evil things that

49

tradition has done for hymnody here. I am very glad you have seen that point, and will set a good example! I have often had students who refer to a hymn plus tune by the tune-name, thinking of ST. ANNE as a synonym for 'Our God our help in ages past'. I don't allow them to do that a second time! I doubt whether the people on the Harvard Dictionary of Music thought hymns worth being precise about. Big-time musicians never do.

I think you are now in business with the Commandments Hymn [p. 48], and wish it every success!

Yours ever -

ERIK ROUTLEY
6 June 80   929 Route 518, R. D. 1 :: Skillman, N. J. 08558

Wow! More temptations most gladly received and yielded to. I am just back from Britain (2 weeks) and found them waiting. We are enjoying them immensely. Thank you so much!

Will you be at Garrett soon? I'm sorry I shall miss you: my greetings to the faithful.

Yours ever,

June 30th, 1980

Dear Dr. Routley:

At last I'm getting this written! And you're probably at sixteen workshops all over the country so you won't get it for an age until I'm up North July 26th and then I won't know .... oh well, delay is not a thing to dwell on, I do enough of that already in the delaying itself!

I thought to ask your ideas on the enclosed text. The hymn writing seminar (or whatever it was called) was really very interesting, but there couldn't be too much in-depth discussion of the original efforts. Gracia Grindal assigned Psalm 16 to paraphrase, and the efforts (brought in the next day) were Xeroxed and discussed anonymously in class. With 30 texts to go over, it was admirable that we got through them at all (we didn't on the tunes the next day).

About all she said was that it's "pretty clean." She didn't like the word "position" which I hadn't liked either. And she didn't hear the anapest foot at the beginning of each stanza, which "made her nervous" (she kind of heard the first syllable stressed, instead of unstressed).

As I read it over this morning, I still like it; would you offer any comments? No tune for it that I can think of, of course, with the irregular beginning.

One of the things she mentioned about another text I accosted her with (on a walk to the Student Center) which relates to God's law, she said didn't sparkle because it lacked imagery - it came off very didactic. Does this one do that too? I was figuring a paraphrase would stick closely to the text (even though I skipped the "hard" part, and rearranged the thoughts).

I didn't go to Garrett this year; I confess to going last year solely because you were holding forth - I'd never considered going before. It was worth it, too. And I was going to sadly mention that the HSA was not interested in any of my texts or tunes in this last search.....

Best wishes and thanks for all,

51

PSALM 16 (no edits)

My inheritance is from the Lord;
      no worldly wealth can win my praise.
True riches bless me in His Word,
      His counsel guides me through life's ways.
If earth's confusions bring a night,
His heavenly law restores the light.

I have set the Lord before my face,
      and He has held me safe, secure.
His own right hand bestows my grace,
      His love makes my position sure.
My heart is glad, my joy is free,
I glory in His care for me!

God is showing me the path of life,
      my steps depend upon His care.
No hell of turmoil, pain, or strife
      can harm; His love is everywhere!
The pleasures He bestows are mine;
I trust myself to His design.

                A M. Tindall

June, 1980

App. C. p. 333
ER below

Erik Routley
929 Route 518, R. D. 1
Skillman. NJ 08558
Tel. (609) 921-7806

5 July 80

Dear Adrienne -
      Thank you for your letter. I can't earn ten bucks on this hymn text because I simply think it is very good. Yes, perhaps 'position' is a little cold - but then the language of metrical psalms tends to be that way, and I certainly can't think of an improvement.
      The metre is interesting. I don't think it's impossible. The point is that the opening syllable is unstressed, which apparently your tutor didn't see: you rightly call the first foot an anapaest (even if you can't spell it...). Indeed, there is in existence a tune that fits it exactly.

If you have an <u>English Hymnal</u>, it is at no. 359 in that book. I enclose a scrap of paper with the melody.

You are in good company if the Hymn Society turned you down. They did the same to me. They are a funny bunch. . . .

However, I am actually not travelling any more this summer. I have a job in our summer session which runs through August 8th, and am quite glad to have it because it keeps me here and off the planes, but leaves me some useful spare time. Since I have just been appointed editorial consultant to the new hymnal for the Reformed church I am glad to have a little more time than usual. But some weeks I am teaching 30 hours. Lask week was one but next week isn't.

Don't worry about imagery too much. If you are paraphrasing, you have to stick with the imagery of the original. You might, by the way, be interested to compare your version of Ps. 16 with the one at <u>Congregational Praise</u> 483, if you ever see a copy. That is a 20th century one, though made some time ago by an author now dead.

Greetings!

as ever,

SOUTH CERNEY   Henry Hadow, 1906.   7/5/80

My in - he - ri - tance

July 12, 1980

Dear Dr. Routley:

. . . The last letter has been duly and gratefully received. I have the English Hymnal and found the tune which you'd copied out for me - thanks for that! It is always interesting to note the difference - the "complete" feel one gets when a hymn intended to be sung is set to a tune.

I wanted to ask you a couple of questions about that tune particularly, though. For instance, the high note is hit several times, and the general range of things seems to stay somewhat the same (is that the way to say it? I mean, it seems to be sort of static from line to line.). . . .

Would LOVE to have a Congregational Praise!!!!! Where can one order one? I got my British Baptist and Hymns Ancient and Modern from sending for them, plus the related books, but I don't have an address for Cong. Praise. How much does an editorial consultant do? And I don't even know what denomination (?) the "Reformed" church is.... is that also from the Congregational background?

Really appreciate your patience and letters. And your typing too - mine would look worse except I have this IBM Selectric II that one can correct with by simply backspacing.... I know you're not "fussing" and I don't want you to take more of your time than necessary .... besides, there's something rather endearing in the word "parapjrase" - and a thought-provoking insight - showing how trivial mechanical slips are....

ERIK ROUTLEY
929 Route 518, R. D. 1
SKILLMAN, N. J. 08558
Telephone (609) 921-7806

18 July 80

Dear Adrienne -

Well, yes: you are quite right to notice that SOUTH CERNEY is in fact a rather stodgy tune. But I suppose it would be possible to adapt something else in 6 x 8 for your purposes: how about COLERAINE #333 in the English Hymnal - with two half notes instead of a whole in the first phrase? It's a much better melody really. What you want is a 6 x 8 tune with a long opening note that can be divided, or two short ones that can be untied. You might get a better idea. Hadow, the composer of SOUTH CERNEY, was a learned musicologist at the time EH was published and the tune was commissioned: but perhaps it wasn't a very inspired effort.

You get <u>Congregational Praise</u> by writing to

Tavistock Bookshop
86 Tavistock Place
London, England, WC1H 9HT

I don't know what happens when one pays in dollars but I am sure they will tell you. Alternatively you might try the RSCM, but I don't think they actually stock it: Tavistock is the bookshop of the United Reformed Church, one of whose official books is CP, so you would have no difficulty about getting it. Be sure to ask for the <u>full music</u> edition: otherwise you'll get one with words only.

The Reformed Church in the USA is what used to be the Dutch Reformed Church; it's a small & intelligent body, with two seminaries, one in New Brunswick, NJ and the other in Holland, Michigan. They are calvinistic in theology and presbyterian in church style: so they have something, but not everything, in common with the English Congregationalists. Indeed, I fancy they have a lot more in common than the American Congregationalists do. I was President of the Congregational Church in England (a one year Archbishop) 1970-71 but I have had virtually no contact with the ex-Congregationalists over here. However: the main thing is that these Reformed people are theologically unfussy and sane. . . .

Yes: my typewriter is a shocking speller. I wouldn't do any better on an IBM. I am a self-taught operator. And in too much of a hurry always!

Have a good summer -

as ever,

[signature]

Missing AT letter covering :

"an opposition" [reference lost]

Old Regular Baptists at WCC - my discomfort at the suddenness of the "greetings" to us (after zero eye contact with each other or with congregation), and then requiring our greetings to each other?

Denominational beliefs in a hymnal?

BANGOR being named because it was whistled? [I had heard that a man was going to "register" the name of the hymn tune, which he was whistling. The "registrar" asked him, what is the name of your home town? His home town was Bangor, which he stated. The question had actually been , what is the name of the tune you are whistling and are registering?]

ERIK ROUTLEY
929 Route 518, R. D. 1
SKILLMAN, N. J. 08558
Telephone (609) 921-7806

21 July 80

Dear Adrienne -

When I wrote 'is this an opposition?' [background for this is lost] I meant, 'are you opposing spectatorship and participation?' I don't myself. One must listen before one can participate - remember the Parable? Remember also - what I must have quoted there - the epigram of Joseph Poole, 'Worship is a conversation that began long before you were born and will continue long after you are dead: so don't be surprised if you don't understand everything at once.' Personally I hate gymnastics in church & should have been revolted by all those party-games involving stretching arms upwards and what not. Did you crawl about on the floor to express penitence? If not why not?

Yes, I do think a hymnal should come clean about the beliefs of those who produce it - and I am sure the Christian Science one does, though of course I don't hold some of those beliefs so it wouldn't be one I would use much. But it's right to do so.

No, I don't think BANGOR began by being whistled. I think you may be thinking of HELMSLEY (1765) which apparently did come into someone's head after hearing a hornpipe being whistled in the street.

Temperature here is 105 at the moment - excessive for New Jersey. I am not disposed to write - or do anything else - at length! But always nice to hear from you.

Yours ever,

(signature)

August 14th I think

Dear Dr. Routley:

The enclosed will undoubtedly request some suggestions (I refrain from using the word "require" as I hope you will never feel pressed into response.... please don't let me impose).

It's probably quite clear that my understanding of the Holy Ghost is not yet complete - that's the point where I feel least comfortable with the text. Remembering in John that Jesus said the Comforter would "teach you all things" was part of the background, and in Acts where the Apostles spoke in languages that all the devout men could understand is the background for "reaching all." But I don't feel convinced that the sense of those words "teaching" and "reaching" come across acceptably. Also the word "reaching seems rather ---clinical? It doesn't jell (gel?) I fear.....

It would be appropriate to have a couplet involving "inspiring" and "firing" ... except that firing recollects a kiln.....

And also perhaps the totality of the text is too repetitive and doesn't say enough (not belittling gratitude in that "not say enough" - just that the repetition does not best serve the concept, somehow....)

Oh well, your patience has been proved in the past, and I have set this aside now for several weeks (3) and still think I'd appreciate your looking at it - the tune I did away from the piano, harmonizing it later. A couple of spots I query... I've penciled in another melody note because I realized I'd incorporated a tritone, which probably is not desirable for congregational singing, even though it seems easy once one knows the tune...

A local restaurant - The Flame in Lac du Flambeau - has place mats with Indian lore and local facts on them. Lac du Flambeau was named that by the French who came to this area - "Lake of Torches" - because the Indians would fish at night, using torches to attract the fish. I'm kind of glad to know it's something so beautifully picturesque, rather than a portrayal of Gehenna....

We've had gorgeous weather up here this year - and I've had much fun with my camera (I've become somewhat of a snapshot addict in the past couple of years...). Only two trips to the fudge store so far (what self-restraint!) but be forewarned that it would be best if you cool your weather down a bit out there, as next week I shall indulge in the pleasure of sending various much-appreciated friends some English toffee.... it will of course freeze nicely, once it gets there (to encourage some self-restraint (in which I rarely indulge)), but it must of course arrive in the right number of pieces first... and hopefully not melt into one immense block....

We are due to go home Saturday next week - I'll play Sunday - so if perchance it's easier for you to send your answer to the enclosed to Kenilworth (60043 - how does one sing that with the two zeros?), I'll understand quite well. And of course if you send it here, the mail gets forwarded home after we leave anyway.

Thanks again for your kindness. I do feel that I'm learning about hymns in lots of ways from lots of angles - and hope someday to write a couple that communicate with people in a tangible and good way... your summation that a hymn says something that a person wanted to say only says it better, is a lovely goal to strive for....

Sincerely,

JENNEL
A Tindall 1980

Thank you, heavenly Father,
Thank you, only God.
Thank you for your giving life,
For your holding me in life.
Thank you for creating all,
Ordaining all,
Sustaining all
With your own heavenly power!
Thank you, heavenly Father,
Thank you, only God!

Thank you, heavenly Father,
Thank you, only God.
Thank you for your loving Son,
For the Christ, Emmanuel.
Thank you for his healing all,
Esteeming all,
Redeeming all
With your own heavenly love!
Thank you, heavenly Father,
Thank you, only God!

Thank you, heavenly Father,
Thank you, only God.
Thank you for the Holy Ghost,
For the promised Comforter.
Thank you for its blessing all,
Its reaching all
And teaching all
With your own heavenly law!
Thank you, heavenly Father,
Thank you, only God!

MANUSCRIPT PAPER

Adrienne M. Tindall
July, 1980

Note: Originally "Father-Mother" in place of "heavenly Father".
As references to God are becoming more inclusive, "Father-Mother" would be the preferred form; I don't recall discussing the term with Erik.

ER harmonization p. 62; Rev. pp. 64, 65; App. C. p. 369
ER p. 60

Erik Routley
929 Route 518, R. D. 1
Skillman, NJ 08558
Tel. (609) 921-7806

19 August 80

Dear Adrienne -

Thank you for this last one [p.59]. It is attractive and friendly, and I like it a good deal. I think it's a good text, and its simplicity doesn't trouble me. I don't like things that pretend to be simple but are merely silly: this is not like that.

In stanza 1 you should think again about lines 3-4 which I think don't achieve the effect you were planning. For one thing, I shouldn't introduce the first person singular just there unless you propose to make the whole hymn a first-person hymn. It would be just as good if you said 'holding us in life.' Then, I don't think two lines ending with 'life' are quite what you want; I can see that you wanted to throw the emphasis back on the participles 'giving' in one line and 'holding' in the other: but although this goes nicely in reading, the music will kill the effect because it is rising form 'A' on one _life_ to B on the next, so all the emphasis will be thrown back to the repeated word. Since there's no rhyme scheme at this point I would compose a new third line at this point. Anyhow 'your giving life' is a bit gawky.

In stanza 2 I am not sure about 'your loving Son', and want something like 'your mighty Son': you are going to have 'love' a little later in the verse.

Stanza 3 has something I can't wear but which is easily alterable. We never refer to the Holy Spirit as IT. I know the Greek word is neuter: but the Hebrew word is feminine, and Christian theology insists that the Holy Spirit is a Person: so IT won't do. HE is normal, and if you want to go out way ahead you can perhaps write 'she' (in this case, 'her'). But not at any price, IT.

The tune is very pleasant indeed. I have produced a harmonization revised at a few points for the sake of smoothness, and suggest that you consider one or two modifications of the melody. The point with a long tune like this is to make it easy for a congregation to remember. This is a point which modern American composers often overlook because they always think of a congregation as a choral society reading a score. Real hymnody thinks of a congregation as a

60

group of non-musicians singing by ear and writes melodies accordingly. Repetition of phrases is important, though there isn't much we can do about that here: but intervals are important too, and you are quite right to suspect that tritonal melodic phrase, not because it's 'incorrect' - it isn't necessarily - but because singers won't get hold of it easily. I suggest a B rather than the A you thought of because it leads nicely towards the climax-note via the following C#. Another thing congregations don't take to is leaving a note by a leap and returning to it at once. I am suggesting at two points what might be done to avoid this.

But the whole thing is shaping up nicely. It will make a most useful simple hymn on the Trinity and I don't want to lose track of it.

So glad you have had a good summer.

Yours ever -

September 2, 1980

Dear Dr. Routley:

"Thank you heavenly Father" has been percolating on the back burner all week, even though many things have precluded my giving it undivided attention until now. We've sent two girls off to college, one for her final year at Duke and one to start as a transfer sophomore at Rockford College, squared away the high school sophomore who starts back tomorrow, spent Labor Day (appropriately) painting the kitchen ceiling and washing windows, curtains, louvers.... I can see why women, who've given priority to household-homemaker type things, have not really contributed so much in the way of massive creative efforts in art, etc..... Not a takedown on homemaking there, either - just an acknowledgment that the art of homemaking is time- and effort-consuming.....

I love your harmonization. At first I baulked (sp?) a bit at the e-f#-g-f#-g of the third line of text - seemed treadmilly. But there was an awkward place right after that spot in my version, which your pattern resolves nicely. And of course the stepwise motion is easier to sing. I do like to bear in mind the congregation's ease in singing, particularly as my own church has no choir to help them....

The several possibilities for the ending really all seem not bad. I think perhaps I would opt for a-f#, f#-d-b-c#-d. The harmonization of that seems uniquely satisfying. That does sacrifice the musical device of the descending fifth on "Thank you" but it makes singing easier too, which seems well worth it... I had already taken out the descending fifth on the second-to-last "thank you" because things were seeming a little uninteresting.

Textwise I'm still feeling not quite settled. . . . The double "s" is stanza 2 is probably bad, eh? One could mention other things there; I didn't put in "mighty" because the tone of the text comes over to me as a gentle thing - but perhaps I'm only feeling that, thinking about an individual singing? Maybe my "gentle" feeling isn't really inherent in the text or tune (or harmonies), but is just in my own inner ear....

The third stanza I've thought about a lot. . . . I read the article in the Interpreter's Dictionary of the Bible to get a feel for the use of the term "Holy Ghost" or "Holy Spirit," and today looked at my interlinear translation of John's Gospel.... I can relate to the "he" even though I personally would not think of it that way. There are so many biblical passages that "feel" different from that to me! Not that I feel the "he" is denied; it's just that it's more a spirit of inspiration and insight into things spiritual that lifts and moves people to understand and speak out to their fellows about God and His will for all.... . .

I'm thinking that the Holy Ghost / he parallels to the temptations in the wilderness where Jesus was tempted "of the devil...." I don't really personalize that devil, even though there is scriptural reference made to a "person" of devil. Is all that theologically unacceptable to Christian teachings?

I've sent off for information about getting <u>Congregational Praise</u>; if only I would be efficient about studying all the material I get, I'd be extremely well-informed.....

Have Xeroxed [and enclosed] your harmonization, as I don't know if you had a copy or not.... I really like it a lot.... and am pleased that you like the text too, that's a great compliment, and a great encourager....

Queenie

Thank You! (Final Version)

Thank You, heavenly Father,
  thank You, only God.
Thank You for the gift of life,
  power to live and move and be.
Thank You for creating all,
    ordaining all,
    maintaining all
with Your own heavenly power!
thank You, heavenly Father,
  thank You, only God.

Thank You, heavenly Father,
  thank You, only God.
Thank You for Your gracious Son,
  for the Christ, Emmanuel.
Thank You for his healing all,
    esteeming all,
    redeeming all
with Your own heavenly love!
Thank You, heavenly Father,
  thank You, only God.

Thank You, heavenly Father,
  that You, only God.
Thank You for the Holy Ghost,
  for the promised Comforter.
Thank you for embracing all,
    for reaching all
    and teaching all
with Your own heavenly law!
Thank You, heavenly Father,
  thank You, only God.

A. M. Tindall

App. C p. 369
ER p. 66

Tune: Adrienne M Tindall
4/80
Harmonization:
© Erik Routley
8/80

App. C p. 369
ER p. 66

ERIK ROUTLEY
929 Route 518, R. D. 1
Skillman, N. J. 08558
Tel. (609) 921-7806

5 September 80

Dear Adrienne -

First, thank you very much for a handsome parcel of figure-expanding things that arrived the other day. We are enjoying them shamelessly.

I am glad you felt kindly towards what I said about your hymn, which I still think a very nice one.

All I really have to say in answer to your letter is about this theological business. The real point is that we all have our hangups about Christian Doctrine: there are parts of it which we all wonder if we go along with, and for each person those are different. But beyond a certain point it isn't a good idea to let one's hangups show in public! I mean - there are things one discusses with friends and people one knows well: but it's something else when you're talking to, or writing for, people you've never seen, and that is the field in which hymns work. So one either has to go along with orthodox Christian doctrine or keep one's mouth shut. There's no doubt about the Holy Spirit's being a Person of the Trinity, so in public conversation about him we simply have to go along. If we are saying what we really don't believe, then we should say nothing; but if it's a case of 'I don't believe it yet', then it's safe & proper to behave as if one did. Indeed, that is the way one grows in the Faith. After all, it's all inexpressible anyhow, and human language can only approximate to an expression of the whole truth: but if we're in the human language business, as teachers and hymn writers are, then we have to make the best of it.

It's interesting about the Devil. I think it's impossible to think of the Devil otherwise than as a person - I think even of my dog and my car as people because I am like that. But I know they aren't people really: and I know also that the essence of the Devil is malignant nothingness; so he's the archetype non-person. (Does that offend the sexists to refer to the Devil as HE? Never thought of that. Must send a note down to the Seminary). I happen to think - and I suspect it's not theologically disreputable - that it's better to think of too many things as persons than too few. Too abstract an approach to life tends to breed highbrow sentimentality - a condition which I find abominable! I go along, in fact, with St. Francis at that point.

Still, I know that I'm calling across a bit of a chasm here, and I could be saying what doesn't appeal to Christian Science, so I put it a bit tentatively.

I am putting your hymn where I can lay hands on it easily when occasions arise. Thank you again for it.

As ever,

Missing AT letter re

        question re: send Thank you to Boston with ER harmonization?

    text enclosed: "Dear God, I would be holy"!

    integrity in editing, with a list of situations

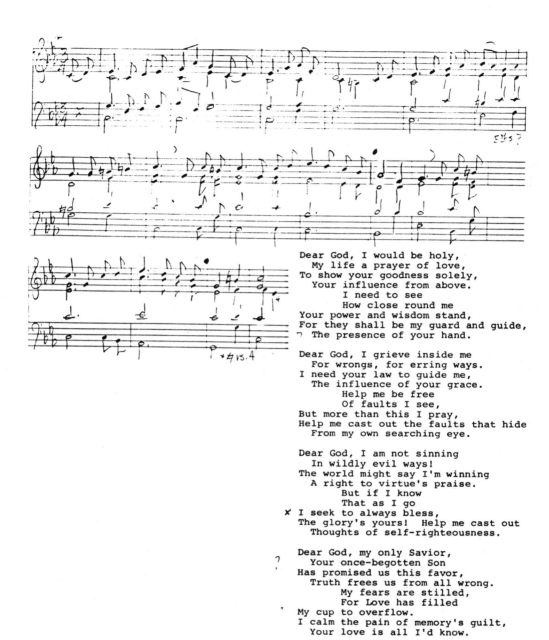

Dear God, I would be holy,
    My life a prayer of love,
To show your goodness solely,
    Your influence from above.
        I need to see
        How close round me
Your power and wisdom stand,
For they shall be my guard and guide,
    The presence of your hand.

Dear God, I grieve inside me
    For wrongs, for erring ways.
I need your law to guide me,
    The influence of your grace.
        Help me be free
        Of faults I see,
But more than this I pray,
Help me cast out the faults that hide
    From my own searching eye.

Dear God, I am not sinning
    In wildly evil ways!
The world might say I'm winning
    A right to virtue's praise.
        But if I know
        That as I go
I seek to always bless,
The glory's yours! Help me cast out
    Thoughts of self-righteousness.

Dear God, my only Savior,
    Your once-begotten Son
Has promised us this favor,
    Truth frees us from all wrong.
        My fears are stilled,
        For Love has filled
My cup to overflow.
I calm the pain of memory's guilt,
    Your love is all I'd know.

                    Adrienne Tindall
                    September, 1980

Rev. p. 76; App. C p. 368
ER pp. 69-70 [green spot: system 2, measure 4-5; red spot penultimate measure]

68

ERIK ROUTLEY
929 Route 518, R. D. 1
Skillman, N. J. 08558
Tel. (609) 921-7806

19 September 80

Dear Adrienne -

Yes, it's very nice in most ways, though I think I share your doubts here and there. I am not sure that we need too many more of these highly devotional pieces; in any hymnal I edited (if it were for my own sake alone which it never would be) there would be just a few real classics of that kind, but no more: it's profoundly difficult to write a hymn of first-person devotion that becomes universal in its application. 'Shepherd divine' does it, and so does Donne's 'Wilt thou forgive?' but I can think of precious few during the last 150 years that really do: so you're taking on a considerable task here. And it is certainly better than most. There are two technical points which need looking at.

(a) I 8 - 'the presence of your hand' - what is the syntactical force of this phrase: it seems to be hanging loose. What verb does it govern?

(b) III 6 - 'to always bless' obviously will have to be altered - it's a shameless split infinitive.

I am also in trouble with 'your once-begotten Son': 'only begotten' yes, but did anybody ever think He was twice-begotten? Surely that phrase doesn't mean quite what you meant it to mean. 'Filled my cup to overflow' isn't really English either, - 'to overflowing' is a legitimate phrase, if a little antique: - 'to' being there a preposition going with 'overflowing' a noun: but 'to overflow' is an infinitive: and that can't follow a verb like 'fill.' Sorry to be pedantic, but one has to be.

The tune is nice too; I react thus -

(1) I am a bit sorry it comes home to the tonic at the half way point, and on the same note that you finish on. This makes the whole a bit key-tied.

(2) In every stanza the end of line 4 is a full stop: and at the mid-point of the tune you hurry us on with only a half-beat's

69

breath, whereas after phrases 2 and 6 you give us a longer pause. I thought that slightly odd.

(3) No, there are no offensive 5ths at the point you mention and the harmony is quite all right: but there is a case of 'hidden 5ths' at the point where I have put a little mark; hidden 5ths are dodgy and difficult to identify, but this is a clear case - don't you feel that the descent from treble B flat to C over the bass A flat to G is a little unsatisfactory? (The problem is that A flat, which isn't written in the treble interval but is implied).

(4) I am slightly unhappy about the point I have worked with a green spot. I wouldn't myself end a phrase on a dominant 7th, or, except in unusual cases, on a discord at all. I'd put an F minor chord there.

Now to the other things. By all means send 'Thank you' to Boston, and use my harmony if you like. Strictly you ought to tell whoever you send it to that the harmonies are mine, and my copyright: but I shall certainly not make a fuss about it.

Your general question about integrity is an awkward one. The principle is, I think, that while it is right for an editor to respect what a poet or composer writes, the poet or composer, if they go into the field of hymns, must be ready to accept suggestions and amendments. We sing so many well known hymns otherwise than as their composers wrote them that that has to be regarded as an accepted convention. So (a) if the author or composer is alive one always asks if one may make an alteration when asking for the permission to reprint, and doesn't alter if the author doesn't agree; (b) if the author or composer is dead, but the work is still in copyright, the person acting as executor has the right to say, 'as he/she wrote it or not at all': they have to be asked. But (c) if the whole thing is out of copyright, then the thing is simply a matter of the editor's judgment. What then decides whether it's done in good taste or not is the result of two lines of inquiry - (a) did the person who altered it really take the trouble to understand the original before altering it?, and (b) does the altered version make as good music, or as good literature, as the original? If it's yes to both, it's a legitimate alteration. So to your specific questions -

(a) a poem metrically smoothed out to make a hymn: not many examples of this but 'Let us with a gladsome mind' is certainly one. The later versions of 'Be thou my Vision' are another.

Both, in my view, successful and sensible because the writers of the originals didn't in either case expect them to be sung.

(b) Adapting from "thee' to 'you' seems to work with early 20th century hymns but not with earlier ones. Westminster Praise 41 ["You, living Christ, our eyes behold"] has had that treatment and so has WP 51 ["You that know the Lord is gracious"], and I think both work: WP 41 was actually praised by the author, and WP 51 was authorized by the copyright holder. But I know of only one earlier hymn which seems to me successfully adaptable in that way, and that is 'We praise and bless thee, gracious Lord' translation from K.J.P. Spitta which I expect you don't know. Certainly it's foolish to do this with 18th century classics and most of the time it isn't necessary at all.

(c) Change because of doctrine: there I can't think of a case where this has been done either well or legitimately. No. If there are nits of Christian doctrine you want to avoid, I think you must undoubtedly give up the hymns that imply it. I think 'Dear Lord & Father' is very close to being good writing & bad doctrine so I never in any circumstances choose it. (Does the chasm begin to show?) I don't know - especially after what you kindly furnished me with in your letter - where the shoe does pinch in your own case; but I'd say, if the doctrine won't do, the hymn won't do. Personally I don't have many hangups, though I suppose I might be uncomfortable with some of the 19th century Catholic hymns about Mary. My troubles are with hymns that state too little doctrine, not those that state too much. But there I would be firm. Let those who differ from Christian orthodox doctrine write their own hymns.

(d) Very small changes in a hymn tune for the sake of metre: usually that is no problem at all, provided that one doesn't upset the melodic line. There have been a lot of such changes which have upset the melodic line, or altered the cadences, and I would rule those out: but hymnals use FOREST GREEN for 76.76, DCM, and 7.6.8.6 D without damaging it. Pratt Green writes a hymn for CHRISTE SANCTORUM, 'Christ is the world's light' (Westminster 7) which is in 10. 11. 11. 6 instead of 11. 11. 11. 5, but it doesn't in any way upset the tune which it requires one slur to be put in and another to be taken out.

There is always a point beyond which one shouldn't go; and the discerning of that point is a matter in which we often need second opinions because we may have crossed the line without knowing it. But from a distance it's easier to see the line than when you're close to it. (Roman roads in Britain are often traceable from an aircraft and not on the ground). The line represents the boundary of that territory where good taste, good manners, and, in the end, charity, are in control. The worst errors and trespasses are committed by people who say, as almost everybody does nowadays, 'I don't understand this, so I will alter it.' That's <u>fatal</u>. It's the way to drain off the hymn texts and tunes so much of that special quality which gives them tang and individuality and excellence. It's the 'Reader's Digest' mind and one must watch for its influences, and fuss when one detects them!

But when one has said all that - there's always this: that hymn writing and composition are very much a community business. I wrote a tune in 1972 and sent it to Gelineau, and he sent it back saying it was very nice, but why didn't I write that, instead of this, in its last phrase. I at once saw how right he was, and it is published like that. One phrase in Gelineau's 'By gracious powers' (<u>EP</u> 48) is actually mine. One measure of <u>Westminster</u> 41 [VINDOLANDA / Routley] is by John Wilson. One line in the words of <u>Westminster</u> 56 ["All who love and serve your city"] is by - I forget whom now, but it's better than what I first wrote. And so on. It is always happening. I suppose one could say that it's one thing to tinker unasked with somebody else's work and another to accept, after asking, a suggestion which is obviously right. It's one thing to invade somebody else's privacy, and another to be hospitable yourself.

Always glad to hear from you: you do it in such a kind way!

Yours ever,

<u>WKRoutley</u>

October 21, 1980

Dear Dr. Routley:

If you are opening this the day after you come to Brookfield I shall have to say "I told myself so..."

And it doesn't seem possible that a month has elapsed since your last letter. No, I've not been sitting here with a crushed spirit because of the many flaws in the hymn and tune you looked at then. A couple of them are easy - "The presence of your hand" was a careless error from trying to type the text without a copy in front of me, and was supposed to be "The holding of your hand," which, of course, means virtually nothing to you out of context anyway. Split infinitives are easily changed. I wonder what usage is doing to the language. Probably I'm preceding use in my ineptness - I just wasn't thinking about it - but aren't "people" splitting more infinitives these days? Don't bother to answer; a hymn should be correct in any case. And the last stanza I'm thinking over. I really kind of liked "my cup to overflow," although it was merely poesy and not thought-through verbiage at all.

The total text I must reconsider though, because it really was aimed a little differently than I think it came across... At least from where it ended up aiming.... The first stanza was kind of general, and then 2 and 3 were so specifically aimed that 4 had to follow, and 1 be revised. So perhaps just 2 - 3 - 4 would be enough (now I'm going to have to include some form in the letter ... it's really not polite to go on and on about something without being more specific). Probably it relates to that chasm -- but the thrust is more or less the acknowledgment of mistakes and errant ways, but not in the sense that man is a sinner no matter what he does. You see, it's often given me uncomfortable feelings to read together a confessional prayer with a congregation, which talks

73

about my grievous sins, etc., which infer that I would have been one of the ones shouting "Crucify him!" Maybe I would not have recognized the Messiah... but maybe I <u>would</u> have, and maybe I'd have been following (even pretty closely, maybe), and I can't just accept the idea that I would have participated in the desertion / crucifixion of the Lord.

On the other hand, God forbid that I claim human perfection! Of all the people I know, I'm the one most acquainted with my own shortcomings.....

So that's where the text was coming from.....

And as for Brookfield, well, it's a long drive away, an hour plus some, but I plan to be there. Unless the crowd is overpowering I shall make myself known - I'll be the one who asks you to autograph a brand new (from Tavistock) <u>Congregational Praise</u>...! I told them you "sent" me, and your name was as good as 100% endorsement -- I haven't even gotten the bill yet....

Thanks so much for the rest of the letter - extremely helpful as an insight into honest alterings of texts or tunes .... your analogy(?) of being hospitable vs. intruding on someone's privacy is particularly appealing and clear to me.

<u>WORSHIP Magazine</u> came to other day. As usual, I opened it to the Table of Contents, scanning for your name.... and this time there you were .... and I delight in reading your style, because I can with an aural memory of Garrett almost hear you speaking it (is that verb too split? I'll bet it is.... sorry!) I've written a couple of things that have been printed and I always feel that the editing "smoothed out" some of the individual style, so that it doesn't sound like "me" any more. Not that sounding like me is all that vital (as I'm only me...) but you have a very enjoyable style, and humor is always peeking through and I find it pleasing to "encounter" you in such articles.

And you said everything I was trying to say in July [about the Old Regular Baptists' greetings] and got into hot water trying to verbalize..... so I can just quote "one of the world's leading hymnologists" (BACCM Newsletter Sept 1980) that I was trying to say something like, "Where is the line drawn between 'community' and 'gang,' 'shared living' and 'invasion of privacy,' and 'liturgy' and 'organized games'? I really don't want to be curmudgeonly about all this, but I [did] feel a bit suffocated [and uncomfortable] by all this contrived cheerfulness." (WORSHIP pp. 449-450). I remember thinking since that time (in Princeton) that it was kind of like walking into the telling of a punch line, and being expected to laugh - when the main body of the joke, and therefore the "punch" of the punch line, had been missed. . . .

I am looking forward very much to Brookfield, as I have been ever since I heard it was going to be, and shall see you there (shall have seen??).

Oh yes, I would really like to follow up one quote - well, maybe two while I'm pestering.... Thomas Poole "Religion is a conversation..." I don't know where I would find out about him or who he is..... Also, in your Sept. 5 letter you said, "Too abstract an approach life tends to breed highbrow sentimentality.... I go along, in fact, with St. Francis on that point." How would I most efficiently find our what St. Francis (of Assisi?) said?

Sincerely,

(Revised form)

O God, I grieve within me
      for faults, for erring ways.
I need Your law to guide me --
      The influence of Your grace.
        Help me be free
        of faults I see!
      But more than this I pray:
help me cast out the faults that hide
      from my own searching eye.

Dear Lord, I am not sinning
      in wildly evil ways!
The world might say I'm winning
      a right to virtue's praise.
        But if I know
        that as I go
I always seek to bless,
the glory's Yours! Help me cast out
      thoughts of self-righteousness.

Dear Lord, my only Savior
      is Jesus Christ, your Son.
He promises this favor:
      Truth frees us from all wrong.
        I will not fear!
        For Love is here
to govern me each day.
Faults purged through gracious words and deeds:
      for this, O Lord, I pray.

AMT 1980

That's not a good inversion in the last line, is it.
Oh well, I've got to "on to other things", so this has to be finished for now....

App. C p. 368
ER p. 81

Hymn Festival

Erik Routley

with

Richard Proulx, Organist

Sunday, October 26th 3:00 p.m.
St. Barbara Church

HYMN SINGING, 26 October 1980

PRELUDE

Introduction

1. Praise the Lord, ye heavens adore him	Worship II 229
2. Praise, my soul, the King of heaven	Worship II 228

OLD TESTAMENT: Sirach 35

God's generosity to us and our duty to Him

3. For the fruits of his creation	Cantate Domino Supplement-876
4. Jesus my Lord, how rich thy grace	Manuscript

EPISTLE: II Timothy 4

Christian Courage

5. Christ is the King	Worship II 44
6. Awake, our souls, away, our fears	Manuscript

GOSPEL: St. Luke 18

Penitence and Prayer

7. Jesus, name all names above	Festival Praise 5
8. As the bridegroom to his chosen	Festival Praise 4 Worship II 26

Epilogue

9. Lord God of hosts, whose purpose never swerving	Presbyterian Hymnbook 1955-288
10. O praise ye the Lord	Worship II 210

POSTLUDE

Text	Tune
English Evangelical 1798	AUSTRIA European Catholic 1797
Anglican 1834	Anglican 1867
English Methodist 1973	Anglican 1970
English Congregational 1740	GRAEFENBERG German pietist 1653 W-II 256
English Ecumenical 1930	Lutheran 1609
Isaac Watts 1707	DEUS TUORUM European Catholic 1753
Greek 8th century	J.S. Bach 18th century
Medieval mystical poem	English 1968
American Protestant	English Catholic (WELWYN)
Anglican	C.H.H. Parry

AS THE BRIDEGROOM TO HIS CHOSEN

from John Tauler, 1300-61
Tr. Emma F. Bevan, 1858

PETER CUTTS, 1969

8.7.8.7.6.

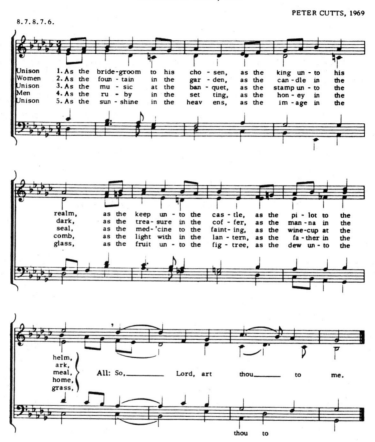

Unison 1. As the bride-groom to his cho - sen, as the king un - to his
Women 2. As the foun - tain in the gar - den, as the can - dle in the
Unison 3. As the mu - sic at the ban - quet, as the stamp un - to the
Men 4. As the ru - by in the set - ting, as the hon - ey in the
Unison 5. As the sun - shine in the heav - ens, as the im - age in the

realm, as the keep un - to the cas - tle, as the pi - lot to the
dark, as the trea - sure in the cof - fer, as the man - na in the
seal, as the med - 'cine to the faint - ing, as the wine - cup at the
comb, as the light with - in the lan - tern, as the fa - ther in the
glass, as the fruit un - to the fig - tree, as the dew un - to the

helm,
ark,
meal,   } All: So,_____ Lord, art thou_____ to me.
home,
grass,

thou to

-8-

ERIK ROUTLEY
929 Route 518, R. D. 1
Skillman, N. J. 08558
Tel. (609) 921-7806

29 October 80

Dear Adrienne -

How good to see you on Sunday - especially brandishing your copy of <u>Congregational Praise</u>! The sight of it takes me back a long way now: for when the editing committee first met, 13 October 1944, I was not quite 27! I could go on a long time about the experience of monthly editorial meetings over four years. I was of course the youngest member of the committee of fifteen, and the eldest was 47 years older than I. I still think it is a good and lively book. Curiously enough I only had seven years during which I actually used it as minister of a church, because when it was published I was on a campus, and when I returned to the pastorate in 1959 I went to a church that didn't use it! So I only had a real chance to see how it worked between 1967 and 1974. Ah well: I hope you enjoy it. I warmly appreciate your acquiring it.

I am happy now about your hymn [p. 76]. I think a colon after 'favor' in stanza 3 would be right - line 4 defines what is announced in line 3. I now think it is very nice.

And I agree with you 105% about confession of sin. I am always complaining about written-out prayers of confession that make me admit to sins I can't afford, haven't time for, and am not interested in! Your lines touch the right spot.

Poole: I think you're referring to my friend the Reverend Joseph Poole (b. 1909) who from 1958 to 1977 was Precentor of Coventry, and who is personally responsible for the quite remarkable liturgies they have in the new cathedral there. He is my master in all liturgical matters. He has written hardly anything except what he did for the cathedral. I understand that the Evensong booklet from which the quotation came - 'Evensong is a conversation which began long before you were born and will continue long after you are dead' - is out of print. I know he has recently written a book, and I have heard that he can't get it published - probably because it is not trendy enough. If I ever hear that it has come out I will tell you. It is he who pointed out to me the alternative to that awful modern response - 'The Lord be with you' - and ALSO with you', which I always find clumsy and inept. He made his people reply, 'The Lord bless you' - which is exactly what is written in the Book of Ruth, chapter 2 v 4. That is the sort of thing he noticed. (I insist on that response at Westminster!).

81

St. Francis. If ever you come across G. K. Chesterton's book, St. Francis of Assisi - published ages ago, about 1920 I think - snap it up. I don't know other books about him though there must be many. But that's the one that really interprets him. See if any library near you is intelligent enough to have it. My copy disappeared long ago, I'm afraid.

I didn't get a chance to see you after the show at Brookfield . . . I thought that bunch were very responsive; and having run such things in other RC centres I was agreeably surprised by the way they took it up. Richard Proulx, playing a perfectly shocking instrument, did us proud, I thought. He is very good news indeed for Chicago - a delightful person and a first-rate musician.

Anyhow it was very good of you to drive all that way on a Sunday afternoon. That Dr. Iris Zahara, by the way (who introduced me) is a very fine musician indeed and somebody well worth knowing. She lives at Flossmoor - not exactly next door to you. But she's doing a great deal to help Catholics appreciate good music.

I must now turn to the rest of the heap of mail I found waiting after 9 days away from home!

Yours ever,

November 14, 1980

Dear Dr. Routley:

Normally I don't allow pestering without some hymnic effort to include -- keeps me working, and cuts down pestering. But I ran across the enclosed text in an old hymnal I got and recalled your mention of "simple hymns on the Trinity" I think you said. Had you run across this one? The word "children" specializes its use of course, ...well anyway I thought I'd send you it just for interest.

And also because I wanted to be the 17th person (or maybe even a higher number...) to look forward to your memoirs or autobiography or whatever would interest you to write.... I'll bet hymn enthusiasts in particular could get wonderful insights into all things hymnic through the various things you've done. Like the story about Peter Cutts and your nap [ER wanted a nap, so to keep his guest occupied for the length of a nap, suggested writing a tune, which took Cutts only 20 minutes ... the nap was <u>very</u> short...]. Were you the minister at the time? That hymn and tune I find uniquely satisfying -- amazing how a tune can so fit the text, can have so perfect a "feel" to it, as to take an already exciting text (or perhaps satisfying text is a better description) and turn it from black and white into living color.... And your background in pulling hymnals together (<u>Congregational Praise</u> -- wouldn't you like to write down your recollections? And <u>Ecumenical Praise</u> would've been very different, with just four of you all very experienced... and whatever other projects you've worked on...), all that would be informative, interesting and enjoyable reading for church-interested people. No question about the fact that you write books readily, so <u>that</u> part couldn't cause undue effort. The style could be so relaxed as to make the material appealing - I mean comments like you made in Brookfield, where the first hymn "has two stanzas, which is just right for this hymn.... some hymns would be better if they had no stanzas at all..." -- I have to admit that your sense of humor almost invariably grabs me (shocking slang?) and this tired old world needs all the laughs it can get....

But all of that in relation to a specialized field a lot of people don't even think about, an area - church and church music and hymns - which perhaps epitomizes Christian life at its potential best, focused on God and God-centered, recognizing, acknowledging and feeling the gratitude to God for His love, for His Son, for everything ... (I guess I'd certainly better include the Holy Ghost in that list - and with a much more comfortable sense of it because of my hymn and your letters). So next time you have a weekend free....

from   THE SABBATH HYMN BOOK: for The Service of Song in the House of the Lord. New York, Mason Brothers, Boston, J. E. Tilton & Co., 1858.

> Hymn 1076 (credited to Montgomery)
> Children's Praise to the Trinity
>
> Glory to the Father give,
> God, in whom we move and live!
> Children's prayers he deigns to hear;
> Children's songs delight his ear.

Glory to the Son we bring,
Christ our Prophet, Priest, and King!
Children, raise your sweetest strain
To the Lamb, for he was slain.

Glory to the Holy Ghost!
Be this day a Pentecost;
Children's minds may he inspire, --
Touch their tongues with holy fire.

Glory in the highest be
To the blessed Trinity
For the gospel from above,
For the word that "God is love."

ERIK ROUTLEY
929 Route 518, R. D. 1
Skillman, N. J. 08558
Tel. (609) 921-7806
19 November 80

Dear Adrienne -

Yes, indeed, that hymn is by Montgomery, and was written for the Sheffield Sunday Schools in 1825. It's not bad, though not vintage Montgomery, I think - 'to the Lamb, for he was slain' is a sort of cliché which I should have doubts about now. And I'm not sure that it is about the Trinity so much as about each Person separately - which a lot of so-called Trinity hymns are. The best stanza is the last, I think. It's quite nice but possibly a bit dated - which the best of Montgomery isn't.

Well well - I doubt if many people are as nice as you are & would be interested in my autobiography! Since I still have a rather useful memory it would probably be too long for anybody to stand; and whatever I've done, somebody else has done better. Perhaps when I retire, if I ever can.....

But yes, I was indeed the Minister at St. James's Newcastle when Peter Cutts stayed with me and wrote that adorable tune. He'd been with me to church in the morning, and our organist was looking rather ill, so I told the organist to stay home for the evening service (he lived, and indeed still does, 15 miles away) and Peter Cutts played the service. He is, among other things, a first-rate organist. I agree with you that his BRIDEGROOM tune simply lights up those words.

Congregational Praise takes me back a long time: 13 October 1944 was our first meeting. A wonderful experience, monthly meetings for four years - I was 26 when we started on it. Much more peaceful and delightful than any such meetings would be now! We didn't all agree, but in true Congregational style we never took a vote, and didn't make a single decision until everybody was prepared to go along with it. In one case a hymn which a clear majority wanted was omitted because one member felt he couldn't stay on the committee if we included it: we felt at that stage that no hymn was worth that. That same member - who would have been 106 if he were still alive and in fact died in 1948 - and who started out by thinking of me as a rather conceited young upstart - towards the end of our deliberations passed across the table a book of his: 'I shan't be needing it for much longer - you'd better have it' and it was a first edition of the collected hymns of Doddridge! Good days, those, when somebody 43 years older than oneself behaves like that. Goodness - history! when I think back I find that the members of the committee were born in, let's see, 1871, 1873, 1874, 1884, 1900, 1901, 1906, 1908, and 1917 (me): I have left one or two out - but a 46 year span wasn't bad! Among the actual contributors, committee members were Eric Thiman (music chairman: lots of tunes), J. F. Shepherd, the Grand Old Man (no. 710), Eric Shave (tune 466, rattling good one, too), Marjorie Renton (720 [edited the French tune?]); and oddly enough not a single text was written by a member of the committee. But I thought at the time that every member contributed something which made the book better. I think one of the best texts in the book is 532 ["Give me, O lord, the strength that is in Thee" by Henry Child Carter]: they love it on our campus - we sang it last Tuesday (but as set in Westminster Praise [26, set to KINGSTANDING / Routley]).

Blessings!

December 1 already

Dear Dr. Routley:

I daren't look too closely at the calendar in an analytical way; not only do I have a vague feeling of what the next three weeks include, but realize your own schedule may well have a greater sense of superabundance....

So I am dashing off the enclosed. The text is one I've known for several years, and have loved the thought ever since... And I hoped that for our carol sings for neighbors and friends this year (two sessions around the organ) I could perhaps set this text somehow and share it with them. Could you look it over, and comment on any and everything? Which tune do you think is better for it? When I attempt a carol I still find myself harmonically a bit embarrassed, although the thought of lyricism and / or simplicity seems the most important consideration.... The 6/8 tune might well be better with a naive "story" text rather than this text, perhaps [other tune lost]....

Also, sometime around Christmas will come a box from the English Toffee Source - I didn't have a card enclosed, as two daughters were the emissaries - but you'll realize why it's coming, won't you? And a second (egad!!!) box of English toffee will be coming about the same time - with an all-winter-long source, and which I think might just be a bit tastier, in my estimation. In any event, I hope your enjoyment is still in effect.... for the whole quantity!

I'm always keenly aware of how grateful I am to be able to get your ideas on things hymnic... thanks so much!

Sincerely,

[Note: I've found only the final version of "Christmas 1970": see p. 90]

ERIK ROUTLEY
929 Route 518, R. D. 1
Skillman, N. J. 08558
Tel. (609) 921-7806

4 December 80

Dear Adrienne -

Thanks for this [p. 90]. I think the 6/8 tune in all
ways preferable to the other. A carol is essentially a dance, and that
tune sounds like one. I have pencilled in a few suggestions you might
consider - simply to make the counterpoint run a little more smoothly,
and to avoid the thump of major on the first strong beat of line 2, which I
think gives a slightly key-tied impression. But they are only the merest
details, and the whole tune is very nice and innocent. You can probably
use the other for something else, but the 6/8 one is the one for these
words.

To be honest I wouldn't alter 'his' to 'their' because 'their'
isn't English; and since there's a 'men' in the next stanza it isn't worth it.
(Do you realize - I was told only to-day) that somebody is heading up a
new revision of the BIBLE to avoid language that offends feminine
militants. Need I say this is emanating from Princeton Seminary. I am
beginning to regret even the concessions I have made to this gang.

It's a nice poem: I am not sure that I really understand the
opening stanza: the total message, of course, comes through quite
clearly in the succeeding stanzas. If I were amending the poem at all I
think I would also question the word 'large', which, except in its original
sense of 'generous', is, I think, a rather prosaic word - and 'large city' is
very awkward to sing! I should also wonder whether everyone keeps
Christmas nowadays. I seem to recall that there is quite a bunch of
people who keep Hanukkah (if that's how it is spelt). I wonder if one
could say, 'In this our city now, where Christians all in their own ways....'
Perhaps the author doesn't want to confine Christmas to Christians:
but I can't really take 'everyone'. Maybe you would think about that - but
it is worth resolving! You certainly need to revise the original stanza 1
because the first line is deficient in one syllable.

Ah, toffee! My figure is beyond praying for anyhow. How fortunate that is!

Have a blessed Christmas in your own home anyhow!

yours ever -

[Note: I've found only the final version of "Christmas 1970": see p. 90]

December 18, 1980

Dear Dr. Routley:

Thanks for the help with the carol! I certainly preferred your harmonization of the second line's beginning -- in fact you can tell I liked all your suggestions... I 'm going to enclose a copy of the "final" thing tomorrow when we get it from the printers. . . .

The enclosed carbon copy [paper about the Shroud of Turin] I've thought of sending to you to read over ever since I typed the original (and copy) at Thanksgiving. Nothing in it to ask about actually, it's Jenny's (daughter #2) paper for her computer course, and the subject I thought might interest you . . . .

I also plan to enclose a little gadget which you may recognize. If you do, a second one won't hurt. If you don't, try it! It's to hold recalcitrant hymnals open....

Have a joyous holiday, with Christmas everything it should be. How easy it sometimes is to join the rushings around! We are doing a bit of both -- rushing around until Sunday (after I play in the morning), and then heading up to Wisconsin for almost two weeks. How about the "our" in stanza 1 avoiding the "everyone" problem in the carol? Seeing as "we" are singing the carol doesn't that seem rather workable? Thanks again for your help -

Best wishes,

Adrienne

P. S. I'm afraid the carbon copy of Jenny's paper exposes how much I rely on this correcting typewriter; I did that on my old SCM....

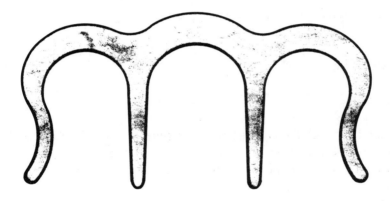

It Could As Well Be Bethlehem

DUNAWAY
Max Dunaway, 1970
Adrienne Tindall, 1980

1. It could as well be Beth - le - hem, year one, With
2. And there could be to-night, as there was then, A
3. It could have been that star that shines a - bove Which
4. And there could be in us a ho - ly birth Of

qui - et shep-herds watch-ing o - ver sheep, For in this ci - ty
mul - ti-tude of an - gels sing - ing praise To God, and pro-mis-
shone up-on the man - ger babe that night. And it could lead as
Christ- li-ness here in this pres - ent place To bring a - gain up-

now we lis - ten still, And in our ways a Christ - mas
ing sweet peace to men, If we would seek the Christ in
sure-ly to his love, If we let rays of truth make
on this trou-bled earth The glad na - tiv - i - ty of

vi - gil keep.
all our ways.
our lives bright.
truth and grace.

App. C p. 364
ER p. 88

[missing ER letter dated January 9, 1981]

January 31, 1981

Dear Dr. Routley:

Your letter of January 9 ended with that lovely encouragement to keep up the
"good work in hymnody." Well, at the very least you're not telling me to not
bother you any more! . . .

In any case, I ventured down to my little file of favorite potential texts, and
found this one which I think is quite appealing. And perhaps I varied the text
too much in taking out that one "servant" line, but I think I got carried away... I
was thinking a little of that Peter Cutts tune [see p. 80], which has such a
lovely sense of building to "So Lord, art thou to me."

Could you comment on the tune, the harmonization, whether it fits well with
the text, whether you like the text, would it be better to keep the line that I took
out and go for a more symmetric tune? Are the harmonies too much creeping
chromaticisms? I like the minor key I think, and I'd like a tierce at the end; the
funny little motif in the "tenor" (which of course it isn't as the tune is to be
unison) is to be played on the manual, with pedal holding. Kind of a pace
keeper for the singer, through notes longer than he could conveniently count
out. Is 8/4 a logical meter?

So that's what you get for kind words.... more pestering..... But as usual, I'm
deeply grateful for the opportunity to do so!

I wish there were something I could do that could help you in return....

Best wishes,

SERVITOR
11.11.8.11.
A. Tindall, 1981

a minor chord on repeat

The greatest man that walked this earth
Was servant;
He knew the highest, deepest worth
As servant.
    Who better knows how work is blest,
    To whom belongs the sweetest rest?
The servant.

May mankind heed this glorious call
For servant; *
Not unto one but onto all,
Be servant.*
    May we each know humility,
    Forsake all else, dear Lord, and be
Thy servant.*

Max Dunaway, 1970
Christian Science Journal, p. 254

* possibly plural

ERIK ROUTLEY
929 Route 518, R. D. 1
Skillman, N. J. 08558
Tel. (609) 921-7806

7 February 81

Dear Adrienne -

This 'servant' poem is very effective indeed. I have just one suggestion to make which involves you adding only three letters! Why not put 'servant' in stanza 2 into the plural? This would (a) point the contrast between the uniqueness of Christ and the plurality of all his followers, and (b) avoid the slightly awkward expression 'for servant.' Perhaps the author could be apprised of this suggestion?

The tune runs very nicely. I'd mark it 4/2 myself rather than 8/4, which suggests a very slow tempo: and if one wanted that I'd write it in four-quarter measures and call it 4/4. I don't think there really are eight beats in every measure. And the second time round I'd play a C minor chord at the opening of the tune - but since the tune is in unison there's nothing you could do to stop me!

Otherwise I think the tune is a most effective setting. Your instinct to set a very short line to slow music and longer lines to fast music is quite right; after all, it's what RVW did in 'Down Ampney' so you are in excellent company.

I have just included your Psalm 16 in a package of new texts to be sent round the committee of the Reformed Hymnal project. It's up to them whether they approve it but I thought I would try it out. I shall certainly put this one in the file.

You're doing very nicely!

Warmest greetings -

93

February 17, 1981

Dear Dr. Routley:

I'm delighted you like the "servant" hymn! ..... The c minor chord is delicious - to begin the repeated line of the music each time?

I don't know if I sent you the original poem Xeroxed - the only query about pluralizing the second verse perhaps is in relation to a revising of mine: the second use of "servant" I put as "Be servant." The original was "A servant." That makes the whole line "Not unto one but unto all a servant." As I rethink that, it more implies the active doing of serving, such as Jesus demonstrated when washing the disciples' feet. To revise to "Be servant" kept the command in the future, and therefore not yet fulfilled..... In any case, the original "A servant" couldn't be pluralized. But I can certainly relate to what you're saying about the contrast Jesus/us, servant/servants.

Max Dunaway I think passed on but the copyright is held by the Christian Science Publishing Society in any case. . . .

I've enclosed a batted-off-and-I-hope-it-doesn't-sound-it text which I've written for a particular purpose. Maybe it'll not weather well enough to use it thus, but would you look at it? It's Psalm 34, D.C.M. If you could point out things that bother you about it it would be very helpful.... rhymes that are too obvious, awkward lines/structures/ideas statements, etc. I'm pursuing a couple of other D.C.M. texts and planning to incorporate a little section of new and very new hymns (this may not be good enough!) in a hymn sing, showing how texts and tunes can be married up for better or not-so-better, using a rousing text set to FOREST GREEN as one to be re-examined.....

Thank you as always for your patient kindnesses...

[Question about sending to the Episcopal hymnal committee?]

Psalm 34 (1st Version)

I will forever bless the Lord,
       His praise shall be my song.
My heart is filled with confidence
       that He will save from wrong.
Together let us praise His name
       and glory in His power!
It is His hand delivering us
       in every saddened hour.**

O taste and see the Lord is good,   (that God is good,)
       our trust is always blessed.
Let faithful followers stand in awe,
       and in that awe find rest.
What man is he that loves long life
       with days peace-filled and bright?
Keep words and actions heavenly
       and feel the Lord's delight!

There is no fear in righteousness,
       for God is everywhere.
No heavy steps along the way   (steps along the upward way?)
       can be beyond His care.
So let us call upon the Lord
       and humbly ask His aid.
His love redeems, His power restores.
       Trust, and be unafraid!

              A M Tindall 2-23-81

D.C.M.

      **   "testing hour" -- or
              "saddened" per crying (v6) &
                  broken heart (v18), etc.

Rev. p. 132; App. C p. 336
ER p. 97

ERIK ROUTLEY
929 Route 518, R. D. 1
Skillman, N. J. 08558
Tel. (609) 921-7806

20 February 81

Dear Adrienne -

Thank you for Psalm 34. [p. 96]

I am not sure about 'saddened hour' because it isn't an hour that is saddened but a person. I should seek for another adjective. I certainly approve 'testing' because that is what Isaac Watts wrote, or anyhow it is often a thought of his: that does describe the hour, not the person.

'O taste and see that God is good' certainly: the omission of 'that' for metrical reasons is always a pity, I think. 'Faithful followers' I wonder: followers are supposed to move, not to <u>stand</u>. I prefer 'all the faithful' or even 'all his faithful.'

'Man' is uninclusive, I'm afraid: no getting away form it. To my own mind it doesn't matter, but I think we have to roll with this particular punch and try to find some way round 'man' and 'he'. 'All you (or we) who hope for length of life....' omitting the ? at end of line 6 and running straight on - something like that.

Not 'upward way' on any account! very 19th century! I think you have a good thought here and only want a more positive word than 'be' in the next line. How about 'stray'? Heavy steps can do, though they suggest 'lag behind';. Wayward steps? That would go with stray, but not, I now see, with 'way.' 'Wayward steps along the road...'? You do it!

It's very nice, though.

Oh yes, by all means send things to the Episcopal Commission. They are worth it, though nobody in heaven or earth can guarantee their acceptance. Church Hymnal Commission, 800 Second Avenue, NYC 10019 will find them.

Renewed greetings -

as ever,

[signature]

February 23, 1981

Dear Dr. Routley:

The US Mail can't be <u>all</u> bad - here I sent you Psalm 34 Wednesday afternoon, you answered the letter Friday, and I have the response in hand Monday.... not even time for anticipation!

And I was considering the enclosed, hoping not to <u>overlap</u> and have two letters requesting your attention at once, only to find that the enclosed wasn't quite in shape to send by the time overlapping was no longer a threat.

In any case, would you consider this one? It's a favorite psalm of mine and as usual I don't feel confident about my own judgment of it.... I think the first and last stanzas, which don't fall into the meter well, would be better served staying the way they are, even though one could sort of squash them into the other meter. And before I type up the copy which you will have in hand as you read this, I must eliminate "man" again - honestly I have grown up with the term "man" used generically, and must flex my muscles of Christian caring to avoid the reference, but it seems so much a tempest in a teacup.....

Most of the wording comes pretty directly from the psalm. Is "I am humbled and..." too quaint? Does "but unafraid" the first time seem to come from nowhere, reasoning-wise?

How do sexists read that question, "What is man, that thou art mindful of him?" <u>Surely</u> a feminist doesn't get self-satisfied feelings of superiority....! Does "angelic heights" lean so heavily on the psalm as to not make enough sense in syntax? Also "God's will obeyed" is kind of a jump with an inference, rather than clearly worded sentence structure.

The music . . . shouldn't the "O Lord our Lord" stanza be more different in character perhaps?

Thanks again.... how <u>amazing</u> your promptness! Don't let me impose, though, okay?

Psalm 8 (First Version)

O Lord, our Lord, how excellent is Thy name
  in all the earth!
And higher than the highest stars in heaven
  (is) Thy glorious worth.

When I look up to the heavens, the moon and stars,
        the endless sky,
I am humbled and astonished in my heart,
        for who am I?

Yet with Your own power You've given unto us all
        angelic heights,
and Your glory and great honor make a crown
        each wears by right.

It is Your ordained dominion that we have,
        that is our place,
Care of all the world, the birds and creatures too,
        with Godly grace.

I am humbled and astonished in my heart,
        but unafraid,
for the power which gives the task gives wisdom, too:
        God's will obeyed.

O Lord, our Lord, how excellent is Thy name
  in all the earth!
And higher than the highest stars in heaven
  (is) Thy glorious worth.

                                    Adrienne Tindall, 2/20/81

Rev. in App. C. p. 330
ER p. 100, 106

Rev. p. 136; App. C p. 330
ER p. 100

ERIK ROUTLEY
929 Route 518, R. D. 1
Skillman, N. J. 08558
Tel. (609) 921-7806

28 February 81

Dear Adrienne -

Thank you for your latest letter - followed so generously by a second. Your Eighth Psalm [pp. 98-99] makes a very pleasant antiphonal canticle, I think. Do you envisage the antiphon as being sung after all stanzas, at the beginning and end, or at the beginning, after stanza 2, and at the end? I should make it optional, though I would myself in performance use the third of those patterns.

I have only one suggestion about the text, which is very faithful. In stanza 3 I think we have to sing 'care of' rather too fast for so emphatic an expression. You notice that in the other three those two quick notes are sung to the words, 'I am', 'and your', and 'for the' - which they carry very well: but I think the word 'care' ought to have a strong beat and a full length note. I wonder if that phrase can be adjusted in the text? By the way, 'Godly' should be spelt with a small g: but is it exactly the word you want? Are you not really saying 'godlike'? That would be a perfectly proper thing to say; but even so it would be a small 'g', I think, since it refers to us, not Him.

The tune runs very well.   I hear it as a vigorous melody, especially with that high finish in the antiphon, and therefore I just wonder whether the harmony doesn't make it sound a little key-tied. There's absolutely no need to be 'clever' in a piece like this: but I think that antiphon and verse together have just one too many home-key cadence[s]. I wonder if we couldn't have a clear movement to B minor in measure 4 of the stanza; of course, if we did, one melody note would have to be altered - the first of the second phrase: and you might think that F-D-E going upwards is a less easy phrase than A-D-E, so I don't press it; but the longer upward leap does, I think, impart energy, and you then move onwards through your dominant and back home. I thought, secondly, that you might possibly consider a 2-1 cadence rather than a 5-1 cadence at the far end of the stanza: I thought maybe it expressed the words 'who am I?' rather well, and once again

100

removed the impression of monotony that a long series of 5-1 cadences gives. Thirdly, I think we might remove those parallel octaves at the end of the antiphon in the way I suggest at (3): when you have a 5-1 movement in the melody at a cadence, contrary motion produces the right effect - indeed, it's the only thing to do if you want a 5-1 bass as well as a 5-1 melody; furthermore, I wouldn't anticipate your tonic at that point but leave it to the very last chord.

I must tell you that recently I sent suggestions round our hymnal committee for our section of metrical psalms (of which I think we shall have about fifty): and the first letter has come back with a note that the writer very much likes your Psalm 16. Don't hope too much but it's a good omen!

Warmest greetings -

as ever,

I want to keep
care if
ponible

March 2, 1981

Dear Dr. Routley:

Unbelievable!!! My middle name was "Parallels" in Harmony 105, but now I check so carefully .... soprano with tenor, alto with tenor, etc. etc. Who would think to look at the final cadence, soprano and bass? . . .

Acknowledging my almost complete lack of any acquaintance with liturgics, I would much appreciate your telling me a little about a canticle - what it is and where it comes in a service, etc. I just wrote this true to the form of Psalm 8, which has first and last verse in this repeating form.... Two versions of change possible ... does it bother to have both third lines of 3 and 4 end with "too"? I don't much like it, and leave it for now as I didn't even notice it last time, so maybe it's not too bad. Would prefer not to repeat the word like that, though.

Your harmonic help is always appreciated, and as usual adds great color to my vanilla tonic-dominance.... . . .

"The Servant" is also enclosed for a re-check... when I asked the Publishing Society for permission for something else (for a hymn sing I'm doing May 21), they gave it, saying, "When giving permission for poems ... we ask that ... no changes be made in the capitalization, punctuation, or wording of the poems...." So what do you think of the unaltered form with the version of the music? Okay? Do you think it's easy enough for sight-reading at a hymn sing of not too large a group? And actually, is the music more than just okay? Do you like this symmetric form of it? Is the added cadence fine / interesting?

The tune name SERVITOR came for obvious reasons. Now I'm thinking it ought to come for good reasons.... I've just started up work on my hymn index again, and am at "Behold, the Lamb of God" (appears in four of my books, three times set to ECCE AGNUS). And when I pursued it, I found that one of the ECCE AGNUS tunes comes from a Dresden collection, early, and the other (in two books) from a 19th century pen! Not too much help.... So is that why it's desirable to come up with names that are completely independent of texts? Of course if ecumenically endorsed hymns and their marriages to tunes becomes the way things are done, perhaps this won't be so big a factor. But how inconvenient to have two entirely different tunes with the same name, linked to a text that's the same, so the unwary would think only one tune is being used. I guess the same thing evolved with SCHÖNSTER HERR JESU and "Ah, holy Jesu" (I think is the text); one tune Münster 1677 and the other Leipzig 1842.

In short, should I find a different tune name?

I have found what I think to be a most peculiar hymn... I wonder if you've noted it or seen it? It's in the Hymnbook for Christian Worship at No. 375, "Before thee, Lord, we join our hearts / And hands in marriage now; ..." As a congregational hymn that seems strange ... and yet surely the bride and groom are not to sing it alone, are they? It goes on in the same personal vein, about building the home ... although much of the rest of it could be taken as general, and fitly applying to a whole congregation attending a wedding. Well in any case that's the only book that has included it in my little collection. It was copyrighted 1961 by HSA. I guess they were looking for a wedding hymn pretty hard..... I must look and see if I have that group of "Thirteen Marriage and Family Life Hymns" to see what were the other alternatives.... It's helpful though to realize that not every text necessarily speaks to me.... Helps me to not feel crushed when my texts don't speak to others....

I am so interested (and pleased!) to hear of what Psalm 16 (my version) is doing.... If you were to start your autobiography piecemeal, that would be the part most interesting to me at this point - how does a hymnal get put together? Your own experiences must include the whole gamut of possible ways, and I'll bet would be educative and fun reading! What are you doing for this Reformed hymnal, and how do you go about it .... (in 1,000,000 words or less.....)

It is always good to get your kind replies, but does make me more aware of the innumerable demands on your time (Since I end up demanding rather much!) I'll try not to write again too soon....

Many thanks,

A.T.

Er... P.S. There's another text here ...
to ... um ... could you please..
ah ... well .... -
you know.....

SERVITOR 11.11.11.11.
Adrienne M. Tindall, 1981

The great - est man that walked this earth was ser-vant;
May man - kind heed this glor - ious call for ser-vant;

He knew the high-est, deep-est worth as ser-vant.
Not un -to one but un - to all a ser-vant.

Who bet-ter knows how work is blest than ser-vant?
May we know the hu - mil- i - ty of ser-vant,

To whom be-longs the sweet-est rest? The ser-vant.
For-sake all else, dear Lord, and be Thy ser-vant.

Text: © 1970, Christian Science Publishing Society
Used with Permission

Tune: © 1981, Adrienne M. Tindall

App. C. p. 367
ER page 107

104

PSALM 51 (1st Version)

O Lord, my God, I look to You
       and Your great lovingkindness,
for deeply do I feel my faults --
       my waywardness, my blindness.
Let floodtides of Your graciousness
       now cleanse me of mistakings.
My inmost heart should be Your shrine!
       Guide me in that shrine's making.

Your hands will wash to purity
       and holy are Your purgings.
Restore to me Your gladdening joy,
       help me obey Your urgings.
Create in me a heart that's clean,
       renewing my right spirit,
and like a Father, keep me close
       to love Your word, to hear it.

To teach transgressors of Your ways
       and lead them from damnation,
my tongue shall ever sing Your praise,
       O God of my salvation!
The sacrifices You desire
       are meekness and contrition.
I offer them with my whole heart!
       Dear Lord, hear my petition.

Adrienne Tindall, 3/3/81

Rev. p. 113, App. C p. 340
ER page 107

ERIK ROUTLEY
929 Route 518, R. D. 1
Skillman, N. J. 08558
Tel. (609) 921-7806
14 March 81

Dear Adrienne -

Sorry: I have left your last letter too long unanswered; but I left on the 6th for journeys to Los Angeles and Winnipeg - a considerable round trip! - and got back only last night. I suppose your letter of the 2nd came in on the 6th and I just missed it.

We seem to have quite an agenda here.

(a)   You ask what a canticle is. It is, strictly, a biblical passage for singing which doesn't come from the Psalter: if you get hold of a copy of the current new Episcopal prayer book you'll see that they have included a number of canticles from the Old and New Testaments; there are lyrical passages from non-psalter sources which are as suitable for singing as the psalms are. In English Congregationalism we've been singing them since 1887: it's good to see the Anglicans getting the message. Of course, Magnificat and Nunc Dimittis, and Benedictus have long been in the Anglican rites (and the Catholic ones before them). That's what we mean, anyhow, by canticle. Anything non-biblical is a hymn, if it's anything: so Te Deum is a hymn. The place for a canticle in the service depends on which Testament it comes from. If it is OT, then it has the same place as the psalm - in association with the OT Lesson (after it or before it), if it's a NT one, it is associated with the NT Lesson (after it or before it) - so the one between Epistle and Gospel, if one has them, would properly be a NT canticle. Your Psalm 8 [p. 98] is an antiphonal psalm, not a canticle. A Psalm is a psalm whichever way it is set - plainsong, Anglican chant or antiphonal.

Specifically, I do think that two successive endings with the word 'too' are a bit tiresome. I don't quite know how you can get round it, but suspect that it is stanza 4 that might be modified: I think 'God's will obeyed', though theologically admirable, is a bit abrupt. I love 'humbled and astonished' - don't disturb that!

Your instinct about the verses and the antiphon is right, I think: they are rather similar in their texture. I suspect that you ought to use E in only one, and that the <u>verse</u>: the antiphon is what everybody sings. I think I would put the whole thing down to C major actually, with that high finish for the congregation. But your antiphon cadence is perfectly sound as it stands.

I wonder if it's a good idea, still in Psalm 8, to have no paUSE IN THE WORDS OF STANZA 2 BETWEEN THE SECOND AND THIRD LINES. (Pardon me - I seem to have sneezed on the wrong key on this machine: I didn't mean to shout).

> It is your ordained dominion that we have;
> earth is our place;
> the plants, the birds, the beasts are ours to guard
> with godlike grace....

Perhaps not - unfair to fishes: but I do want a stop at the end of line 2 to correspond with the music.

(b) The Servant. Very good, I think. Actually I mean the music: . . . . 'Than servant' is a bad phrase: and I am a bit impatient of all this 'servant' stuff because it provides occasion for people behaving like shabby scullions. Never mind that: your tune is very good. I am not quite sure about the join of phrases 3 and 4, and enclose a scrap which I would like you to consider - but to reject if you don't care for it. My point is that at that important point in the tune I feel uncomfortable with an emphatic dominant 7th harmony, and wonder whether you might not gain impetus if you used that long held melody note as a pivot for a modulation (C minor back to F). I don't want to do anything else to it. Of course you can call it SERVITOR.

(c) Schönster Herr Jesu isn't the original of 'Ah holy Jesus' but of 'Fairest Lord Jesus'.

(d) Oh, I hate wedding hymns. So much that I have written one myself - and it takes a lot, believe me, to get me writing a hymn text. Your instinct about 375 in the <u>Hymnal for Xn Wp</u> is quite right; what are they supposed to do: sing it as a duet? I don't like hymns which the two <u>can't</u> sing any more than hymns which only they can. A wedding service, in my book, is an ordinance of the church, and a hymn sung at it should be singable by all present. . . .

107

(e) Psalm 51. Very good, almost all of it. It is a profoundly difficult psalm to set in metre. I think you might reconsider 'mistakings' - especially rhyming with 'making': you could put it in the singular, of course, but is it a very good word anyhow? I don't think <u>damnation</u> is 19th century: I might expect to encounter it in the 18th - in fact there was an anonymous hymn that began

> My thoughts on awful subjects roll,
> damnation and the dead.....

But I think that only Chesterton really gets away with using it. I am a little bothered by 'purgings': to me it sounds <u>medical</u>! I don't think we ever use it nowadays, in that participial form, for any other purpose. And what on earth are we to do, in these multiracial days, about washing whiter than snow? I know the Bible says it (and interestingly: the Hebrews are only <u>just</u> technically white: they must have been thinking of linen rather than skin) - but it's awkward at the moment. But all the rest is very good - you might just consider those small points.

(f) Don't get me going on how a hymnal is made. There are a hundred ways of putting a hymnal together and they're all wrong, so far as I am concerned. However: broadly speaking editors start out from a decision about what means most to their church or constituency. So <u>Hymns Ancient and Modern</u> is based on the <u>Prayer Book</u>: Morning Prayer comes first, and so forth. The <u>English Hymnal</u> (and the <u>Hymnal-1940</u>) is based on the church's year and the Eucharist: so Advent comes first. Protestant hymnals tend to be based on the Creed, so God the Creator comes first. But whichever bunch you are working for, you begin by having in your mind an overall scheme, and then find the hymns for the various sections. The scheme I have sold to the RCA is a quite new one, based on the Bible: so that although like other Protestant hymnals we begin with the Creation, it's a much longer time before we get to Advent and Christmas. I myself feel that a hymnal is a manual of lyric doctrine: and that the one thing we all have in common is the Bible. So broadly speaking our arrangement gives you a book which you could read through and you'd find things becoming more mysterious and ecstatic as the book went on. Nearly all the marvelous things of Charles Wesley are near the end. Without going into too much detail, what we offer is this:

I. God the Father.
      Creation (Genesis)
      Revelation (Exodus)
      Law (The rest of the Pentateuch)
      Praise (The Psalms)
      Prophecy (the prophets)

II. God the Son
      Advent through Ascension, with a large section on the Ministry, Miracles, and Teaching: the Character and Glory of Christ.
III. God the Holy Spirit
      Pentecost - The Bible - The Church (foundation, mission and ministry, prayer and worship, including marriage, and a few morning and evening hymns)
      The Christian's life: as citizen and a member of society, national and international: then in his personal sanctification (this is where Wesley comes into his own)

IV. The Beatific Vision
      Heaven - Christ enthroned in Glory - Christ's Second Coming - The Blessed Trinity.

Whatever else happens the last lines in the book are from Watts's hymn on the Trinity: 'Where reason fails with all her powers / there faith prevails and love adores.' Wow!

But of course there's more to it than this. I myself think it's criminal when people edit hymnals who don't know the hymn-literature; this is happening more and more often now. What they do is to decide what to include from the old book, then slam in the hymns they happen to know. So you get a wadge of traditional stuff and another wadge of self-conscious contemporary stuff. I think a hymnal is a work of art and a teaching tool: and I want to see our hymnal published in a full music edition and in a paperback words-only edition for people to read. But I don't know if I shall get away with that!
      What we are actually doing involves homework for the committee mapped out by me. . . . Committee meetings tell me what I must add and omit; I know a lot of hymns but these characters have directed me to quite a few which I hadn't properly recognized. So we continue to add sheets and subtract sheets from the loose-leaf binders

I have put together, and in the end we'll come up with something they can use in some pietistic dump in Iowa and in Princeton University Chapel. Oh yes, we'll have 'Blessed Assurance', but any time they do that to me they'll be charged a fee - namely, the acceptance of half a dozen of my suggestions! At present the committee has a 20-page memo on metrical psalms (including Tindall ps. 16); if they send in comments in time I consider them; if not, that's our psalm section. I am being firm about the need for them to do their stuff, and I resigned from the whole project last November because somebody wrote to me that I was being too fascist about it. I am reinstated with a licence to be reasonably fascist. And that's about all I can say at the moment - thank you for asking.

I hope I haven't left anything uncovered: tell me if I did. Must stop now.

Yours ever -

March 20, 1981

Dear Dr. Routley:

This letter is sneaked in.... I normally don't let me write unless I have something new to ask about, which keeps me going and doesn't pester you forever on the same material. BUT....we're going to visit Mickey Mouse next week, and I really thought to send a couple of things to the Episcopal committee, which means they have to go before we leave Friday morning, and so I just thought I'd see what you think of these....?

Besides, your letters are such a riot to get, how can one resist??! After all, the indelible memorability of "I seem to have sneezed on the wrong key on this machine: I didn't mean to shout," .... "licence to be reasonably fascist." (N.B. I am giving you that back in your own British spelling, not even MENtioning that it's "license" in American....) I won't mention to Iowa that "pietistic dump" but it's also a delicious phrase....

I love the Bible base for the hymnal! What's Watts' hymn on the Trinity - first line? And you pique the curiosity (I'm not going to look up the spelling; I'll just hope) about hymn texts you've done. My index is progressing so slowly I haven't even gotten to "Blessed Assurance" yet, so I've only run across "All who love and serve...." Is your wedding text somewhere I can find it? About how many have you done (texts)? Just curious though, although it does sound nosy!

As I reread - add above the delightful sentence, "there are a hundred way of putting a hymnal together and they're all wrong...." Really, no one else's letters are more interesting to get.....

I should think any self-respecting reasonable fascist could get a words only paperback endorsed....the Christian Science church has the full music edition in all sorts of bindings and sizes, and a small paperback words only, and a larger hardback words only. The paperback words only I'll bet is the most commonly carried-around version; I called my friend who works in the CS Reading Room and she says that she sells more of those than any other hymnal edition. And in the case of American interlined formats in hymnals, it's uniquely pleasing and good to have the hymn printed as a poem on the page. First Readers in CS churches always read the whole first verse of a hymn before it's sung in service, and most readers I've worked with use that words only book, rather than the

111

hymnal, for that reading of the text. I should think you'd find acceptance of the idea - a book of sacred poetry and prayer could surely bless all.....

In glancing back I see I've "linked" your "city" text with "Blessed assurance" did that cause you pain? Unintentional, but I have to imagine you writhing just a bit.... As a matter of fact I rushed to my index and looked up latter text, and did some writhing when I "savoured" it. Oh my! Only two hymnals in my index use it - your group isn't exactly within the mainstream with it..... I can relate to Alec Wyton's comment at a talk he gave about their project, though, when he said that if 95% of Episcopals want to sing "How great Thou art," they should be able to do so....

I shall stop because I don't want to take too much of your time. And if you've gone away again don't worry about it. I think I shall send these enclosed to the Episcopals along with a couple of others, before I leave, so if you've no comments or no time to comment, it'll be fine anyway. I'd like to know if the changes seem good, though. I worry about blundering into some theological unacceptability....

Thanks as always,

P. S. Grigg Fountain (he's going to buy your two books from St. John's Lutheran because I told him to give me mine back) is doing an interesting project - a hymn tune index. So far I think he's got 25 hymnals coded into a computer setup, which will give back information however one wants it. Includes a system for indicating the melody notes precisely. I haven't seen what it's like yet, but plan to next month. He's chapel organist at Northwestern.

P.P.S. I do wonder now and again about that third volume - the hymn tunes - and St. John's.... I can still recall the neat harmonization to BEECHER. Oh, and thanks for the cadence in SERVITOR - I found that it pleases more and more....

PSALM 51 (Revised)

O Lord my God, I look to You
      and Your great lovingkindness,
for deeply do I feel my faults --
      the waywardness, the blindness.
Let floodtides of Your graciousness
      forgive this heart that's praying.
Let inward truths instruct my sight,
      let wisdom guide obeying.

Create in me a heart that's clean,
      renewing my right spirit,
and like a Father, keep me close
      to love Your word, to hear it.
Yours hands will wash to purity,
      will blot out wrong and sinning.
Restore to me Your gladdening joy
      in Christ, my new beginning.

Lord, open now my lips to speak
      Your words of revelation,
to sing Your praise in all the earth,
      to tell of Your salvation.
The sacrifices You desire
      are meekness and contrition.
I offer these with all my heart.
      Dear Lord, hear my petition.

              Adrienne M. Tindall 3/20/81

Meter: 87.87.D.

App. C p. 340

March 21

eGADnononoNoNoNONO!!!!!!

Next time I'll look it up!!!! In my clumsy inaccurate vocabulary, "pique" has always meant friendly teasing... and there's absolutely nothing in anything your letters include which stir anything but gratitude for your time, expertise, etc. and patience with correcting things I struggle with.... and tremendous enjoyment of a subject becoming more and more interesting to me, and as I said also in that letter - accurately - a great enjoyment of your sense of humor....

So please forget the meaning of "pique" in this case. You can probably tell from the context that I wasn't knowing the dictionary definition..... What an incredibly sour note it sounds when I think back over the letter!

I hope this gets there simultaneously with the offender... lucky I ran into the word used properly in a book last night - how vexed I would be to recall it years later, and think of its implication going uncorrected....

[Note: I was so horrified by the negative connotation of "pique" in the book I had read, that I called Erik on the phone, my call preceding both letters, I am sure, just to be absolutely *positive* that he knew what I had meant when I used the word....]

ERIK ROUTLEY
929 Route 518, R. D. 1
Skillman, N. J. 08558
Tel. (609) 921-7806

24 March 81

Dear Adrienne -

... Actually your use of 'pique' wasn't out of line really. In French the word originally means 'prick' or 'puncture'. So I suppose one's curiosity can be said to be piqued if it's alerted. The meaning 'annoyed' isn't French but English, though a tertiary meaning (I have looked it all up!) is 'punctured' which means 'deflated.' I suppose one is piqued if somebody has put one down. Anyhow I wasn't and wouldn't have been.

I haven't written very many hymn texts. I suppose Westminster Praise has the largest sample because I put into it a few which I had done for Cantate Domino by way of paraphrasing hymns from other languages: 27 [Father, with all your Gospel's power], 30 [There in God's garden stands the Tree of Wisdom (The Tree of Life)], 35 [Happy are they who walk] in that book [WP] are examples, respectively from German, Hungarian and Thai, none of which languages I know well (Hungarian and Thai not at all!).   Others did a prose paraphrase of the original for me to work on. I have also versified two metrical psalms in Cantate Domino so that their Genevan tunes could be sung (Pss 42 [Seeking water, seeking shelter] and 98 [New songs of celebration render]); and one of these, 'New Songs of Celebration' has got into several books including Ecumenical Praise and More Hymns for To-day. I have done one more for the Reformed book (p 68 [sic. But this is a harmonization of SLANE . There are three psalm versions in Rejoice in the Lord: "Happy are they who walk" at #82, "Seeking water" at #101, and "New songs of celebration" at #119]).

Three churches in various parts of the USA have commissioned texts from me; in each case they specified certain lines they wanted taken. The University Methodist Church in Austin Texas

115

wanted something on the text 'The Truth shall make you free' to go to the tune RHUDDLAN; that was a stinker because I had to find three rhymes in each stanza and I am no good at rhyme. A Presbyterian place in Atlanta asked for a hymn on stewardship . . . . This year another Presbyterian church in Pennsylvania asked for one using the two texts they have written up in the church and another which the music director liked, so I wrote one to carry Howell's tune MICHAEL, and rescued back the original tune for the words he wrote it to ('All my hope on God is founded'). Then there's the wedding hymn. Those and a few translations of French canticles in <u>Cantate Domino</u> are about it, I think. I never find text writing easy. 'All who love & serve' is the oldest (1966) and has travelled the farthest. I may have the odd copy of the inaccessible ones: if so I will enclose what I have.

Watts' hymn on the Trinity is "We give immortal praise' (originally, 'I give...') It is in the doxologies after the Communion hymns Its last lines are the point:

> Where reason fails with all her powers,
> there faith prevails and love adores.

You have certainly done me a huge service in telling me that the CS church has a paperback words only edition. Wow! JUST what I want for the Reformed Church. When next you write, could you possibly give me the name & address of the publisher? I should like to get hold of a sample copy, and sell the idea to our people. This is splendid news.

Did Alec Wyton say that about 'How great thou art'? Oh dear, to think that more than 95% of us want to do things we really oughtn't to do!

Good luck to Dr. Fountain if he can come up with a tune index: but he will have to work on much more than 25 hymnals if it is to be any use: because one never looks up an index or dictionary for something everybody knows about. You look it up for the <u>odd</u> ones - in this case, for tunes that perhaps appear in only one or two hymnals. So he has a fine big job ahead of him. He can start by going through the 400 or so tune books I have here....

No, I am not away for more than week-ends until May: but May 13 to June 4 we shall be away on our first real vacation since we got here in '75, for which we've been saving up. A friend is moving to Portland, Oregon and we are going to drive one of their cars from here to there via Yellowstone and whatever else stands in the way, then spend some time between there & Vancouver. Wow! After that, back to the grindstone.

As ever -

[signature: WKRoutley]

[handwritten note:]
ny; copies sum to have run out,
will make sme more o send you
e.

April 4, 1981

Dear Dr. Routley:

Well, I sent off the Psalm 8 as you indicated, including the antiphon, with a note saying it could be omitted - I think I'd want it included myself, just because that's truest to the psalm.

Would that qualify as a hymn on ecology, or stewardship? . . .

Your fastest source for a words only hymnal would be your local Christian Science Reading Room. I think the church in Princeton is small - I used to attend it when I dated my now-spouse (and only one I hasten to add, in these incredibly flexible times....). . . . If you wanted any information about it, you could write to:

> Mrs. Rowene Tennant, Manager, General Publications
> Christian Science Publishing Society
> 1 Norway Street
> Boston, MA 02115

She's very kind and very efficient, and could redirect your letter if she's not the one to answer it. But I would think a percentage of hymnal sales which are words only could be revealing, and particularly if hymnals sold to churches themselves were taken out of the figures; in other words, I'll lay odds that the words only outsells the music editions many times over, when just considering sales to individuals.

You'll notice that the hymns are alphabetical by first line. Not nearly as imaginative as a method, but it does make finding a hymn rather more easy, if one knows how the hymn starts. And I daresay that's the main way they're used, as the user will be looking up something half-remembered, wanting to study the rest of it. A lot of hymns are quoted in the testimony sections of the periodicals, as having helped keep thought from being overwhelmed by dismay or distress in trying times. Now that I think of it, I did the same myself last night, when a rather major digestive upset kept me awake half the night down in Disney World .... the hymns I could call to mind were very helpful stabilizers during the dark hours when I didn't want to wake up the rest of the family by having a light on - a real help in praying about it all....

"How great Thou art..." oh dear, indeed. . . . one of the humbles ones.... I remember a mental image I had in the little church (log cabin style) up North. They had needed a new organ, and I'd written them a rather lengthy letter (and you know what that can mean!) about not getting another spinet electronic. The new organ was there the next spring - a Hammond spinet electronic. I shall spare you a lengthy disquisition on electronics and my far from silent attitudes about them. But as I attended church that spring morning, I thought, Adrienne Tindall, what are you going to do if you get up to heaven and find that the church there has an electronic organ???? (Don't look for theologicality in that! I knew I was using a parable-type query...) And as I sat there listening to the to me raucous incredibly harsh and un-blessing rending of harmonies, I decided that my "heaven" would probably have a lovely possibly chiffy Baroque organ, which would fully adapt to the repertoire I love. And I decided that, God being infinitely loving as well as infinitely wise, that would be true of my heaven even if the person sitting next to me was hearing (and wanted to hear) something very much like that morning's music... Sometime when I'm choosing music for church, I have to realize that erudition and what may be intellectually pleasing to me is not necessarily what would be "played in heaven"; the pearly gates open to more than the scholarly, I daresay, and playing exclusively the masterworks of Bach (which I'd love to do if I knew them all) is probably more pharisaical than anything else.... But then on the other side of the coin, I watched a smidge of one of the TV church presentations this morning before we left Florida - that big glass one in

118

California? - what do you think about such? A friend of mine is so thrilled by that particular show that I really expected to like it....

Grigg Fountain's project is, if he gets grants from NU, aimed at prodigious proportions. The 25 hymnals were a pilot project to show that a computer could digest and give out the material in a useful way. He talked to Dr. Ellinwood about it. I know he has a bunch of tune books - been collecting for a while, I understand - but I doubt if he has 400! What a number! . . .

How big your trip sounds! Coast to coast is a huge thing! Are you an enthusiastic mountain driver? Be sure to have the brakes checked!!!! I am definitely cowed by passes and the like, and have done a lot of needlework at that time, in order to avoid looking out the window. We went out that way in our motorhome when the four girls were smallish; I liked the passes in Canada a lot better - they had wide shoulders on the roads, instead of the straight down stuff.

In any case, you'll undoubtedly be going through Chicago, and if there's something we can do to help - your staying here, or whatever - I hope you'll let us. . . . If you're flying back and want to stop over for a day or two or whatever, that would be fine too. We have lots of daughters' rooms, and the one who lives in California is not going to be around in any case, so there would be space if it would help. Or anything else like that.... for both of you.

It's beautiful country out west - the feel of Montana's space is something else. And Idaho - just immensities of sky! When we went to Yellowstone, we somehow circled around a couple of times, ending up at the same place. Things really looked familiar -- the second time.... I'm not a very good navigator; I think that one got me fired for the duration of the trip. . .

I am working on another text to bother you with, but wanted to 'dash off" this to tell you about the words only hymnal. Too bad I can't do it in less than three pages, eh?

Best wishes,

April 5, 1981

Dear Dr. Routley (my, I seem to be writing in couplet letters these days!):

I wrote you a time ago about how much revising is desirable / permissible / tasteless, etc. And I recall without looking up the letter that there is indeed a point beyond which one really should not go. So I hope you will survive looking at the Words Only CS hymnal.... All I can say is that it has been a source of amazement, the occasional wholesale "adapting"... One can say ah well that was way back in 1932, . . . In any case, hang on to your hat, because the revising doesn't at all affect the desirability of a words only hymnal and its potential usefulness and ability to bless.

Some of the texts, as I researched them all, were not "findable." In fact I just found "Behold, a sower from afar" the other day, which turns up to be our "O Lord of Life, to Thee we lift..." with the first stanza deleted. Maybe I should send you my list of first lines that I've not found, eh? You'd probably recognize them cold....

But the main point of this letter is to query the adaptings of the two enclosed poems. The second one really isn't all that wild in any case, but what do you think of setting it to FOREST GREEN? For this hymn sing I'm doing, I'm going to use several CMD texts for FOREST GREEN and for ELLACOMBE, to introduce new texts to the people there (I mean the CS Hymnal being already 50 years old surely a change is due sometime! Maybe this will prepare a few for the happy reception of a new book....) . I thought I'd use this "If I have lightened..." and that Psalm 34 I asked you to look at - "I will forever bless the Lord," which really goes with both tunes and lets one realize how the music affects the feel of the texts. Then I want to try the text found with FOREST GREEN (CS 5 - "A voice from heaven we have heard") with ELLACOMBE, . . .

The first poem here has much more revising, and perhaps too much. I did write the author and she has given permission to alter it, recognizing that the sense of it is not changed... I asked Austin about it when I was pursuing using GLENFINLAS with it, and inquiring about the marriage in his estimation - and he suggested the "let me" changes, which I kind of don't like all that much. They sound sort of un-humble and demanding. But he thought it better not to repeat the "May I" in the two consecutive lines. . . .

If I were including this in a collection, and now knowing that the final lines of the two stanzas were 4's, I might look for a 6.5.9. tune (for someone to write??). But by then I'd heard GLENFINLAS, and I loved it so much, and it seemed to fit the feel of the text so well, that maybe judgment was overridden... Haven't heard about GLENFINLAS yet, though I asked for permission (Austin had the address, which had taken him months to find!). Would you tell me what you think about revising, revision, tune, marriage, any better solutions? . . .

I am pursuing your texts a tich - I have a few here, included in Westminster Praise and More Songs and Hymns, and Ecumenical Praise. I suppose that Cantate Domino is the one I've written England about twice, and still have not heard anything about? I asked Cokesbury to find it for me, and they decided that it doesn't exist.... Is that an immensity of a collection? The first I heard of it was from a list Austin put together for me, saying these books would be interesting to me (I asked him what collections would be so) ... published by Barenreiter, I think? But in any case the couple you mention as commissioned are very piquey (hahaha) and so when and if you have the time and the copies ....????? (!) In the meantime I shall see if I can finish this text because I'd like to end up with a pleasing usable one on this one. I'm sure no tune exists for it as yet - weird stress pattern I'm letting evolve, straight from the psalm. . .

A Chosen Vessel (by Margery Cantlon, in CS Sentinel)   Adapted to 6.5.6.5. meter

As a chosen vessel let me do my part, in bringing water to a desert heart.	As a chosen vessel let me do my part, may I bring cool water to a desert heart.
As a chosen vessel may I hold sweet oil, and pouring, ease another's toil.	As a chosen vessel let me hold sweet oil, may my pouring lighten someone else's toil.
As a chosen vessel, wrought of gold or wood, in healing work O use me, Lord.	As a chosen vessel, wrought of gold or wood, may my work bring healing; Use me now, O Lord.

Words used with permission of The Christian Science Publishing Society.
Rev. p. 134
ER p 123

PSALM 139 (1st Version)

Search me, O God, and know my heart,
try me and know my thought,
and tell me if some wicked way
makes paths of truth unsought.   23,24
Everything I would say or do,
everywhere I would go,
Your hands possess my reins of life   13
and lift from sin and woe.   6

Where could I ever hide from You?
Where could I flee away?
In heaven I am by Your side,
in hell You are my stay.   7,8
Taking the wings of morning's beams, (rays)
dwelling in farthest seas,
Your hand is even there to guide,
Your right hand, holding me.   9,10

Darkness can have no power to hide,
night brings no threat too near!
Your presence is my shining light,
Your truth dispels my fear.   11,12
Precious are all Your thoughts to me,
glorious is their sum!
They number more than endless sands,
they bless the dawns that come.   17,18

Surely Your Word will vanquish sin!
Surely Your power will reign!
I'll raise a standard to Your rule;
I'll hate all evil's stain.   19-22
Search me, O God, and know my heart,
try me, and know my thought,
and tell me if some wicked way
makes paths of truth unsought.   23,24

AMT 5/81

This is undoubtedly a nonexistent meter, tunewise ... what would you call it? It can also, of course be 8 four-line stanzas, but somehow that makes it seem longer.... It really seemed that the verses slipped into this meter readily, but what do you think of it?

Rev. p. 158; App. C p.360, 361
ER pp. 123-124

ERIK ROUTLEY
929 Route 518, R. D. 1
Skillman, N. J. 08558
Tel. (609) 921-7806

9 April 81

Dear Adrienne -

Before I get to your agenda, I have a message to convey to you. Only two days ago our hymnal committee was meeting, and they were looking at your version of Psalm 16. They liked it very much indeed but they had one point to make, which was to ask if by any chance you would consider adding another stanza right at the beginning. The Reformed Church is very much a psalm-singing body - and they really do appreciate the psalms. Somebody said, and we saw the point, that one of the great things about Psalm 16 is the dramatic way in which it rises from the depths to the heights. Now your version starts out at verse 5: and goodness knows verses 1-4 contain pretty unpromising material. But what they wondered was whether you felt like providing a first stanza which, as it were, sketched in the dark background against which the real message of hope stands. Now don't fret if you find you can't do it or don't want to. Your version may well get by without any alterations, and we might even supplement it with another which took care of those points: we are certainly going to offer two versions of certain psalms and we may do so with this one. But I pass on the message. The tune SOUTH CERNEY, which I mentioned to you, works perfectly well and they approved it.

Now your material. In "As a chosen vessel' I think your version certainly makes it singable: the one word I doubt is in the original - a 'desert heart'. I doubt 'desert': is it supposed to mean 'deserted', or 'a heart that feels like a desert?' In either case I think the word is being forced into a shape it doesn't naturally have, and I'd prefer 'thirsty' - a bit obvious no doubt, but less awkward. Your slight revision of 'Holy Purpose' [see p. 131] is entirely sensible, though I share your doubts about FOREST GREEN. There are several good CMD tunes available - there's no need to sing everything in that metre to FOREST GREEN. How about HALIFAX (Pilgrim 294)?

The version of 139 is fine. The metre is no problem, surely, being once again CMD, but with a trochaic opening to the

123

second half. I wonder if a slight adaptation of the OLD 137th would meet the case? (Enclosed)

Some points. I 7 - 'reins of life' won't, I think, do. 'Reins' are kidneys. I shouldn't use the word nowadays because people think it means what you use to guide horses. II 4 - 'in hell you are my stay': humph. I think hell for Christians is precisely the absence of God, so God can't be there. What the AV translates 'hell' is <u>Sheol</u>, which is something entirely different: the supposed place where everybody goes when they die, but not a place of punishment or grief. We usually now translate it 'in the grave' or something neutral like that. IV 7 'endless sands' try 'countless': you mean grains of sand, of course, which don't really have ends. V - 4 "I'll raise a standard' - I am not sure what this means: what sort of standard? A flag? If so I think perhaps it should be re-thought: 'raising standards' has quite other connotations in English. 'Makes paths of truth unsought' - not quite what we mean, I think, and a slightly weak finish. Small points but you might ponder them.

Your other letter - thank you very much indeed for putting me in touch with the hymnal publisher. I shall follow it up.

You mention the Crystal Cathedral - which I think is officially Garden Grove Reformed Church in Los Angeles or somewhere. No, not my style at all. One of the members of the Reformed Hymnal committee is an able choirmaster, and he had his choir on tour in March; they went and gave a concert there. They were required to submit the texts of everything they proposed to sing, because the authorities wouldn't allow anything that didn't chime with their idea of 'positive thinking'. I imagine they never allow reference to Calvary. . . . . As soon as a church begins to aim at pleasing vast numbers of people I'm afraid it becomes intellectually corrupt, and purveys something which people like but which isn't Christianity. I've seen it again and again, and virtually any organization which gets on to nationwide network TV on Sunday morning seems to be like that. I keep well clear of it. Of course, you may well say (well, I don't think you would but some might) that this is a sour-grapes remark of an Englishman who never had a regular congregation of more than 150 and serve him right: but I am bound to say that when I attended a certain church in London on the first Sunday of this year where the congregation numbered about 45 and the organ was one of those pestilent electronics, I was more thoroughly nourished by the Gospel than I ever expect to be by the Schulers and Falwells: I would rather sing Watts to bad accompaniment than Joyful Joyful to an accompaniment by Gerre Hancock . . .

As for electronic organs, I forget whether I have told you about the one at St. James's Newcastle (where I worked before coming here). It is the exception to all the generalization: but in a general way I think all <u>small</u> and mass-produced electronics are an abomination, though <u>that</u> one, 4 manuals, 100 stops, is astonishingly good. Cathedral organists were lining up to play it and walked away looking very thoughtful. Dem pearly gates sure are open to other than scholars: but within them there dwells nothing unclean, and the cheap and pretentious is unclean.

I shall not overlook your very kind invitation to stop over on our journey. Plans are not yet fixed but I shall advise you at once if we are able to take you up on that.

Warmest greetings as always -

Old 137th

Adapted from Ps. 137 in Anglo Genevan Psalter 1556

M - 790   12 Stave

THE BOSTON MUSIC COMPANY
a Division of Williamson Music, Inc.
116 Boylston St., Boston, Ma 02116

App. C p. 361

April 14, 1981

Dear Dr. Routley:

Because you've asked, I'll try .... but I surely can understand why I didn't try at first! Sitting in a dorm room at WCC, armed only with my King James Version, no wonder I didn't want to work to understand that segment of the psalm!

However, my lack of confidence in what the passage means is based evidently in difficulties of translation; I've pored over several translations, and there isn't all that much agreement about the Hebrew and what it actually says. So after coming up with a stanza 1, using mainly Jerusalem Bible and New English, I went back to KJV. And now as I read it, I wonder if it has more of a clue than I thought. If vs. 2 is outlining hypocrisy - to saying God is "my Lord," but that "my goodness extendeth not to Thee (Lord) but to the saints that are in the earth, and to the excellent" (whom I already know and know that I delight in) .... However, I 'm vastly uncomfortable at reading so much into it without scholarly confidence and background to justify. Interpreter's Bible introduced me to the word "bathos" which I looked up [ludicrously abrupt transition from elevated to commonplace], and which describes perfectly my reaction to the RSV translation.....

So that's part of the problem. Your comment, "one of the great things about Psalm 16 is the dramatic way in which it rises from the depths to the height," does that refer to rising from idolatry to conscious monotheism? . . . Using the two questions was "endorsed" by the tune (I am happy with the tune now, too . . .), and permitted the negatives to be introduced without perhaps detracting from the affirmative so much.

Is it okay to have "power" two syllables this time? Usually I think of it as one.

Would my heart make temporal sacrifice?
    My refuge is in God above!
Have idols power to entice?
    God only will I serve and love.
There is no goodness found on earth
Except to mirror God's own worth.

I'm not sure how well this joins to st. 2 .....

N.B. only 1 pg!

127

ERIK ROUTLEY
929 Route 518, R. D. 1
Skillman, N. J. 08558
Tel. (609) 921-7806

23 April 81

Dear Adrienne -

Just a short note on the run (exam week!) to thank you for your addition to Psalm 16. I will work on it and circulate it & see whether the committee [members] think it meets their need. I am not sure actually that we ought not to keep your original & add another version of the psalm which begins at the beginning. But we will ruminate on it. I am most grateful to you for taking the trouble.

What I had in mind - but I am not sure it was exactly what they [the committee members] did - was the drama in Ps. 16 turning on the protest in it against the old Hebrew doctrine of eternal life: which of course as you know was that there wasn't any. Once you were dead you were filed away in Sheol and that was that: and here and there the Psalmists say 'That <u>can't</u> be true!' It happens again in Ps. 30. In Ps. 16 it's in such a phrase as 'Thou wilt not let thy holy one see corruption; 'You can't let anyone You value have no future...'

Thank you, by the way, for putting me on to the Xn Science hymnal: Mrs. Tennant was extremely kind and sent me a copy of both words-only editions, and said that the words-only edition represents 37% of their sales. Just what I needed, especially the paperback. Shows how practicable it is, and that people do buy it.

Must hasten away now:

As ever -

May 19, 1981

Dear Dr. Routley:

I'm dashing this one off - leave in the morning for Wisconsin. But seeing's I recall that the 24th you're leaving for points west, I figured I'd better get this off .... because if there's anything around Chicago that might help or be nice for you, we'll be home the night of the 25th and thereafter, and I hope you'll let me know....

I'm enclosing just in case you have time, but will you please just leave it till you get back if things are hectic? And I would suspect they are, but I wanted to get the above paragraph in the mail, so these come along with....

"Search me O God" I changed all per your suggestions except the heaven / hell construction - and even though I saw the "Sheol" in other translations, I still like the way I have it.... theologically I would think that if God is everywhere, then there's no hell anyway, which suggests His absence, but even in one's mortal imaginings that God is not everywhere, still perhaps knowledge of His being-ness is a "stay".... well, what do you think of the other changes in any case? [no version included here; see p. 158.]

The other two may be awful, but I wrote them on the way home from Jenny's graduation from Duke, and one is a very favorite passage type, and the other just kind of came .... you don't mind looking them over <u>when you have the time</u>, and being very frank? Thanks.

Gave a practice hymn talk last Sunday, and will give the "real" one on Thursday in Ripon, WI (the 21st). I really kind of enjoyed it! In spite of the fact that, in the words of a friend, I have an awful lot to be humble about..... Even though it was an hour and 20 minutes, it seemed to move right along and not bog down or seem boring (at least to me....). Program enclosed. Kind of a one-man-band, though, doing it all. The console was out in the open, so I could stay at the keyboards and talk from there....

All for now - imagine only one page! Have a really lovely trip.

HYMN FESTIVAL

Adrienne M. Tindall
Hymns Old, New and Very New

I

Fantasie over het lied, "heilig, heilig, heilig"   Piet Post
HYMN 117 *"Holy, holy, holy"* (NICAEA)

Trio on "Wordsworth"   Austin Lovelace
HYMN 135 *"I know no life divided"* (WORDSWORTH)

Chorale Prelude on "Quem Pastores"   Healey Willan
HYMN 237 *"O may we be still and seek Him"* (QUEM PASTORES)

HYMN 107 *"Help us to help each other, Lord"* (WINDSOR)

Praise God from Whom all Blessings Flow   Paul Manz
HYMN 63 *"From all that dwell below the skies"*
    (OLD HUNDREDTH)

II

"Hymns New and Very New"

III

Wer nur den lieben Gott lässt   J.S. Bach
    walten (Orgelbüchlein)
HYMN 216 *"O he who trusts in God's protection"* (NEUMARK)

Pastorale on "St. Columba"   Jack Goode
HYMN 300 *"The King of Love my Shepherd is"*
    (sung to ST COLUMBA, at 339)

Prelude on "Hyfrydol"   Flor Peeters
HYMN 175 *"Lo, He sent His Word and healed them"*
    (HYFRYDOL)

HYMN 305 *"Shepherd, show me how to go"* (SHEPHERD)

HYMN 283 *"Praise we the Lord, for His mercy endureth
    forever"* (LOBE DEN HERREN)

Lobe den Herren, den mächtigen König der   J.G. Walther
    Ehren

First Church of Christ, Scientist, Ripon

The Manz and Peeters credits should be reversed.

FOREST GREEN   CMD
Traditional English

Holy Purpose

If I have lightened someone's cross
Today by word or deed;
If I have loved sufficiently
To sense another's need
And answered it unsparingly
From heaven's boundless store,
Then I have used God's talent well
And am prepared for more.

If I have shed a ray of Truth
On someone's doubts and fears
So that he sees the rainbow glow
Through trembling, hopeful tears
And knows that God has sent that bow
For him, then I shall be
Found worthy of the holy plan
That God ordained for me.

Naville Hoogs Rutledge, 1961

Psalm 34

I will forever bless the Lord,
His praise shall be my song.
My heart is filled with confidence
That he will save from wrong.
Together let us praise his name
And glory in his power,
It is his hand deliv'ring us
In ev'ry testing hour.

O taste and see that God is good,
Our trust is always blessed.
Let faithful hearts acknowledge awe,
And in that awe find rest.
Let all who hope for length of life,
With days peace-filled and bright,
Keep words and actions heavenly
And feel the Lord's delight!

There is no fear in righteousness
For God is ev'rywhere.
The hardest steps along the way
Are not beyond his care.
So let us call upon the Lord
And humbly ask his aid.
His love redeems, his pow'r restores.
Trust, and be unafraid!

ⓒ Adrienne M. Tindall, 1981

131

ELLACOMBE C.M.D.
"Gesangbuch," Württemberg, 1784

Psalm 34

A voice from heaven we have heard,
The call to rise from earth;
Put armor on, the sword now gird,
And for the fight go forth.
The foe in ambush claims our prize,
Then heed high heaven's call.
Obey the voice of Truth, arise,
And let not fear enthrall.

I will forever bless the Lord,
His praise shall be my song.
My heart is filled with confidence
That he will save from wrong.
Together let us praise his name
And glory in his pow'r,
It is his hand deliv'ring us
In ev'ry testing hour.

The cause requires unswerving might:
With God alone agree.
Then have no other aim than right;
End bondage, O be free.
Depart from sin, awake to love:
Your mission is to heal.
Then all of Truth you must approve,
And only know the real.

O taste and see that God is good,
Our trust is always blessed.
Let faithful hearts acknowledge awe,
And in that awe find rest.
Let all who hope for length of life,
With days peace-filled and bright,
Keep words and actions heavenly
And feel the Lord's delight!

Irving Tomlinson, 1932

There is no fear in righteousness
For God is ev'rywhere.
The hardest steps along the way
Are not beyond his care.
So let us call upon the Lord
And humbly ask his aid.
His love redeems, his pow'r restores.
Trust, and be unafraid!

© Adrienne M. Tindall, 1981

"The Lord is my Shepherd"

The King of love my Shepherd is,
    Whose goodness faileth never;
I nothing lack if I am His
    And He is mine for ever.

Where streams of living water flow
    My ransom'd soul He leadeth,
And, where the verdant pastures grow,
    With food celestial feedeth.

Perverse and foolish oft I stray'd,
    But yet in love He sought me,
And on His Shoulder gently laid,
    And home, rejoicing, brought me.

In death's dark vale I fear no ill
    With Thee, dear Lord, beside me;
Thy rod and staff my comfort still,
    Thy cross before to guide me.

Thou spread'st a Table in my sight;
    Thy Unction grace bestoweth;
And oh, what transport of delight
    From Thy pure Chalice floweth!

And so through all the length of days
    Thy goodness faileth never:
Good Shepherd, may I sing Thy praise
    Within Thy house forever.

                    Sir H. W. Baker, 1861

GLENFINLAS 6.5.6.5.
Kenneth G. Finlay

As a cho - sen ves - sel let me do my part,
As a cho - sen ves - sel let me hold sweet oil,
As a cho - sen ves - sel, wrought of gold or wood,

may I bring cool wa - ter to a des - ert heart.
may my pour - ing light - en some - one el - se's toil.
may my work bring heal - ing, Use me now, O Lord.

SERVITOR 11.11.11.11.
Adrienne M. Tindall, 1981

The great-est man that walked this earth was ser-vant;
May man-kind heed this glor-ious call for ser-vant;

He knew the high-est, deep-est worth as ser-vant.
Not un-to one but un-to all a ser-vant.

Who bet-ter knows how work is blest than ser-vant?
May we know the hu-mil-i-ty of ser-vant,

To whom be-longs the sweet-est rest? The ser-vant.
For-sake all else, dear Lord, and be Thy ser-vant.

Text: © 1970, Christian Science Publishing Society
Used with Permission

Tune: © 1981, Adrienne M. Tindall

App. C p. 367

O Lord our Lord how ex-cel-lent is thy name in all the earth! And
high-er than the high-est stars of heav'n Thy glor - ious worth!

1. When I look up to the heav'ns, the moon and stars, the
2. Yet with your own pow'r you've giv'n un - to us all an-
3. If your will gives us do - min - ion's care for life that
4. I am hum-bled and as - ton - ished in my heart, but

end - less sky, I am hum - bled and as - ton - ished in
gel - ic heights, And your glo - ry and great hon - or make
fills this place, Ev' - ry crea - ture of the earth, and earth
un - a - fraid, For the pow'r that gives the task, gives wis-

my heart, for what am I?
a crown each wears by right.
it - self, must feel our grace.
dom, too; God's will o - beyed.

App. C p. 330

PSALM 131 (1st Version)

Lord, let me be a child
    who knows humility --
who trusts Your wisdomed plan
    and follows steadfastly.

Lord, let me be a child
    unlearned in evil's way --
obedient to Your laws
    rejoicing in each day.

Let me have childlike faith
    unmoved by worldly cares,
relying on Your good,
    uplifting thought in prayer.

Let every ray of light
    show me Your light of truth
seen in simplicity --
    seen as with eyes of youth.

Let trusting love be mine
    as felt for parents' arms,
to know that You are close
    in dangers or alarms.

Lord, I would be Your child --
    see Fatherhood above,
see in Christ Jesus' life
    an eldest brother's love.

Lord, I would be a child
    who knows Your constancy!
Your lovingkindnesses
    are mine, eternally.

A M Tindall 5/11/81

Rev. p. 143; App. C p. 357
ER p. 139

137

PSALM 133 Original Form (no revision)

How good and how pleasant it is
    when the children of God
      dwell together in love and unity!

How good and how pleasant it is!
    like the sweet morning dews
      when they kiss every flower tenderly!

How good and how pleasant it is!
    like the ointment of grace
      which abundantly pours its loveliness.

How good and how pleasant it is
    when each heart opens wide
      to embrace all the world in Christliness.

How good and how pleasant it is!

A M Tindall 5/11/81

App. C p. 358
for tune - POLLSTIN - see p. 146
see also p. 256 (solo setting)
ER p 139

ERIK ROUTLEY
929 Route 518, R. D. 1
Skillman, N. J. 08558
Tel. (609) 921-7806

7 June 81

Dear Adrienne —

I am now in Bloomington, IN — Indiana University: we got home from vacation on the 5th, and so it was a quick turn round and all I could do was to throw all the mail into my bag and bring it with me. Hence the handwriting — and I don't know which is worse - my holograph or my typing! The holiday was the experience of a lifetime — driving a friend's car to Oregon, leaving it there, and eventually returning by train from Vancouver to Montreal. We saw enough scenery, including the Tetons and Yellowstone and the N.W. volcanoes, to keep us talking for the rest of the year.

Nice to have your two psalms. ψ 139 is excellent now except for the split infinitive which we really can't have. Perhaps the last quatrain, ought to be reconstructed: 'let truth & love guide thoughts & acts' seems to lack something. It could refer to anybody's thoughts & acts, but the psalmist was thinking only of his: I think we must have a 'my' somewhere. While you are about it you can clean up the infinitive.

ψ 131 is very nice. Why 'eldest brother'? Wouldn't 'elder brother' do? The whole thing is very personal - just you and He, as it were. If you have several brothers older than yourself you can speak of all of them as 'elder brother.' I suggest 'elder'. Otherwise - very nice indeed.

So is ψ 133. It suggests attractive musical possibilities. I have no criticisms here.

Congratulations on your one-woman-band: a very nice program cunningly devised. I am sure everyone enjoyed it, and I hope you carry on with this work. Do you know the organ chorale preludes of CHH Parry, Charles Wood, and Basil Harwood? Some very good things there — although perhaps they don't feature tunes your people

→

139

know. Novello used to publish them, I think. They might enrich your repatoire.

Very nice of you to suggest our calling in the Chicago area, but that's one place our train didn't call at. On the way out we passed South Chicago on I 80 about 7 am in a tremendous rainstorm — on the 14th, and soldiered on until we were clear of it. That was the only rough weather we had — though we escaped the massive floods in Helena, Montana, about which maybe you heard, by one day!

Have a splendid summer.

As ever —

CR Routley

140

July 1, 1981

Dear Dr. Routley:

Your letter of June 7 has been on my desk ever since and I've been anxious to answer it. But perhaps this is a fuller, more interesting letter because of the delays and their enrichments..!..

Austin Lovelace has been at Garrett for summer school - he did an hour each morning last week on modern hymn texts. A lot of things I never saw, of course, and quite a few of great interest. I also showed him a couple of things and pursued ideas about them..... . .

Showed him 133 [p. 138] - "How good and how pleasant it is," and the meter at the end didn't gel with him.... so I was "challenged" (not verbally, just by implication) to see if I could come up with a tune that would keep the motion going through the "missing" unaccented syllable at the end of the second line. The version is included. The first ending is Austin's harmonization; I wanted to have a half cadence first ending [and a full cadence for the ending of the last stanza], but had ended up on the dominant too soon to do so. His A# to b to f# are harmonically nice and interesting and I like them 100%, even though I hope and wonder about not confusing a singer by having the initial note of the next stanzas not even in the chord....

Psalm 131 [p. 137] he didn't care for several things wordwise - and I think I had little mental nudges about them already - . . . I shall cogitate (on) those lines. The elder brother is of course right, as you point out. I had originally used that, and then was getting "clinical" about it. The first time I recall running across the concept was in Wither's cradle hymn (if I remember the words right) "Hush little one .... your elder brother is a king...." and I just loved the beauty of that recognition!

Psalm 139 [p. 122] vexes me a tich. This morning's possibility for the last four lines . . . - oh I'll just "try them out" on you.... [not included here; see p. 158]

Psalm 42 is enclosed - three queries are Austin's, one my own now that I look back.... One of the things Austin said in the class sessions caught my attention and seems a relevant issue in my own efforts, and that is the need for the whole thing to sound _impelled_ enough - the author "must" say it, rather than something that he just "could" say, or had time to write down, or sat down and diddled the time away with.... I just "decided" (in the "could" category) to work on the psalms, partly for practice, mostly for the joy of the material and working with it, understanding it better, etc. . . . So even though I'm basically thinking of being close to the original, with some interpretations interpolated once in a while, still to be literally close verse by verse becomes less relevant when the ideas don't seem to go in that channel to me,....

And of course that relates to the why and where-it's-going of all this.... there is nowhere "it's" going, consciously, so there's no tailoring to fit a particular need. I wonder if there's a "where" that's relevant? I tend to get ambitious projects started which don't offer that much promise of being "finished," as they're merely personal goals, and other commitments preclude consistent endeavor. For example, when I finished a year's introductory coursework to the Bible, I bought the Interpreter's Bible, deciding to read all the material except the bottoms of each page - thereby getting the text itself and the direct commentary. Never even started, though it's great to use the books for reference....

Well anyway, if you have any insights that relate, would you mention them? I do feel like continuing to work with psalms....

Psalm 130 I was trying to use a shorter meter than the same old one (which is the way it gets to seeming...), and Austin thought I really chose the wrong meter for this particular one. I can sense an inconsistency in having so many stanzas - 7 times through a short musical idea would be awful! ... But as I explained to Austin, when he mentioned the long rolling phrases (my words, not his) of Luther's version of this psalm (which I don't know), this one is more in the spirit of the publican's brevity, as opposed to the Pharisee's longwinded assertions.... And it seems to me that if Luther has a long one, why not feel free to not emulate a version so well-known? Well what do you think about the "exhorting" meter with this text?

Glad your trip was good. Hope Indianapolis was too - the handwriting was fine! Beats my husband's any day. ... I've used four of Parry's chorale preludes with some regularity - whenever that hymn tune has been chosen for the particular service. Shall have to pursue Basil Harwood and Charles Wood - any particular chorale preludes ? I love the SLANE of Willan I just learned about at HSA meeting there at Westminster ... but then I love SLANE anyway...

PSALM 131 (Revised Version)

Lord, let me be a child
　　　　who knows humility,
who seeks and trusts Your plan,
　　　　and follows steadfastly.

Let every ray of light
　　　　show me Your light of Truth
seen in simplicity --
　　　　seen as with eyes of youth.

Lord, let me be a child
　　　　unmoved by evil's way,
obedient to Your laws,
　　　　rejoicing in Your day.

Let trusting love be mine,
　　　　as felt for parents' arms,
to know that You are close
　　　　and save from all that harms.

Lord, I would be Your child --
　　　　see Fatherhood above,
see in Christ Jesus' life
　　　　an elder brother's love.

Lord, I would be a child
　　　　who trusts Your constancy!
Your lovingkindnesses
　　　　are mine, eternally.

　　　　　　　　A. M. Tindall, 5/81

6.6.6.6.D.

App. C p. 357

PSALM 42 (1st Version)

My soul is longing for my God,
        When shall I see his face?
Like thirsting deer by waterbrooks,
        I thirst for his pure grace.
The tears that fall in night's dark hours   (night time? darkest?)
        Have mocked my constant prayer --
To feel God's presence with me here,
        Sustaining with His care.

Why have I turned my thoughts to gloom?
        Why is my heart laid low?
My hope is in the Lord Himself,
        Whose goodness overflows!
I know from all the days gone by
        His saving love was known
In acts of powered deliverance   (powered?)
        Of those he called his own.

The might of worlds still tells the tale,
        How can I doubt or fear?
From oceans' depths to mountain peaks
        I feel his glory near.
No enemy can shake my faith
        with words of subtleness.
I will not doubt because of them!
        My God will always bless.

So will my heart be anxious now?
        And will it be dismayed?
With God forever at my side
        How can I be afraid?
My heavenly Father sent his Son
        that I be saved and healed:
I am redeemed from earthbound fears
        Through heaven's love revealed.   (heavenly)

A M Tindall 6/29/81

First line is not very captivating - could work to get the deer first, but then my questions pattern
is aborted ....

Rev. p.153; App. C p. 337
ER p. 147

144

PSALM 130 (1st Version)

O Lord, don't count my faults!   (count not?)
        They seem immense...
They plunge me to the depths
        Of anguished sense.

If You would count all sins
        And judge each one,
Lord, who could stand at last
        Before Your throne?

*The heralds watch for dawn,
        See the sun's face.
Much more I wait for You...
        Wait for Your grace.

Deep in my heart I know
        You hear my prayer.
Your hand will lift from sin,
        Not hold me there.

*My heart is filled with awe
        That You forgive.
The good news of His life
        Stills doubts within.

The deepest shades of gloom
        Can cause no fear.
I feel the love of God
        Around me here.

A M Tindall June 1981

Meter too short for subject?
Too many stanzas? An even number of sts. would permit double format.... a couple of [starred]
sts. could be omitted...

ER p. 148

145

App. C p. 358
ER p. 148

ERIK ROUTLEY
929 Route 518, R. D. 1
Skillman, N. J. 08558
Tel. (609) 921-7806

6 July 81

Dear Adrienne -

Good to hear from you: thank you! I am so glad Austin Lovelace was at Garrett: he is a very reliable critic as well as being a most delightful person, and you should certainly take his advice seriously. I think the Garrett summer school should introduce the class to lots of different people of that calibre, and not go on round the same circle: that's partly why I said I wouldn't come any more for a while: our summer session with its new job for me (1980) provided the occasion but I should have said it anyhow. Why, if I'd gone on & on you might not have met Austin. I like him and admire him very much.

Well now: Ps. 139 [p. 158]. You answer your own question really. 'Makes paths of truth unsought' is just like a metrical psalm. Maybe that isn't all bad: but it's the sort of thing the metrical psalm writers of 1650 might have written. I don't know. I have just been completing the metrical psalm section of our hymn book and I think that where we do use a metrical psalm of the old kind (Scottish 1650 or American 1912) there's something to be said for the occasional quaintness or gawkiness of the original. I have been studying the Murrayfield Psalms, 1954, a book nobody knows, which was produced for an Edinburgh parish and fell more or less dead, and have found it immensely helpful in tidying up the old Scottish psalms. All this makes me less worried by 'unsought' than I otherwise might be. The only thing is that the rest of the psalm is of a sufficiently poetic standard to make it possible to recommend that you do take one more look at it. I am quite happy with the "Search me' verse, the second in your letter. That is fine.

Ps. 42 [p. 144]: here's a problem. It's one of the 2 metrical psalms I have attempted myself: but [as] both these have been done to carry the Genevan tunes, they don't really compete. Your stanza 1 I should leave as it is without incorporating the bracketed words. Stanza 2: you can't rhyme overflows with low, I'm afraid. Fred Kaan might but you mustn't! I am not sure about 'powered deliverance': you probably mean 'powerful acts' but I am afraid it reads

147

a bit unnaturally. 'In powerful delivering grace for those....'? No: you want ACTS. 'In liberating deeds of love'.... Your problem.

I didn't quite get the message of 'the might of worlds.' Do you mean the power of God suggested in the cosmos? Are you sure you've got hold of what the psalmist has in mind? I take it that you are here in the 'deep calleth unto deep' passage. Well: what he means is (say the commentators) the cataracts in the rather picturesque country the psalmist was exiled to. He'd been at work, as it were, in Illinois, and had been bundled off to Wyoming as an exile where the scenery was marvelous, but what use was it to him? The cataracts didn't tell him how good God was - rather they mocked him. What I rather want to see is a more eloquent rendering of the enemies saying 'Where is now your God?' In the last stanza I am equally happy with 'heaven's' and 'heavenly'.

Ps. 130 [p. 145]. I am unhappy about this for reasons that may be personal. For me Ps. 130 is second only to 103 in glory: it is one of the very greatest. 'For there is mercy with thee - therefore shalt thou be feared.' - What an august thought! That tremendous crescendo from the beginning to the end of so brief a psalm! So yes, I do think the shortness of the stanzas, and the lines, is against it. 'For he shall redeem Israel from all his sins' - too broad and universal for an intimately personal ending as you have it. Of course, you are up against monumental competition in Luther (Panorama 2). Your lyric is graceful in itself. But I wouldn't have 'don't' in the first line. Or 'seem immense' in the second: they are immense when seen against that Perfection! And I think you might look again at Luther and see how he 'Christianizes' the Psalm. I am far from sure about 'the good news of His life' in your st. 7. Certainly if you made it 6 or 8 stanzas you could give it more apparent substance by joining two stanzas together each time: but the rhyme scheme keeps the lines short, and that wouldn't really make much difference: besides, I don't know of a tune in the 6.4.6.4. D which would adequately express the subject.

Tune for [133] [p. 146]. Very nice. I am most interested to hear that ACL stumbled over the b you marked. Didn't he point out your 5ths between treble and tenor at that point? It's the oldest of traps - a 4-5 progression in the bass simply invites a 6-5 in the tenor and a 3-2 in the treble and we're always doing it - the most famous example (which has always been allowed to stand) is the first cadence of ABBOTS LEIGH, and who can argue with that? Answer - I can! (Cyril Taylor's a very dear friend of mine): have you thought of using an alto E to provide 'salt' - as indicated? Then you've got 5ths bass / treble at the end of measure 2, which I'd rather you avoided. All the rest is nice.

I'd toss out the intrusive 2nd tenor F# in the last-time final chord, and have you considered how you would persuade a congregation to hold the final f# for ten beats? I would shorten those closing bars so that you got your f# cadence on the fourth beat of the penultimate bar (and correspondingly your D chord at the end). But if ACL advised you to have your ending as you have it who am I to complain? (ACL can tell his choir what to do. I feel less authoritative over a congregation, if a congregation is singing this.)

Back to the Hymnal: I am recommending that we have your Ps 16 as you originally did it, plus a version by Nichol Grieve (Congregational Praise 483), which brings out the other colour. I think that will be ideal. Nobody takes any notice of my memos to the committee so I am concluding that they approve but of course we haven't got anything set in stone yet.

Oh the Pharisee and the publican. The minister who shoved me into the ministry - a preacher of superb originality and fascinatingness - once gave a sermon on the Pharisaism of the Publican. He often did things like that! It wasn't quite kosher, I suppose; but it did remind us that if the publican knew the Pharisee was there, he might have been making a parade of humility.... Isn't life difficult?

Basil Harwood's chorale prelude on the hymn tune GRAFTON is beautiful: I forget what it's actually called, but I think it's called TANTUM ERGO. It's in his set published by Novello. Wood is always interesting. You'll be clever if you find them in print, but persevere. So glad you use Parry. About 2005 AD he's going to have a revival. I shan't be here but I'm sure of it.

Warmest greetings!

as ever,

149

July 27, 1981

Dear Dr. Routley:

I'm breaking with "tradition" -- never do I bother you with correspondence from yours truly unless there's something new I've been working on and am ready to ask about. This time I think I'll just go ahead, perhaps on the excuse of the enclosed joke from "Cantate Domino" I think is the name of the Chicago Diocese newsletter I get....

But it's my favorite!

And to follow through on the couple of things from my last letter, and to touch on things from your letter.

Yes it is nice to have different people at Garrett, for a varied approach. Not having you twice is not particularly great, though.... Austin's I enjoyed, but *in toto* all we did was look at new texts; I liked your framework, which would permit fresh materials in more of a context than we had this year. Of course, you had twice as much time as he in which to cover material.... And also I think the creative aspects of hymnody - writing things, or pulling together hymn programs - is possibly the most eye-opening of all. Austin I have known for innumerable years, having been his Publicity Chairman while he was Dean of the North Shore AGO for a Regional Convention (very successful, I am sure partly due to his indefatigable (sp?) little black book.... he is really a very organized type of person (wish I could learn some of that!)). It was fun seeing him again, and Polly too.

His looking over the tune for 133 was very brief, just a few minutes before class, with a couple of other people sitting there, so it wasn't very concentrated. I have a bit of a hard time with rules about parallels that are not permissible vs. those that are okay. I recall heaps of rules from pedagogy classes, at which time my middle name was undoubtedly "parallels" because of the quantity I left undiscovered.... I suppose that parallels in four part texture, when the effect thins the texture, are still bad, although in unison hymns (examples in Chicago's <u>Cantate Domino</u> I am sure ... I remember lulus!) one can "get away with" quite a few. I seem to recall Austin has some like that that shocked me, in his HINMAN...

Anyway I changed the tune at the spot of POLLSTIN (I don't much like trying to name tunes -- this one came from Polly and Austin, obviously, because of Austin's "challenge"...) where there were parallel fifths between soprano and bass - that V-VI progression, I think. Also changed the tenor, as the modal doubling and the lowness of the tenor and the overlapping of parts didn't thrill me much ... honestly! Melodies that jump up so drastically, as this one does, really cause difficulties in harmonizing!!! Then the next score where there are the close harmonies (for textual reasons, as you may have guessed) there are parallel fifths again between soprano and tenor. I'd rather leave those though; avoiding can be through using the note in ( ).

Psalm 139 is included here also [see p. 158]. I've left "unsought" because it doesn't bother me all that much, and I like "thought" and need a rhyme.... the second suggestion for the line seems a little smoother perhaps, although the "paths of truth" fits nicely with the "everlasting way." Do four "truth"s seem too many for the four verses?

Psalm 42 with this last letter to you I must have really blown the deal (as the saying goes); I don't know where I put my copies of what I sent you. But I don't really need them anyway ... I just can't remember what words I had bracketed.... anyway I think this version I rather like. The "might of worlds" I took right off an early version because as I recall I couldn't find the most recent version, which didn't include that... I think I was referring to awesome things in nature, and not at all tuned in to the psalmist in Wyoming.... Certainly do like the "Where is your God?" in there though ... do you? Except for "confidence" perhaps, per note....

Tune for 133 - now I have reread your comments, so I guess the final extra F# [doubling the soprano] is still not as nice as I think. But without it sounds hollow to me - the problem is holding the superlong melody note which is also the third of the chord. Well I'll leave it... I see what you mean about the congregation holding the last notes so long. Actually I wouldn't at all care if they let go and breathed comfortably for most of the time ... and then came in at the beginning ... but maybe that's not logical or notate-able....

Are your two metrical psalms somewhere that one can see them....?

How does one "tidy up" the old Scottish psalms?

Part of my problem with things like "unsought" is that very little bothers me; I remember in that Hymn Society class [WCC- 1980] with Grindal and was it Parker? that a lot of the texts all the class members wrote seemed just fine and quite usable.... maybe the most obviously "bad" thing was when modern or too secular words were used. "Old" forms and thees and thous really didn't seem offensive to me...

You've got another of those funny lines in there -- "Nobody takes any notice of my memos to the committee..." I think they're spoiled, if they don't just make a couple of we-know-how-fortunate-we-are noises once in a while! Do you send around lists of hymns or xeroxes of texts for them to study over? What do you think about subject indexes? I'm still convinced that the CS Hymnal should have one - it's the only American hymnal I know of that doesn't, and even the concordance to the hymnal doesn't tell the topics hymns are focused on....

I've been delving into my hymn index in a new way - very interesting! I'm taking the Unitarian hymnal and comparing it to others ... it has a very high % of hymns unique to itself, which I shall look at en masse up north (along with writing several dozen psalm versions [haha]) ... etc. etc. (and visit Dan's Minocqua Fudge, of which visit you'll be aware in a couple of weeks, so be warned...). And bearing in mind that a hymnal is a layman's book of theology, I can really relate to how very very different are some of the ideas in Unitarian hymns. It's going to also give me a clearer sense, when I look at the non-unique hymns, how they've treated revising... because certainly their ideas are off the mainstream. Must end: no one should have to get more than two pages of my ramblings! Please forgive? Oooh forgot the Pharisee (next time....)

PSALM 42 (Revised Form)

My soul is longing for my God!
      When shall I see his face?
Like thirsting deer by waterbrooks,
      I need His love and grace.
The tears that fall in nighttime hours
      have mocked my constant prayer --
to know God's presence with me here,
      to feel His loving care.

"Where is your God?" Must doubting fears
      destroy my strength and peace?
God is my Presence, and my Rock,
      His loving does not cease!
No enemy can shake my faith
      by words of subtleness:
"Where is your God?" My heart of hearts
      knows God at hand to bless.

Why should I lose my hope to gloom?
      Why do I struggle so?
God's goodness is a fountainhead
      which will forever flow!   (orig. "with ceaseless overflow!")
I've seen in all the days gone by
      His saving love is shown
in acts of power and might, to save
      the ones He calls His own.

So will my soul be anxious now?
      And will it be dismayed?
With Love forever holding me,
      I cannot be afraid!
My heavenly Father sent His Son
      that I be saved and healed.
I am redeemed from earthly fears
      by heaven's love, revealed.

A M Tindall

Meter: CMD

App. C. p. 337
ER p. 154

153

Erik Routley
929 Route 518, R. D. 1
Skillman, NJ 08558
Tel. (609) 921-7806

31 July 81

Dear Adrienne -

Thank you for your last one.

Glad you had a good time at Garrett. We are in the middle of the busiest period here. Two days ago my class composed a tolerable hymn tune. To-day (the last of the week) we shall be looking at their personal compositions. Hectic, but quite fun.

You are quite right: it's in SATB texture that parallels are offensive: and always between treble & bass whatever the texture. But in unison tunes it's a different story. I think you can regard your Ps. 133 [p. 146] tune as finished - it is very agreeable now.

Not too much to be pedantic about in Psalm 42 [p. 153] now. I am a little restless about 'fountainhead'. I think that means really the source of a river: and that's the one part of the river that can't be said to <u>overflow</u>. It flows all right, and if you filled up that line with 4 adjectival syllables & ended it with 'flow' everything would be fine. Your 'confidence' is, I think, quite all right. So, I think, is your 'enemy': and as for Presence - it's elegant, but in the AV - the Hebrew scholars tell me (I am not very subtle about Hebrew) - the sense is blunted. Hebrew implies, definitely, 'see God.'

In Ps 139 [p. 158], one metrical problem: 'glorious is their sum'. If sung to an ordinary DCM with an upbeat, the effect would be tiresome because most of the time the middle syllable of 'glorious' isn't even sounded: so 'glor-EE-ous' would bump badly. Anyhow, is the sum <u>glorious</u>? You really want a synonym for 'countless'. I should re-cast the whole quatrain, because you might need something like 'How countless is their sum!'. Otherwise, apart from a residual touch of doubt about 'makes paths of truth unsought.', I am happy with it.

My two attempts at psalms can be found, for what they are worth, at 4 and 6 in the World Council's <u>Cantate Domino</u>. Ps. 42 is really a paraphrase or summary of those two psalms, designed to carry

154

the Genevan tune: Ps. 98 has travelled a bit and is in <u>Ecumenical Praise</u> (9) and <u>More Hymns for to-Day</u> (165).

I enjoyed the cartoon. You know what <u>my</u> favorite would be! [Probably Watts' "We give immortal praise" - last hymn in <u>Rejoice in the Lord</u>?]

I don't really complain about my committee - except when they fail to answer letters & then say I am making decisions without consulting them! Oh yes, I send round all new texts in full, with melodies stripped in above. I have in my own mind more or less finished the hymnal but I have to appear to be going slowly! However, summer session, with 30 hours a week teaching for 8 weeks, has held all that up for the time being.

Subject indexes are most necessary but often hastily and confusedly compiled - I think the best one I know is the one done by Brian Wren in <u>New Church Praise</u>. A good subject index helps a hymn chooser to be both flexible and exact. Even more important is a good Scripture index: and I don't know of even one that is properly compiled. It's usually done by an editor who doesn't know his Bible!

Have fun Up North.

As ever -

August 7 (I think)

What a delight to get a letter the very first day!!!!!!!

It's wonderfully rainy and thundery right now - an ideal time to type away, and even on this ordinary machine, which will undoubtedly expose my typing

155

weaknesses (the enclosed having already been daubed with liquid paper quite a bit....).

Psalm 42 I already felt that way about fountainhead; I think I like the "will forever" even though the order is dated? Maybe too dated? Anyway the four syllables of adjectives would work too, although not carry into the next four lines as well. (or maybe they do....)

Psalm 139 is the one I said I couldn't possibly name the meter of, because in my as-usual inexpertise I was not realizing meter relates only to syllable count (?). Austin looked at this, and asked if I knew I had used a choriambus. Actually, I may not even be able to spell it .... but I did on purpose fit the psalm's "Search me, O God, and know my heart..." So even though I think perhaps "Infinite" would replace "Glorious" it still must carry the stress on the first syllable, to fit with all the other sixth lines.

Psalm 84 what do you think? A few questions I can see are listed at the bottom of the page.....

The other is way off the subject, as it were. It's been in my file for a couple of years now, since it was rejected by The Christian Century.... and I remembered it when I got to thinking about the publican and the Pharisee... and thought well why not ask what thoughts it stirs for you.... just as a curiousness... anyway it relates to the publican and the Pharisee in that any time one thinks about what one is doing in reference to looking for the reward one gets for doing it, one is undercutting if not nullifying the good effect... At least I think that's what I mean; the "doing" is lost to (self-righteous) "appearing to be doing." When I was a kid I'd be thinking about something, and all of a sudden get sidetracked into thinking about the fact that I was thinking about that something ... then I would realize that I was thinking about thinking about something, and could mentally project the situation like a chain of mirrors slightly off parallel....

I daresay "self-humbleness" is of the same ilk as self-righteousness, and if the self-righteous Pharisee, enumerating his double quantity fastings and his superdiligent tithing were not "justified," then if the publican were "self-humble", he too would not be "justified." Certainly a good topic for a sermon - to make each relate to the purest and most sincere motives. For the Biblical account, however, I have no hangups at all. It was Jesus' story (original or not), and if he says the publican was in fact answered in his prayer, then his prayer must have been sincere ... his humility must have been genuine, which was the point of the story anyway, wasn't it ....?

156

Now my interpretations of "Pharisee" may be off the beam, and I wouldn't mind if you said so ... would you if I am? But I kind of associate them [Pharisees] with this human obedience to extensive humanly interpreted strictures for the sake of their own salvation, and often the human obedience did not include anything genuinely loving in it, but rather was self-oriented, to the working out of salvation in an excluding way ..... that's pretty much what the poem's saying anyway, and maybe they rejected it because it is so incorrect....

I wonder if I can put that more clearly -- if I fix dinner tonight for everyone to eat (and I will...), I can do it motivated by Christian caring - loving my family and loving to provide good for them - or I can do it from the "pharisaical" motivation - it's my job to do it, and so I shall do my job well for my sake, thereby insuring my reward for righteous behavior. In either case the family gets the food ... it's just the motivation that's different, the one very obviously better, in my opinion....

A package is on the way but it's not the good one.... they had a run on toffee last weekend and so in the next week or so some of that will be on the way ... this is just some fudge. Not remembering if you had a taste preference, I got you two kinds with nuts. They have vanilla too - do you like that a lot? And please do not feel you must consume instantaneously! All of this freezes well, though it must be wrapped airtight so it doesn't pick up freezer taste.

I am planning to continue psalming up here -- grateful as always for your incredibly immediate responses (you've undoubtedly snowed your committee ... they don't not answer; it's just that you're superefficient and in contrast they seem to stand still.....)

PSALM 139 (Revised Form)

Search me, O God, and know my heart,
      try me and know my thought,
and guide me if some wicked way
      would make Your truth unsought.
Everything I would say or do,
      everywhere I would go,
Your love sustains my inmost life
      and heals all sin and woe.

Where could I ever hide from You?
      Where could I flee away?
In heaven I am by Your side,
      in hell You are my stay.
Darkness can have no power to hide,
      night brings no threat too near;
Your presence is my shining light!
      Your truth dispels my fear.

Precious are all Your thoughts to me,
      numberless as the sands!
Each time I wake I feel myself
      still cradled in Your hands.
Taking the wings of morning's rays,
      dwelling in farthest seas,
Your hand is even there, to guide,
      Your right hand, holding me.

Surely Your power will vanquish sin!
      Surely Your truth shall reign!
May my life glorify Your good, --
      be free of sin and stain.
Search me, O God, and know my heart,
      try me and know my thought,
and guide me if some wicked way
      would make Your truth unsought.

Adrienne M. Tindall, 1981

CMD

App. C. p. 360, 361
ER pp.139, 147,154

PSALM 84 (1st Version)

How lovely are Your dwellings, Lord,
        courts echoing with praise!
My heart is longing to be there,
        to sing each joyous phrase.
The sparrows find themselves a home,
        the swallows find a nest:
Your altars welcome all of them --
        how sweetly they are blessed!

How happy are the ones who know
        their strength is from the Lord.
They triumph as they hold themselves
        obedient to Your word.
Lord, strengthen me, and hear my prayer,
        anoint me with Your grace,
and let me hope to know Your love
        within Your holy place.

I'd shun the tents of wickedness
        whose doorways open wide,
a thousand days of sensual lusts
        would lure Your world inside!
Far rather would I know Your house --
        just let me guard its door...
the task would be my joy! to serve
        my God, forevermore.

A M Tindall 8/6/81

Rev. p. 210; App. C p. 349
ER p. 189

70 x 7

the christian pharisee came down
and (with a tiniest disconcerted frown)
(it didn't match the jovial smile, which, stretching
 upwards, ended just below the nose)
he greeted all with superoverflows
of camaraderie
       helLOthere!!!!!!! how'veyoubeen?
       (and listening then for just one-
       quarter instant, turns)
and you how'rethings?(look there's another one just there)
let's get together soon...........................
                    helLOthere!!!!!!! how've....
      or else with
      duteous touch of
      hand, embraced
      muchclose his
      brotherman (re-
      membering well
      his Lord's com-
      mand) assiduously
      looking neither   right
         nor
left,
      disclaiming care
      or thought to who
      would see him
      cherishing "the
      least of these"...
completes the picture (wonderest now the frown?)
when Slighting Fault affronts the duty-full ami,
he draws out of his wide phylactery
a tightened scroll and pencil stub?
notes carefully a Fact, smile rigidly serene,
"that's okay, friend, ... but now it's ||||-||||-||||-|| ."

Tuesday August 11th

Greetings from the North Woods!

One often learns the most from one's less ept efforts, and I think it is probably in that framework that I take typewriter in hand and write to see how busy you are these days, and mention that we leave the 21st so if you are busy, the home address is the one to use....

Psalm 45 came second, and I think I may have done something I didn't want to .... obviously it starts but does not stay with the psalm, and quite probably loses the inspired abundant sense of the psalm itself .... I know we talked about wedding hymns in the past when I ran across one that bothered me, and at this point I can't recall exactly what was objectionable ... but in any case this one would fall under that category of being sung by the congregation assembled about the bride and groom, without expecting them to hold hymnbooks and participate.

It says quite a few things which I like, whether they are based in the psalm or not, but there are obvious problems with it too.... Music of course would have to be written because of the weird stress pattern I settled in on... and having 9 (!) stanzas is almost unfair! But something that's done with Mary Baker Eddy's hymns would work here too - there are a couple of settings of her 7 verse poems where there are two stanzas of music alternated, with the odd verse accommodated in the way the hymn / tune appears on the page ... 253 and 256 if you have a hymnal...

So tell me what you think about everything? Including as always how appropriate the ideas are for the focus and within Christian theology....

Psalm 147 [see p. 186] I started before I came up here, and then couldn't find the start. But stanzas 4 and 7 stuck in thought so solidly that it was easy to begin again. Besides, I'd not gotten any rhymes to that point at all ... just seen that the incredibly (impossibly?) long line framework seemed to include the lines remarkably readily.... But I recognize that I have probably exceeded the range of possibility (meter 20.20??). The music of course doesn't exist either, and probably the triple meter is too rollicky? Is that only appropriate for joking or secular use? Anyway, I played around only very briefly with a tune which would accommodate the very irregular joins within the 20 syllable frameworks. A congregation would breathe with the sense of the words, and if it moved along that wouldn't be too bad .... and they could of course breathe with the need, which they do anyway...

The music of course seems vanilla and boring to me . . . .[music lost]

There are of course a few spots where a word hasn't settled in yet, and feels a need for revising .... but I may be so off the beam as to not profit from spending time cogitating over them.... And I daresay calling these "psalms" is not logical, they're so different from the psalm..?

Hope your summer is going fine and that I don't tax your patience beyond its great elastic limit....

from PSALM 45 (1st Version)

Father, bless this wedding,
Let the spirit of Your grace
inspire the hearts of everyone
now gathered in this place.

Make this bridegroom kingly --
inner strength a majesty,
his love and truth and meekness show
a rightness all can see.

Faith, dominion, gladness,
human qualities of grace
are God-ordained and God-sustained;
help him to give them place.

Help him as protector
from all enemies' allure,
to keep his home a citadel
defended and secure.

Make this bride as lovely
as a queen of royal line,
her wisdom and her innocence
describing Your design.

Kindness, peace, compassion,
human qualities of grace
are God-ordained and God-sustained;
help her to give them place.

Help her to be loyal
to the home that she will share,
to let her inner radiance   (3 syllables for radiance wrong??)
bless all who enter there.

Christ, the perfect Bridegroom,
and the church, his perfect Bride,
bear witness to two lives made one;
help hearts to open wide.

Help them, and these people
who are gathered for this feast
support and cherish holy bonds
through love of God, increased.

A M Tindall 8/10/81

Accents '-'-
    --'-'-'
    -'-'-'-'
    -'-'-'

Text recast; see App. C p. 338
[No ER comments (possibly just as well) - letter lost in the mails]

Wednesday August 19

Greetings for the final time from the North Woods!

Actually, I wouldn't get so far "ahead" in letters, except that in completing the enclosed three I have fulfilled a mini-goal I set for myself to accomplish during our three weeks up here....

These are quite different from the last two - quite close to the script, as it were... Ps. 65 came out backwards, but that first line is a favorite with me. By the end of these three, I feel that I am overusing a few rhyming words....

Psalm 15 started out in LM because I was feeling very over-CM'd... The last st. I felt a need for, because of the nature of the material above. Its first form had a slant rhyme for lines 2 and 4, but I've squashed the sentiments into "roam" (even though it took some fussing) because I like the conclusion, and "home" had to stay.

So maybe you've answered a letter and I'll find that out Friday when I arrive home .... but in any case please don't feel any pressure to answer faster than is comfortable to you....

I wish I felt some "good" "bad" "indifferent" about these efforts of mine. I think I "like" them better when they get a little "carried away" rather than sticking very close .... but I've long since accepted the idea within myself that I have no taste insofar as what is great and what is not good - much more is acceptable to me than is probably of recognized excellence. Maybe in hymnody excellence is less than the ultimate consideration, but if I were trying to choose from several texts, I doubt if I could even come up with the "best"!

So I've done two of these today, in any case, and perhaps they show overquick underdoneness....

Another thing I am thrilled with!!!!!!! Ever since HSA Convocation there at WCC I've tried to listen to your tapes, and have only been able to hear a couple now and then, forgetting enough between attempts that I always feel a need to start back at the beginning. ...... Such has gone on for these 14 months .... and so I decided to bring them up here and make a special effort to listen at last .... I have had a ball!!!!! I've heard them start to finish in about 5 afternoons, most of the time intensifying my relaxing holiday luxuriousness by sitting in front of a fire (yes, even in August it's pleasantly cool, delightful after swimming, and anachronistically interesting, season-wise, to have a fire), doing thread count embroidery while you tell me in your relaxed way all about hymnody.... Of course it helps to have it my favorite subject, and it's nice having English spoken in a way I'm partial to (bad construction, eh? ending with a preposition when I'm talking about proper English usage....). But the way you go about it, with complete expertise and overviewing combined with in-depthness, ... well, I've loved it all!!!!! I've thought of someone I shall offer to loan the tapes to - a minister in town whose church really needs to look for a new hymnal - but if he wants to have anyone else hear them I shall give him the address of WCC and suggest the church get a set. I don't want mine worn out.

The background you give in the tapes has given me insights I've not had before, and a much more solid understanding of the whys and wherefores. It all fits together so beautifully, start to finish. . . . .

Anyway, thanks, thanks, thanks from a consumer who's loved the end product.....

I shall be back in the saddle at home soon -- you know I can understand how women have contributed minimally to fields of creative endeavor: interruptive regular responsibilities almost preclude focused efforts unless one almost sets up "office hours" and holds the latter sacred....

Many thanks for all you patience - hope writing again doesn't o'erwhelm you .... and do freeze everything that you don't want to eat right away....

PSALM 65 (1st Version)

You crown the year with goodness, Lord,
    abundance is Your way.
The magnitudes of grace afford
    all good today.

The pastures, clothed with flocks of sheep,
    the valleys green with corn,
shout, joyous for the watch You keep
    through night and morn.

Your water's life abundantly
    pours out to bless the earth.
The grains and grasses form a sea
    of lovely worth.

Each tender shoot is in your care;
    is warmed by gentle rain;
the sunlight, shining everywhere,
    brings forth good grain.

The mountains stand upon their base,
    tumultuous seas find peace,
and warrings of the human race
    are made to cease.

At times iniquities prevail,
    mistakes and sins are great,
but Your great love will never fail
    to compensate.

Salvation's righteousness is Yours,
    and Yours all imminence. (eminence)
Each act of love and power stirs
    our confidence.

All prayers will turn unto the Lord,**
    all vows obey His will.
All praise will wait upon His word,
    and flesh be still.

A M Tindall 8/19/81

**"must" or "shall" for "will" in 8:1, 8:3

Rev. p. 175; App. C p. 345
ER p. 169

PSALM 26 (1st Version)

Each day, O Lord, I try to do   1
   what's good and clean and right.
I walk in my integrity,
   but Yours must be the might.

Your lovingkindness shields my path,   3
   Your truth lights up the way,
to show me what is right and wrong,
   to guide me when I stray.

I will not go in vanity,   4,5
   I will not credit lies.
I will not stay with wickedness
   nor listen to its lies.   [typo for cries]

I'll wash my hands in innocence   6
   and lift my thoughts with prayer,
and then approach Your altar's love
   to feel Your presence there.

Thanksgiving moves my voice to sing   7
   the joy that's in my heart!
I'd tell the world of wondrous works
   and blessings You impart.

I love the honor of Your house,   8,9
   its perfectness is pure.
My heart escapes from sin unstained,
   unmoved by sin's allure.

Redeem me, Lord, for Your great love   11
   and mercy fill all space.
I walk in my integrity,
   relying on Your grace.

A M Tindall 8/19/81

Possible alternate for first st:

Each day, O Lord, I try to do
   what's good and right each hour.
I walk in my integrity,
   but Yours must be the power.

Rev. p. 173; App C. p. 335
ER p. 167

PSALM 15 (1st Version)

Lord, those who come unto Your hill
with righteousness deserving praise
have always listened for Your will
to be their guide throughout life's ways.

Their steps are steady, stance upright.
Their righteous works will never cease.
The truth of God inspires their sight
and moves their hearts to words of peace.

Their tongues obey Love's sweet control,
their acts are for their neighbor's good.
Their friendships have a beautied whole,
forgiving faults in brotherhood.

They honor those who feel an awe
of God and His almighty power.
Their vows, like gems without a flaw,
stay valued still, in trial's hour.

They are not careful of their worth,
nor take from those of humbleness.
Their godly ways enrich the earth,
true witness of the God they bless.*

Unaided, Lord, I cannot live
in paths so pure, and never roam!
And yet, before I've asked, You give
The Christ, to bring me safely home.

A M Tindall 8/81

LM

*and witness forth, and image forth, true witness of, the God they bless.

Rev. in App. C, p. 332
ER p. 168

168

Erik Routley
929 Route 518, R. D. 1
Skillman, NJ 08558
Tel. (609) 921-7806

25 August 81

Dear Adrienne -

I wrote yesterday - I explained in the letter why it was so long: and I am afraid my letter has gone to the North Woods. I only hope the post office there will send it back - I had forgotten you would be leaving so soon. If it has had a roundabout journey, I apologize even more. This one, anyhow, shall go to Kenilworth.

I don't know about women contributing little to creative work: look at all the novelists! It's a mystery why there are still so few female <u>composers</u> on the large scale: but there certainly have been some good philosophers & scholars. Don't be discouraged! Certainly time for concentration & reflection has something to do with it. I am finding that: I have just started trying to do what I stopped doing forty years ago - compose something in a larger form that isn't church music. Somebody has asked me to. The thing I most miss is a good tract of time when nothing else interferes: but I am pretty sure that will never happen now, so I am doing my best in bits. But it makes me see what you mean.

Nice psalms: very nice ones, I thought. You will have to look a long way for a decent tune in 8.6.8.4 to Ps. 65 [p. 166]: I don't know one: still, you can always compose it. I hesitate over 'Your water's life': I believe you might be able to say that a bit less contortedly. And I just wonder about the mountains standing on their <u>base</u>. I don't know - either it's almost tautology (what else could anything stand on) or it's a shade affected. Iniquities prevail - at times? Always, I'd have thought, here or there. Can one 'compensate' without anything to follow? I rather doubt the use of that verb as a plain intransitive. Apart from these details, this runs well.

Psalm 26 [p. 167] is mostly excellent, but stanza 3 needs looking at again, because you made 'lies' rhyme with 'lies', which is cheating! While you are about it, perhaps you could dispose of the rather prosy word 'credit' meaning 'believe'. Not a very good word for formal use. Your alternative for st. 1 is not an improvement, because it has, in the first two lines, 'Each day' and 'each hour' qualifying the same verb: stay with the original.

Psalm 15 [p. 170] is always a favorite of mine, so I look at any version with special suspicion. Yours comes off pretty well. 'Stance upright' - does that mean they 'walk tall'? it suggests something crudely physical. 'Their tongues obey' - I want to say 'accept love's sweet control'. I slightly miss what I think the most eloquent phrase in the psalm: - in Coverdale 'He that sweareth unto his neighbour, and disappointeth him not, though it were his own hindrance.' 'In trial's hour' I find a little too formal for that very pregnant observation. And have you coped with 'and speaketh the truth from his heart'? It's an incredibly difficult psalm to versify with conciseness and faithfulness, and I think you have made a very good shot at it. You may have observed that you use more words than the original does: you have 152, the Coverdale 118, King James Version, 99. I wonder about 'take from those of humbleness' - apart from it being a rather stilted phrase, I don't find anything to correspond with it in verse 5: and what about 'He that doeth these things shall never fall'? As I say, I doubt if there is a more difficult psalm to versify than this one.

But keep up the good work; you're developing an easier and more relaxed style, and that is all to the good.

I hope this gets to the right address.

As ever,

170

September 4, 1981

Dear Dr. Routley:

Your letter to the cabin is evidently on its way here, either through forwarding (I called the post office Monday, so they're now forwarding everything), or Jack and the girls will bring it back, as they're arriving up there tonight .... it may be in the box, and the post office won't take it back again... [Letter was never found.]

In any case this of the 25th is fine to be going on with.... I took your "You can always compose it" [for ps. 65] literally ... one a "friendly" (hopefully!) tune, and the other more a straight "psalm" tune. The problem with the latter is 8 sts., I would think. I've checked and checked for parallels, left in one "bad" (I bet) direct octave soprano/bass. Undoubtedly you'll unearth more things .... the beginning of the melody is maybe not very melodious, but I had a bit of fun making a crown there.

I think I got the four things you mentioned about the verses .... didn't I? Does the "Injustices" stanza still bother? The affirming is like Isaiah's "Though your sins be as scarlet...." My OT course thought that should have question marks, instead of periods, to imply that scarlet-red-bad-sins couldn't be white as wool (snow), I guess. Sounds "Lutheran" to me .... "With God all things are possible," even dissolving historical-fact sins.... "Again" can rhyme with "stain" can't it? Just slantwise...

Psalm 26 stanza 3 looked at. The "lies / lies" rhyme was a typo type blunder; the original had "lies / cries" but I dropped it along the way somewhere.

Two new ones - the stress pattern to 61 is regular; I thought I was doing the irregular one first... And of course I may be finding out with the letter that's traveling that '--'--'--.... etc. is not good.

As I look at psalms to think which to do next, I can see part of the challenge is taking similar ideas from psalm to psalm and letting the psalm's individuality still come through ... anyway what do you think of these?

I'm chicken (do you know the idiom?) to look at 15 again ... you should just list your favorites so I don't cause you pain as I mess around with them .... Have you ever composed organ things that one could use? Chorale preludes or something? I'm not too hopeless at reading ms...

All for now - amazing eh? Only one page.... thanks as always....

PSALM 61 (1st Setting) (1st Version)

The ends of the earth hear my cry to the Lord
      when enemies make me afraid.
No fear overwhelms me when I know Him near;
      I stand in my trust of His aid.

A glorious heritage blesses my days
      of love and respect for the Lord.
He hears all my prayers as they pour from my heart,
      and peace is my precious reward.

O Father, Your strength is a towering rock,
      Your love is a covering of wings.
Such power and gentleness fill me with awe,
      my heart leaps with joy as it sings!

Your mercy and truth are preserving my life,
      prolonging the length of my days.
I'll dwell in Your house with abundance of thanks!
      Let all the earth echo my praise!

A M Tindall 9/4/81

Stress pattern:

ER p. 178

PSALM 26 (Revised)

Each day, O Lord, I try to do
   what's good and clean and right.
I walk in my integrity,
   but Yours must be the might.

Your lovingkindness shields my path,
   Your truth lights up the way,
to show me what is right and wrong,
   to guide me when I stray.

I will not give an ear to lies,
   I'll shun hypocrisy.
the subtle snares of wickedness
   will gain no hold on me.

I'll wash my hands in innocence
   and lift my thoughts with prayer,
and then approach Your altar's love
   to feel Your presence there.

Thanksgiving moves my voice to sing
   the joy that's in my heart!
I'd tell the world of wondrous works
   and blessings You impart.

I love the honor of Your house,
   its perfectness is pure.
My heart escapes from sin unstained,
   unmoved by sin's allure.

Redeem me, Lord, for Your great love
   and mercy fill all space.
I walk in my integrity,
   relying on Your grace.

        A M Tindall 9/4/81

App. C p. 335
ER p. 178

PSALM 47 (1st Version)

Clap your hands, all you peoples of God,	1,2
clap, and shout with song!	
For God most high is exalted on earth,	
no enemies triumph long.	

Clap your hands, all you peoples of God,   1,2
    clap, and shout with song!
For God most high is exalted on earth,
    no enemies triumph long.

We are claimed with His trumpet and love,   3,4
    witness, and pay heed!
We each inherit God's promise of old
    as Abraham's living seed.

God is King over all of the earth!   7,8
    Praise, and understand.
He sits upon His holiness' throne
    and rules over every land.

Praise His name, all the ends of the earth,   9,4
    praise, and praise again!
We are His people, inheriting good, --
    the blessings of His hand.*

A M Tindall 9/4/81

*Could be "and blessing from His hand," as a continuation of preceding line. Sts. 2 & 3 carry over like that...

Stress pattern:

```
              '-'--'--'
              '-'
              -'-'--'--'
              -'-'
```

I surely would prefer "ye" for "you" in line 1! "You people" really sounds klutzy.... I had "ye" to start though, and the rhythm has to be maintained... One could say "the" but that sounds kind of remote and non-direct.

Is "earth" ... "earth" too much ending 3:1 and 4:1?

Rev. p. 195; App. C p. 339
ER p. 178

PSALM 65 (Revised Version)

You crown the year with goodness, Lord,
      abundance is Your way.
The magnitudes of grace afford
      all good each day.

The pastures, clothed with flocks of sheep,
      the valleys green with corn,
shout, joyous for the watch You keep
      through night and morn.

Your life-bestowing streams flow free
      with blessings for the earth,
The grains and grasses form a sea
      of lovely worth.

Each tender shoot is in your care;
      is warmed by gentle rain;
the sunlight, shining everywhere,
      brings forth good grain.

Your strength holds mountains on their base,
      commands the seas find peace, --
the warrings of the human race
      must also cease.

Injustices will not prevail,
      wrongdoings will not stain,
for Your great love will never fail
      to cleanse again.

Salvation's righteousness is Yours,
      and Yours all eminence,
Each act of love and power stirs
      our confidence.

All prayers must turn unto the Lord,
      all vows obey His will.
All praise must wait upon His word,
      and flesh be still.

A M Tindall 9/4/81

App. C p. 345

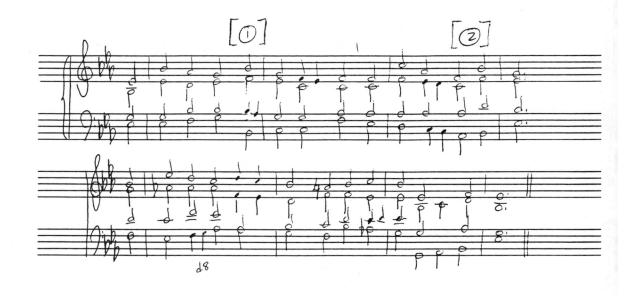

App. C p. 346

ER pp. 178-179 [Copied from the rough draft of the tune; no ER markings.]

ARCHIVES

App. C p. 346
ER pp. 178-179 [Copied from the rough draft of the tune; no ER markings.]

[no letterhead]

12 September 1981

Dear Adrienne -

Thank you for your latest - and I'm not sure
whether I mentioned that the second parcel of goodies arrived safely:
but it did, and thank you for that too.

Psalm 61 [p. 172] is very pleasant. 'Let all the
earth echo my praise' - rather a large claim? But no, maybe it will do.
The metre is much better than the one with the unremitting dactyls.

Pslam 47 [p. 174] - another pleasant & lyric metre.
In II, I am not sure about being claimed either by or with the trumpet,
because I think 'trumpet and love' is a kind of zeugma - unequal yoking
of ideas. I don't think there's enough in common between trumpet &
love to find any verb that will go with both. I am fussy about 'all of' in III,
which is an expression I am increasingly encountering here. It's a
contradiction. I know we often say 'all of you' and 'all of them', and I
expect we have to live with that. But 'of' always means a part, and 'All'
means 'all', and I myself would never use 'all of' with anything stronger
than a pronoun. 'All the earth' is what you mean, - and it's just too bad
that the metre doesn't accommodate it. Similarly, I just wonder about
'His holiness' throne': the genitive of things ending in s, or worse, ss, is
always difficult. ('All hail the power of Jesus' name' - so awkward!); I
wonder if this expression can be put more gracefully. No, I don't think it
matters too much having two earths: but you can always use 'world' in
the earlier stanza if it bothers you.

Psalm 26 [p. 173] is now very nice. No problems, I think.
Nor with 65.

The tunes for 65 [pages 176, 177] both present to me the
same difficulty, which is that I think you're a bit key-tied, and a bit
tentative in your modulations. The first one runs nicely - even if I think
it's a pity in CM (which this almost is) to return to the tonic chord half

178

way through: I know plenty of tunes do, but few really good ones. Details - you don't always prepare your discords very firmly, do you? I think the chord marked (1) would be much better as a plain B flat chord. At (2) where I have put an arrow you move the tenor through a tritone. No way, I'm afraid! You then introduce a leading note that doesn't lead - the D should go to E flat, but you saw that that wouldn't really do. It's the D that causes the trouble. I don't understand the force of the very odd and alien chord marked (3) and perhaps it isn't what you meant. There are two naughty progressions there in the 6th and 7th measures. Why don't you try a plagal cadence on the 6/4? It shouldn't happen too often but it might do here. (Then you wouldn't have that other non-leading leading note in the alto).

The second tune is more ambitious; I think maybe it is a bit folky in style for Psalm 65 which really is rather august; it's the repeated notes that produce this effect, and also the repetition of phrase 1 in phrase 3 a tone higher. At (1) there's an unprepared discord which looks a bit odd. At (2) there's one of these tentative modulations - the C# suggesting that we're going to have a cadence in D minor - which would actually be rather effective. But if you want to rush back home to your dominant, make it a real dominant, not a 6/4 on the home chord (3), which at that climactic point is a let-down. Do be careful of the 6/4, especially unprepared. But the tune has plenty of character and only needs cleaning up a bit. For the life of me I can't detect the octaves between soprano & bass. If they are there I suppose they must be all right!

I don't think I have quite understood your difficulty about sins being white as wool. (Wool it is indeed). Blood stain is very difficult to wash out: and even if it's as it were a permanent stain, the thought in Isaiah is that it can be removed by forgiveness. Not error, mark you, but sin. Sin is unparaphraseable: either one means sin or one means something else that needs another word. Exactly what your OT teacher was getting at I haven't really gathered. Of course what's red can't be white, but it can become so, especially through the Hebrew doctrine of atonement. (KAPHAR - I expect your teacher mentioned that.)

Again does, I think, rhyme with stain in the USA; in parts of England too, though I think not in received speech, where we tend to say 'agen.' But eye-rhyme, in such cases, is usually deemed to compensate for that sort of variation in pronunciation.

I hope my letter to the far north caught up eventually. Yours of the 4th arrived here today (12th), which looks leisurely: letters

179

from our son in Australia usually take 5 days. That, I suppose, is known as relativity.

All best wishes,

as ever,

September 23, 1981

Dear Dr. Routley:

A quick note before we head north to see the fall colors tomorrow. I'll call the post office there to probably put a tracer on this missing letter of late August... [Letter was never found.]

Enclosed please find... and the one I did today is going to gel a while before troubling you with it....

I knew that 8684D [p. 177] tune was not the right flavor; I remember thinking that as I finished it up, but decided to send it anyway. From the dumb mistakes in that one sheet, I think I ought to take some coaching around here in composition... one would never guess I majored in Music Theory, undergraduatewise! The parallels as always plague me; I think my ear does not reject them the way it should; I tried the parts together two at a time, and still didn't turn them up. A couple of specifics: the bad octave you did find - your number 2 in the first tune ... a direct octave soprano/bass. The tritone in that progression was another oops!, but the leading tone resolving down to the fifth of the next chord used to be regarded as okay? JSB does it, and I recall that Piston endorsed it, when handled that way. Such rules, or rather exceptions to general rules (of resolving leading tones) are a little vague in my mind at this point, and could be solidified with review. I recall surprising you with the "hat" rule that was enforced in my harmony classes - no skip between stepwise motion in the same direction, no stepwise motion between skips in the same direction. And although it's not a frequently appearing pattern, I noticed one in the hymn sing Sunday (program enclosed [no copy here]) which gave no one any trouble at all.... (that was the reason to not do it, according to my teacher - hard to sing). I marked it, p. 13 [of the hymn program?]. But maybe there are some "different" rules I'm starting from...

I shall correct these later ... along with Psalm 47...

But a couple of other questions I thought I'd try to get the answer to before doing those ... what kind of candy was in your second parcel? I've gotten some rather confusing thank yous from other friends, and don't like to pursue them with questions.... Could you define error and sin? "Sin is unparaphraseable" doesn't quite tell me whether or not I'm thinking of it right.... My OT teacher did not mention KAPHAR... he was maintaining that one could not wash blood out, red could not become white, and I thought he therefore was inferring that God couldn't "erase" sins either.... And last query, is the group you're editing the hymnal for starting from the hymnal put together by Reformed and Presbyterian groups in the 1950s? Hurray another one pager (barely...)!! Less of your time, eh?

well page 2

P.S. I just have to add that after all that serious (though of course helpful and interesting!) letter, with only a smile [evoked] at trying to hear noway! with a British accent .... that your last word had a remarkable and telling effect! Relativity indeed.... and as your letter was postmarked about 36 hours before I was reading it, there must be, at best, an exciting unpredictability in the US mails .... which hopefully will yield up the letter that still wanders... "Unremitting dactyls" gives me a hint of something though, and I shall avoid them from now on.

And while I'm telling chuckles I must mention that on the way home from Wisconsin in August, when I drove down with my sister-in-law, I took your tapes in the car, and offered to play her one tape to try it, choosing the Watts one. She's rather addicted to England, travels there, appreciates English spoken by Englishmen, and is a teacher, so she relates to learning things. We ended up hearing 5 1/2 tapes, all of which she enjoyed immensely. The winning lines were "card-carrying member of the Church of England," the one about lazy musicians and you knew because you are one (haha) and there was a third one written down downstairs but which I'll not pursue. Are your tapes being advertised to libraries and schools? I still enjoy them, thinking back...

[signature]

PSALM 121 (1st Version; no revision)

My help is from the Lord most high
who makes the earth, the seas, the sky.
His strength is higher than the hills.
He guards me, and my fearing stills.

He keeps His vigil day and night,
no weariness will dim His sight.
No matter where my path may lead
I know He's there to meet my need.

The Lord will cherish me each day,
give gentle shade upon my way.
I'll fear no heat of blistering sun,
nor moon's dark force, when day is done.

No evil overwhelms the Lord,
and He preserves me with his Word.
My going out and coming in
are safe, as they have always been.

A M Tindall 9/23/81

LM

App. C p. 353
ER below

Erik Routley
929 Route 518, R. D. 1
Skillman, NJ 08558
Tel. (609) 921-7806

1 October, 81

Dear Adrienne -
    Psalm 121 is very nice indeed. I have no quarrels or nits to pick at all. Thank you for it.

182

Yes, I know that the leading-note going down at the final cadence is JSB's invariable custom, and my own theory (I haven't checked it with the experts) is that this came of his always writing for instruments as well as voices. (It does happen also in the a capella motets but that would be because the habit was ingrained). I am not sure, but I think that when strings are playing, the common chord without the fifth sounds quite differently from the way it sounds with voices, especially alto voices. On the organ one often adds the 5th to a final chord of, say, G-B-G for a similar reason. The rule about leading notes going up is strictly vocal, and I suppose that if one thinks of SATB hymn tunes as vocal, that's the rule one follows. But it doesn't matter much.

As for the theory of never having skips between stepwise melodic phrases in the same direction, who on earth propounded that? I never heard such nonsense in my life! As if the opening phrase of 'Come down, O love divine' didn't get all its strength from the small skip! As John Wilson has observed, many successful tunes are pentatonic, and in those such skips have a sort of inevitability that gives pentatonic phrases their character. I should forget all that if I were you. Why, come to think of it, even in plainsong you have this phrase in the eighth tone -- G-A-C-D -- and it's marvelous.

KAPHAR. No, you can't wash blood out, but what you did in Hebrew times was cover it: that's what KAPHAR means. And it is also the word for 'atonement' The custom was that when blood was spilt on the ground, you hastened to cover it up 'lest it cry to heaven'. Hence, in Psalm 32, 'the man whose unrighteousness is forgiven and whose sin is covered.'

Myself, I think 'error' is the mistake you or I make on some specific occasion - never mind whether it's a small one or a big one: 'sin' is what predisposes us to make it. A good deal of what used to be attributed to 'sin' has now been re-described in psychological terms, and that, as it turns out, has helped nobody: because while one can say that this fellow was predisposed to mug that old lady in Central Park because he had a bad home background, what one is really saying is that he couldn't help it and shouldn't be blamed for it. If you believe in the existence of sin what you say is that he decided to do it, and, calling on divine power, can be forgiven for it. And of course being forgiven doesn't mean "We'll say no more about it': it means the sin, for which one may properly be asked to make some restitution, can be covered - hidden away, and through being hidden, atrophied: it needn't fester, and it needn't become a permanent source of corruption or bitterness: this character can start again. Since that's in human terms

183

inconceivable, it's one of those things that are impossible with us but possible with God: I think that's what we believe.

The Hymnal. No, that's the beauty of it! The Reformed Church in America has commissioned it solo. But unofficially Presbyterians have been showing interest. One of them, who has been sitting in on our meetings, has openly said, 'We couldn't begin to do it like this,' meaning that a large denomination like Presbyterianism is vulnerable to emotional bureaucracy the way a small one isn't. By that phrase, which I have just thought of, I mean all the baggage of pressure-groups who demand representation and foul up what is essentially a highly skilled operation. We don't have to be like that: a committee of seven can come to a common mind fairly quickly, and can accept responsibility for seeing that the interests of others are represented. In a big denomination no such committee would, nowadays, be trusted. Everybody wants to have their turn at flying the plane. So it's being rather fun. You must have noticed yourself that the most influential and distinguished hymn books of history have been edited by small groups or even by one person! (The English Hymnal, Songs of Praise, Oxford Book of Carols, Congregational Church Hymnal 1887 - one person in that case). We aim to get the interest of anybody who wants an intelligent new hymnal, no matter who it is!

The last batch of candy we got was the sort we like best of all: chocolate covered toffee: sinfully good.

I don't know what promotion there has been for the tapes you so kindly speak of: but the publisher has sold enough of them to get his outlay back and a tolerable profit, so he's cautiously pleased. The price seems to me horrendous, but people have been very kind.

As ever -

184

October 20, 1981

Dear Dr. Routley:

When we went north I called the Post Office, and they said that the sender would properly initiate looking for lost letters... your reference to it merely includes that it is a "long" one - answering two of mine, and you must have sent it about August 20th. . . . [letter was never found.]

Well anyway, I've enclosed two of the efforts that were in my letters to you [I omitted the wedding psalm and the 70 x 7], because I really would like to pester you for at least that much ... Psalm 84 [see page 159] I kind of like and the other, 147, I've taken out some of the '-- feet per the comment in one of your letters since....

I was interested in what hymnal your present effort will supersede... my exploration of the Unitarian was very interesting and contributed also to my hymn index file's being expanded, so I thought I'd explore what you were "coming from" next.... But actually the next month of so looks a bit thick with my being involved in a new organ (Möller) being installed in our church (where I belong, not where I play), so I may not be working on that right away...

Thanks for your explanation of sin and error... and I certainly to agree with the psychological interpretations not helping things much! I have just finished looking over my daughter's potential psychology text, and admit to not being in tune at all with what they seem to be presenting! Some of it is amusingly farfetched, except for the effect that you mention, that people can't help what they do and shouldn't be blamed, etc. etc. Seems to me that a very sad effect of that attitude is that people won't try as hard to do what's best or right.... Ah well, mustn't oversimplify lest I be judged closed-minded. Some of it seems reasonably common-sensical (and some of it not...).

The new effort is one of those meters which doesn't look like there's an existing tune for. Should I be putting little slurs under potential two syllable counts that are to be taken as one? Does that bother you? I love getting your letters,

185

hearing about your current hymnal editing, having the opportunity (and the impelling) to dig in again with a psalm or two. Too many distractions make me put them aside, and I really don't want to stop a <u>little</u> going ahead at least... thanks again as always!!!

Psalm 147 (Revised Version)

Let praise to God fill the music of earth!
Let the beauty of thanks be our song.
Our hearts overflow for blessings He gives (to)
His people all day long.

His understanding is infinite;
listen, Jerusalem, hear and obey.
Commandments are sent in swift cadenced echoes,
His people shall not stray.

Happy am I! for the God who was Abraham's,
Isaac's, and Jacob's, is mine!
His love is eternal; all of His children
are blessed in His design.

God counts the stars, and He calls them by name,
ice and snow, frost and cold show His power.
He covers the heavens with clouds, He sends rains
which bring the fields to flower.

God takes His pleasure in all those who fear Him,
in those who have hope in His care.
He heals broken hearts, He binds up all wounds,
He hears the meekest prayer.

Lives are transformed, for disciples are stirred
and the good news is preached and proclaimed.
The lame walk with leaping, blindness sees plainly,
all healed in Jesus' name.

Happy am I! for the God who was Peter's
and Paul's and Christ Jesus' is mine!
His love is eternal; all of His children
are blessed in His design.

A M Tindall 10/20/81

Stress Pattern: '--'--'--'--
                   '--'--'
                   _'--'--'--'
                   _'-'-'

I may have gotten this backwards; having the last line -'-'-' seem to put the brakes on. Maybe it should aim for starting that way, and then rollicking along at the ends of the stanzas in the '-- feet (if that's possible, of course... who knows? I'm just fiddling around with it at this point....) Maybe the first two lines continuous dactyls (?) are too much in any form...

First line of st. 1 necessitates a strong beat on "Let" which music would have to provide....

App. C p. 362
ER p. 189

Psalm 61 (2nd Setting) (Revised Version)

From the ends of the earth will I cry to God --
    O listen to my prayer!
For you are my shelter, my shield and tower;
    I need Your love and care.

When the enemy's power overwhelms my heart
    with danger's darkening fear,
You lead to the road that is higher than I,
    and keep me safely near.

And my life is prolonged, for Your goodness and grace
    preserve my strength and peace.   (my strength, my peace.)
Your mercy and truth ever bless my years,
    Your loving does not cease.

All my vows have been heard in the heights of heaven:
    what joy this knowledge brings!
I'd live in Your dwellings forevermore
    beneath Your sheltering wings.

A M Tindall 10/19/81

--'--'--'-'
-'-'-'
-'--'--'--'
-'-'-'

St. 3 could start with "Thus" instead of "and" ... but I'll bet I won't get away with that stanza anyway; three lines which all have two nouns linked with "and" seems a bit much when one looks analytically...

App. C p. 344.
ER p. 189

188

Erik Routley
929 Route 518, R. D. 1
Skillman, NJ 08558
Tel. (609) 921-7806

26 October 81

Dear Adrienne -

What a bore about my letter that went astray. All post offices are a bit imprecise these days, though ordinarily I trust the small ones (like Skillman) better than the big ones. Perhaps it will turn up eventually, but I hate to think of your sending all those goodies and never getting the letter. I can't remember what I said, I'm afraid, because these aren't letters I take carbons of. (There was once a man who carboned all his letters & then published a lot of them as a book: I'm not in that league) [AT does not agree!]

Psalm 147 [p. 186-187] is rather nice; I think the metre works quite well. It's odd about the initial word 'Let' - a point I hadn't noticed until you raised it: that in the first person plural imperative - 'Let us with a gladsome mind...' it carries an accent, whereas in the third person plural imperative (or singular) - 'Let all the world in every corner sing' it doesn't. Or it needn't. Yours is 3rd person but it doesn't matter that in this case it is accented. The effect is lyric, and I should think quite easy to set to music.

Ps. 61 [p. 188] is also original metrically, but it would go to one of those early 19th century CMs which have lots of short notes that you can distribute more or less a you like - e.g. WARWICK, which I'll enclose. I don't mind 'And' in st. 3: the old pedantry about never beginning sentences with 'And' is now quite a thing of the past. It shouldn't happen too often because it could become affected: but it sometimes communicates a touch of enthusiasm, even of impatience to get the next thing said, that can be quite effective. As in 'And can it be that I should gain....', 'And did those feet in ancient time....', 'And now, O Father, mindful of the love.....' I see nothing to object to in any of that stanza!

Psalm 84 [p. 159] of course has a lot of competition - especially from Milton, who I think did it very well. What do you think 'from strength to strength' means in this context? I am not sure what it means in st. 2 of yours. The commentators seem to agree that 'they go from strength to strength' means that they get stronger (not more weary) as they go on: I don't think that quite comes through in your

189

version. And I think perhaps you could add another stanza to express the sense of movement and pilgrimage in the psalm; 'Blessed are they... in whose hearts are the highways to Zion', as one translation has it.

The hymnal has already got to the stage where there's too much good stuff for us to use. I was telling our last committee about your words-only hymnal, and about the letter I had from your publisher. It impressed them. They'd never heard of a hymnal printed as a book of poetry. Just possibly we may get away with that. I am certainly surprised, and a bit gratified, to see how some of them are reacting to the sight of hymns thus printed: for when I send a section round for them to work on I always re-type it so that the words are separate from the music, and they say they are appreciating words for the first time. It looks as if our publisher may well be Eerdmans - who are a good firm: they must be because they publish Charles Williams.

These 3 psalms are good. Keep it coming.

As ever -

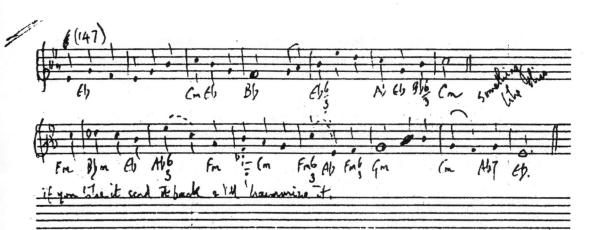

if you like it send it back & I'll harmonize it.

November 10th!

Dear friend....

I've run into you, as it were, several times in the past few days... awe-inspiring all the creative things that you've done!! Saturday I went down to the Episcopal hymnal workshop, to see how things are coming along. Your name came up as the first outside (is that term right?) consultant they asked to look over the book. Then Monday I finally got (after at least two years of trying) the Cantate Domino done for the World Council of Churches, and there, signing for the editors..... Monday night I sat down to write up the minutes for a church committee meeting (Organ Installation - lots of ever-changing details!) and the GIA fall catalog, on top of the printed matter from Saturday's workshop, had bold as imaginable the ad for that third book [The Music of Christian Hymnody, ISBN 0-941050-00-9] which St. John's Press was supposed to print (and evidently missed the boat on....). So I called GIA and have ordered it as soon as it is ready.

So I don't know where you find time to answer letters such as mine, or where I find the nerve to presume upon your kindness, but I shall continue to do so as long as you don't mind.... As to your keeping copies of all your letters... I can only judge from the ones I have here (and do save for obvious pedagogical and enjoyable reasons) that, for someone interested in to the general subject matter, they're well worth saving! Considering your prodigious achievements you'll likely dash off memoirs or an autobiography some month or other in the distant future, and I daresay biographical efforts by others too, would be well served

191

by any and all writings ... oh who am I to tell you what to save anyway? Such intrusion! It's just that you've done so much no one would ever be able to comprehend it all unless your files are full of clues in all the activities in all the directions they've gone! It sounds egotistical to publish all one's letters ... but it doesn't sound egotistical at all for someone else to discover and publish all the letters of important figures in specialized or general areas of creative endeavor.... Anyway, I save them all, refer back on occasion, and am consistently grateful and amazed at your generosity in writing them.

We sang a "Holy Spirit" text to BRIDEGROOM last Saturday. I think I have the words here somewhere in this little packet. Why were they so definitely NoWay! about the bridegroom text? Is it too "personal" for an Episcopalian? I admit that the fit was so perfect between tune and its original text ["As the bridegroom to his chosen"; see p. 80], and the association so close, that I wasn't ready to let go and relate to this new marriage.

A new marriage which I found fabulous - as I did at that Convocation in Princeton - is the Frederick Pratt Green text, "When in our music God is glorified" set to the tune, ENGELBERG. Of course in both situations it was sung by a large group of musicians, for whom the text would have its sweetest and deepest significance, perhaps even the greatest emotional appeal... and the tune has a warmth and a kind of soaring quality, which for me fits this text better than the text in the Hymnal 1940... the latter being a text with a lot more doctrinal points which seem more "formal" than the tune's flavor... oh well, just an observation, but "When in our music" fits so well I'd almost think he'd had the tune in mind as he wrote. What beautiful ideas, one after the other, irresistibly the right ones next, I think, carrying the singer along... (you might guess I like it...)

I'm glad to hear your words-only-book convictions are finding acceptance. I somehow supposed having such a book was typical, rather than rare. But then when I was purchasing American hymnals I was always specifying the edition with the full music score, and I never even asked what else was available. Probably the Christian Scientists got the idea from England anyway, as the committee in charge of the 1932 hymnal was half from England. I was going to rush around and tell you all the English hymnals which I knew of that had words-only volumes, but you probably know all that already... I got the Songs of Praise in a words-only by mistake, before I got the music edition. But they don't print it as a book of poetry, which I think is almost intrinsically necessary to achieve what you're going to achieve; Songs of Praise has printed the texts in as little a number of pages as possible, and some texts will even start with half of a stanza on the bottom right and a page turn for the rest. Kind of a downer on the significance/identity/unity of the individual texts....

Yes yes yes! I do like your tune SOMETHING LIKE THIS (unusual name .... no, I'm teasing of course...)! Chock full of noticeable things to me ... like a IV-I cadence at the end, no key-tiedness, and a "hat" in the third measure! We were singing hats all over the place Saturday, and even though I can still visually recall just how they were marked in my first year harmony exercises, I am letting go of what is obviously baseless restricting... I shall enclose the tune delightedly andticipating the harmonization, as all your harmonizations are, in my estimation... Are the dotted slurs right? Do you suppose the first 2 measures are "excited" enough for the "Happy am I!" stanzas....? But I like it! The tune for 61 I can see what you mean. Was I ever chagrined (sp.?) to find when I went to file that text, that I had already done a text on psalm 61! What a signal example of unmemorability!!!! yccchh!

About SOMETHING LIKE THIS ... my meter pattern at the bottom of the page is much more regular-appearing than the lines are in actuality, and the half notes fall well in three verses, not so well in the other four perhaps; see what you think:

1. on "earth" (good)
2. on "List" (?)
3. on "Ab" (medium?)
4. on "name" (good)
5. on "fear" (not too good)
6. on "stirred" (good)
7. on "Pete" (medium?)

I don't know how much one would want to smooth it out; you're the unquestioned expert so I just mention it.... Would something with this irregularity of the lines' sense still be okay to print separate from the music? I guess if the syllable count is always right (no irregularities between the verses) it wouldn't bother anyone, eh?

I confess with the psalms sometimes I research, and (obviously) sometimes I just kind of "take off" in whatever direction. I shall pursue Psalm 84 later, even though Milton's is so obviously a winner... my "from strength to strength" I can't say I "understand", and certainly I wasn't tuned in to what was really going on in the psalm! The hymn starting "From glory unto glory" is in our book, including "From strength to strength go on," and I was just relating to its being affirmative, I think.

Psalm 47 nothing too unobvious - does it read better now?

Psalm 127 just the meter. Is the word "might" seeming dated at all? It's a handydandy rhymer and crops up often, but the other meaning bothers me a bit - the "I might go, and then again I might not" (I suppose it should be "may" in that usage, but you know what I mean...)

Psalm 93 I have a couple of questions about... what do you think of it? The rhyme scheme may be "wrong;" a,x,b,y,a,b doesn't fit with the line length patterns; I kept finding myself wanting to rhyme lines 4 & 5. Would "unbelief" of natural law being set aside make this a hard hymn for a congregation to identify with?

Psalm 83 I did this morning - just to have enough to send to merit asking you to answer a letter... and in this case I acknowledge having just taken off (93 I researched a bit)...

I'm looking forward to getting to know your <u>Cantate Domino</u> hymnal (difficult to keep having the Chicago Diocese book pop into mind when I say that! But I guess there are lots of hymnals with names the same as others...). Also, my mother-in-law brought me home a hymnal from Ireland, which I have yet to delve into, past trying a couple of the tunes...

Thank you!thank you!thank you!thank you! as always! I wish there were something I could do to help you in return....

Psalm 47 (Revised Version)

Clap your hands, all you peoples of God,
　　　clap, and shout with song!
For God most high is exalted on earth;
　　　no enemies triumph long!

Hear His trumpet, the power of His call:
　　　witness, and pay heed!
We each inherit God's promise of old
　　　as Abraham's living seed.

God the Lord is the King of the earth;
　　　praise, and understand!
His holiness is a wonderful throne!
　　　He rules over every land.

Praise His name, all the ends of the earth,
　　　praise, and praise again!
We are His people, inheriting good
　　　and blessing from His hand.**

A M Tindall 11/11/81

**or:　　the blessings of His hand.

Avoiding zeugma (2:1) conflict (3:1) and an incorrect genitive (3:3) of the first version...

'_'_ _'_ _'
'_'_'
_'_'_ _'_ _'
_'_ _'_'

App. C p. 339

Psalm 127 (1st Version)

God must build the house   1a
or else we work in vain.
His love and truth must move our hands
that labor's fruits remain.   (that labor's works remain.)

Keeping watch for harm,   1b
which threatens in the night,
we know that safety comes from Him
Who holds us with His might.

Striving on our own   1
will never ease our fear;   (will never free from woe;)
to rest securely in His love
will bring us peace and cheer.   (will cause our joys to grow.)

Home is then a place   5
where children grow like flowers,
where hearts are filled with love and joy,
and beauty crowns life's hours.

A M Tindall 11/11/81

Is this meter so short for this subject as to seem terse?

'_-_'
_-_-_'
_-_-_-_'
_-_-_'

Rev. in App. C, p. 356
ER p. 200

196

Psalm 93 (1st Version - No revisions)

The Lord, our Father, reigns!
He clothes Himself with majesty,
     He clothes Himself with might.
The universe and all its worlds
must stand or move as He ordains;
     as He commands is right.

The floods of chaos fail!
The floods have lifted up their voice,
     have lifted up their roar.
Their waves will pound and fade away,
the winds will shriek but not prevail.
     God reigns forevermore.

Earth's laws are set aside!
The cycling powers of birth and life
     must own a primal cause.
Accepted patterns of the world,
its gravity, its times and tides,
     must bow to heavenly laws.

The Israelites were saved.
And as they fled from Pharaoh's hordes
     the waters rolled away.
God sent them meat, gave dews as bread,
became for them the Guide they craved
     with fire and clouds each day.

Christ proved to us God's will.
He told us of our Father's love,
he walked upon the sea.   (waves.)
The sick were healed, the dead were raised,
the hungering seekers ate their fill
     and heard the truths that free. (the truth that saves.)

The laws of earth still bow.
As we are faithful, just, and good,
     obeying God each hour,
dominion is God's gift to us,
all nature's forces yielding now
     to His benignant power.   (all-loving power.)

A M Tindall 11/10/81

App. C p. 350
ER p. 200

197

Psalm 83 (1st Version)

Speak to me, God!
I need reassurance; my fears and pains
would deafen me to heaven's strains...
would bind me close with mortal chains:
speak to me, God!

Help me to trust!
The world and its dangers crowd in too near!
I need to feel Your presence here,
to know Your love, which quiets fear.
Help me to trust!

Speak to my heart!
I know my defense is in Your right hand,
the power of good at Your command:
Lord, help my heart to understand!
Speak to my heart!

Show me Your love!
I need to be confident in its power,
protected, cherished every hour.
Be now my hope, my shield, my tower.
Show me Your love!

Open my eyes!
No kingdom of darkness escapes the fight;
Your Son dispersed all evil's night
and claimed for me the life of light!
Open my eyes!

Thanks be to God!
My heart overflows with a grateful prayer;
I know Your love is everywhere!
My life is safely in Your care.
Thanks be to God!

A M Tindall 11/11/81

stress:

     '--'   6:1 could be "You are my God!" pretty easily, or something else....
   .'--'--'-'
   .-'-'-'-'
   .-'-'-'-'
   '--'

Rev. p. 206; App. C p. 348
ER p. 200

· Erik Routley
929 Route 518, R. D. 1
Skillman, NJ 08558
Tel. (609) 921-7806

17 November 81

Dear Adrienne -

Thank you for your latest letter. I am interested to know that you were at the Episcopal hymnal workshop. Only the other day James Litton - a very good friend of ours and a member of their editorial board - showed me the new text for Peter Cutt's BRIDEGROOM, and I was not pleased at all. Seeing that that tune was (I have probably told you before) composed in my home on my piano because I especially wanted a tune for those words [see p. 80], I don't regard this divorce as legitimate at all. What on earth they found wrong with the medieval text I don't know: but if they didn't like it they should have left the tune alone.

Glad you approve of Pratt Green's hymn for musicians to ENGELBERG. That's a winner: and I think it was <u>Westminster Praise</u> that introduced it in this country. The story of ENGELBERG is in itself an epitome of hymnology. It was written in 1904 for 'For all the saints' and never caught on because the V-W [Vaughan Williams] tune beat it in 1906: then the Episcopals here revived it with Tucker's fine text, 'All praise to thee', which <u>he</u> had written with SINE NOMINE in mind. Meanwhile John Wilson in England had written a new tune for 'All praise to thee', so that its association with ENGELBERG, which <u>Congregational Praise</u> had introduced, following the US Episcopals, was upset. Then John Wilson writes to Pratt Green suggesting that a new hymn for ENGELBERG would be useful - and so that's where we are now. I think it was a happy outcome - FPG's text fits the tune beautifully and the tune is now being sung more often than it ever was before.

Every English hymn book is published in a words-only edition, or in an edition with words written as poetry and the melody over them, as well as in full music. I doubt if there are any exceptions. But of course, as you say, publishers rather often make the result look as little as possible like poetry, to save space and make the result cheap. However, I expect you have noticed that the full music edition

199

Songs of Praise rather often, when it has to interline the words because of fitting-in problems, prints the words out a second time as a poem, as in #196. That's ideal. I wish we could afford that nowadays!

I liked your Psalm 93 [p. 197] very much. I think the rhyme scheme is quite comfortable. I like 'the waves' better than 'the sea' because although it's called the Sea of Galilee, it's not much more than a lake. 'The truth that saves' will do very well. I think your conflation of Ps. 93 with the walking on the water is very good: when we sing Psalm 93 to plainsong our antiphon is always 'Who can this be? the winds and the waves obey him.' And I think you just about get away with the idea in st. 6 that if we obey God, nature will obey us (and if we don't, nature has the right to be awkward with us). All I am not sure of is whether I've seen that because I have long felt that to be the truth, and whether to others it might come slightly obscurely. But no: I think you had better leave it alone.

Psalm 83 [p. 198] is a tour de force: that's one of the psalms most people omit. But you have found something very good and edifying in it. Indeed, the more I see of these, the more I think your collection should have been called 'The Spirit of the Psalms'. It's bad luck that H. F. Lyte and Harriet Auber both used that title in the 19th century: but on the principle that if title's been used twice it won't hurt to use it a third time, maybe you might consider it. I think you usually do get hold of the spirit, and you certainly have done so here. There's a slight metrical bump at 'crowd in', isn't there? In the other stanzas the beat you allow to 'crowd' is a very light one - so it might be difficult to devise a tune that carried both patterns - only a small point, but if you try making a tune for it you'll see what I mean.

Psalm 127 [p. 196] is good too. I think the short metre (SM minus the opening syllable) is very suitable for this domestic psalm. Don't use your bracketed version of III 2 - 'free' without an object isn't all that good; leave it as in the original version. I feel sure there is a tune in SM which would stand the lopping off of its opening syllable.

Talking of titles used more than once - actually it was very naughty, and perhaps ignorant, of that Chicago gang to annex the title Cantate Domino. It's all right to revive a title that hasn't been used for a long time: there was a Songs of Praise published in 1694. Nowadays it's mighty difficult to find a title that isn't already current - we don't yet know what to call our Reformed hymnal. But it's cheating to use somebody else's unless the book carrying it is firmly dead & buried.

Thank you for liking SOMETHING LIKE THIS: I will keep this open until I have a moment to score it for you. Now I must go &

prepare for 3 classes and a chapel service to-morrow. But your psalms are coming along nobly: the set you sent is, both new and revised, the most encouraging yet.

As ever,

PS. ... but you <u>do</u> help - generously and courteously....

December 3, 1981

Dear Dr. Routley:

How fun to read your interview! [Probably "An Interview with Erik Routley," Harry Eskew, in The Hymn, 32:198, October, 1981.] I did so immediately upon seeing the cover ... and I can just hear you, thanks to those tapes which keep the aural memory refreshed....

Almost I want to write, "Tell me the story behind BRIDEGROOM" because I've forgotten the exact wording, but it definitely is a delightful and appealing story - intimate (is that the right word?) like the text and the tune. But you did tell it at Brookfield [how Peter Cutts was at your house between morning and afternoon services, and as you wanted a nap, you asked him to write the tune, and how he finished it in 20 minutes so you didn't get much of a nap...] ... I figure that was one of the most important naps in modern hymnody.... And the "As the bridegroom" text is bound to be a winner, so I would bet the dove graft won't take [see p. 80].

Psalm 83 I've enclosed with just moving "crowd;" does that seem better? Do you really like it? You can take the same credit for it as you should for BRIDEGROOM (if you wanted to, that is -- and my lumping it to so super a tune seems brashly over-confident!). I just wrote it the morning I wrote you, very quickly, in order to have three to send...

I'll be interested to see what you call the Reformed hymnal (I take it it won't be "The Reformed Church Hymnal" or something like that, which does "restrict" it to a denomination....). Some of the not-so-high-class hymnals I've picked up in the past couple of years have non-denominational names, and I guess one must achieve the right sense of .. of something ... that bespeaks a book of more than transient value... I thought around about how you could incorporate the Bible or Scripture into the title, seeing as the format is unique to your book, and that would permit it to cross denominational lines readily, but nothing dignified or "non-transient" enough came to me (I'm stumbling over words

202

again! Anything too catchy looks cheap, I think is what I mean...) Well I know you'll find the right title... it's right there somewhere....

But you've stirred up a miniquestion for me... why is it called "The Pilgrim Hymnal"? Just the sense of man being a pilgrim? (Of course I could read the Introduction to see if it tells....)

Well I've enclosed some more if you wouldn't mind... sometimes I feel like I'm becoming more fluent, and then I bump up against things that convince me I have no idea what I'm doing....

Psalm 126 has a lot of exclamation marks... I don't think of tunes that have that feeling too much...

Psalm 123 - even though it's only four stanzas, it really kind of looks like it should be two double length stanzas, from the sense of the words... what do you think?

Questions on the sheets of these two...

Psalm 137 is certainly a somber psalm!!!! I'm being better, by the way, at doing my minimal research before embarking on writing... it gives me a kind of smile to use a source I just bought recently - . . . "Tyndale Old Testament Commentaries, D.J. Wiseman, General Editor". They're small, which is nice to haul up to the cabin or around in a knitting bag. I also have Dahood's three volumes from the Anchor Bible, and the Interpreter's Bible... (I'm kind of a book-aholic on some subjects, and the Bible is one of them...).

Back to 137. Only in juxtaposing with other psalms could one (i.e., I) leave this with its conclusion! But how clearly it depicts utter dejection! I had a couple of additional stanzas which didn't say much, and so I took them out. One was something I added at the beginning which added to the dejection world-is-full-of-evil feeling, but it was horribly heavy.... Stanza 2 of course is perhaps not even implied in the psalm... and now that I read it over maybe it's too big a jump subject-wise to fit in... I kind of like the meter.

Psalm 84 I do want to finish up, and I suspect am not finished with it yet. .. And here my lack of confidence is rampant. In your letter of Oct. 26 querying "from strength to strength" which I put in without understanding it (therefore in a meaningless way), you say, "The commentators seem to agree by 'they go from strength to strength' means that they get stronger (not more weary) as they go on: I don't think that quite comes through in your version. And I think perhaps you could add another stanza to express the sense of movement and pilgrimage in the psalm; 'Blessed are they... in whose hearts are the highways to Zion', as one translation has it." Well, I'm adding a stanza, but I'm not sure the pilgrimage/travel sense is quite right; it's much more a personal effort to live right... And the last stanza I've changed away from "tents of wickedness" possibly in error, but "tents" don't really seem so relevant an analogy to me in this day and age. And leaving in "a thousand days" may be not good, because it is also psalm-era-specific, like "tents" ... Well if you'll comment I'll work it over again... and I have to <u>not</u> compete with Milton! How <u>could</u> I compete...?

Which brings to another question... and I quote you in your last letter re Psalm 83, when you say "Indeed, the more I see of these, the more I think your collection should have been called 'The Spirit of the Psalms.'" Provocative, tantalizing thought! What collection? I'm just accumulating a file of practice efforts....

Well I love LAC DU FLAMBEAU and look forward to showing the lake and our log cabin to you when you visit northern Wisconsin... just let us know when you're coming! We'll get the guest house opened up and you'll be quite comfortable! Because didn't you say composers named tunes after places they'd been? It's a beautiful spot, and we'd love to have you all come, and I'll bet you've never seen the area either ... and right nearby is this great candy store....

Which reminds me of the next thing to say ... honestly, I think I may have gotten into a rather deep rut, but it's a delicious one, and you can't object too much if only twice a year or so some "sinfully good" toffee wends its UPS-way to your house.... this time I 'm shipping it myself (tomorrow I hope) ... there's another little goody in the box, hopefully in the right number of pieces. It's in the plastic container.... That's homemade ... see if it's tolerable...

And last but not least, a member of the congregation came up after church last night to ask if I would make a tape of a hymn for him. I asked what hymnal and what hymn - JERUSALEM he said, and he's evidently been searching for it (half recollected) for many years now. Yes, I do have <u>Hymns Ancient and Modern Revised</u>, I said (was he surprised!), and came home to try it... well! I think your C. H. H. Parry revival is a sure thing.... You'd already mentioned the "And did those feet" line when I started a line with "And," but I never looked up the text... now I'm exhilarated! If only it didn't exclude the rest of the world by specifying England! Actually though, it's so appealing to me that I can almost identify with England through it.... Isn't there a tradition about Jesus coming to England, - one that's more than a fictional hope, that is? I think I recall a book I read as a child, which I remember loving, called <u>The Bishop of Glastonbury</u> or <u>The Rose of Glastonbury</u> (I may have the words wrong), but I just assumed it was purely imagination....

In the meantime I am all enthused about <u>HAM</u> 578, have left a message for my soloist (gorgeous voice) to come early Sunday, and I will practice (quite a bit; Parry doesn't worry about being easy to play!!) so we can record this, and I think we'll both be delighted with the result... well I hope so, and he should be too, I think....

What a kind, patient, and much appreciated friend you are! I shouldn't ramble on so much; it wastes your time .... but I shall give you a Christmas respite. Have a wonderful wonderful season, with all the good things and important things of the season beautifully uncluttered by all the trivias (triviae?) and impositions of commercialism's heydaying... And thank you, again....

Psalm 83 (Revised Version)

Speak to me, God!
I need reassurance; my fears and pains
would deafen me to heaven's strains...
would bind me close with mortal chains:
speak to me, God!

Help me to trust!
The world and its dangers are crowding near!***
I need to feel Your presence here,
to know Your love, which quiets fear.
Help me to trust!

Speak to my heart!
I know my defense is in Your right hand,
the power of good at Your command:
Lord, help my heart to understand!
Speak to my heart!

Show me Your love!
I need to be confident in its power,
protected, cherished every hour.
Be now my hope, my shield, my tower.
Show me Your love!

Open my eyes!
No kingdom of darkness escapes the fight;
Your Son dispersed all evil's night
and claimed for me the life of light!
Open my eyes!

Thanks be to God!
My heart overflows with a grateful prayer;
I know Your love is everywhere!
My life is safely in Your care.
Thanks be to God!

A M Tindall 11/24/81

*** Or: The world and its threatenings crowd too near!

App. C p. 348
ER p. 212

206

Psalm 126 (1st Version - no revision)

Laugh, all peoples!
and shout your joy!
God ends all captivity.
Sing His praises,
show your love!
As His children we are always free.

Stop your weeping!
lift up your hearts!
Precious seed is ours to sow.
Lift your spirits
to the task!
God Himself will cause the seed to grow.

Join the harvest
of Jesus Christ!
Bring your sheaves into his store.
Preach his message
with your lives!
Righteousness shall reign forevermore.   (Let salvation reign...)

A M Tindall 11/24/81

'-'-
-'-'   I guess salvation doesn't actually "reign..."
'-'-'
'-'-   And I suppose the short lines really
'-'   should be combined to 8.7.8. 9.
'-'-'-'

App. C p. 355
ER p. 212

Psalm 123 (1st Version)

Heavenly God, hear my petition:
growth in grace is what I seek,
standing ready as your servant --   (let my purpose be to serve You,)
patient, loving, good, and meek.

Let me sense Your slightest gesture,
let me hear Your stillest voice,
let me yield my all to Spirit!
Let obedience be my choice.

When contempt and scorn would mock me,
hate and evil bar my way,
let me lean on my Redeemer,
make his love my strength and stay.

For he demonstrates Your mercy;
all his promises are true.
You have claimed me for Your kingdom!
I walk every step with You.

A M Tindall 11/29/81

If the syllable count is 8.7.8.7., is that the meter regardless of the stress pattern? Does the stress pattern ever get figured in to the meter indication in some way?

Does this have too many "let me's" to be desirable and good?

App. C p. 354
ER p. 212

208

Psalm 137 (1st Setting) (1st Version)

Sometimes it seems like Babylon,
  that hostile, rootless place --
Sometimes I feel I'll never rest
  secure in heavenly grace!
      Captive of ridicule,
        exhausted, maligned,
  I struggle to keep pace,
a joyless representative
  of the human race.

There must have been a nobleness
  when time was first begun,
when God proclaimed, "Let there be light,"
  ordaining stars and sun...
      giving His imaged child
        dominion and power --
He spoke, and it was done!
Can God's plan bring futility
  with no victory won?

Dear God, I need to feel Your love
  embrace my world, and me.
I need awakening from this dream
  of sad despondency!
      Jesus has proved for all
        Your love, and Your power;
  his life must help me see
through greatest trials, Your strength sustains
  my security.**

So even when I'm overwhelmed,
  I'll turn from my despair;
I'll look within my heart of hearts
  to feel Your presence there.
      Patiently, faithfully
        I'll hold to this truth:
  Your love is everywhere!
No power can shake my faith in You,   ...my faith in God
  and You hear my prayer.   and He hears...

A M Tindall 12/7/81

** or: tranquillity, or serenity...
Are the contractions all right? Should one
avoid them? Avoid just some of them?

Rev. p. 217
ER p. 213

209

PSALM 84 (Revised Version)

How lovely are Your dwellings, Lord,
          courts echoing with praise!
My heart is longing to be there,
          to sing each joyous phrase.
The sparrow finds herself a house,
          the swallow finds a nest:
Your altars welcome each of them --
          and sweetly they are blessed!

How happy are the ones who know
          their strength is from the Lord.
They triumph as they hold themselves
          obedient to Your word.
Lord, strengthen me, and hear my prayer,
          anoint me with Your grace,
and let me hope to know Your love
          within Your holy place.

Your Son will guide my pilgrimage,
          Your love shows me the way
to make the world a better place
          for those I meet each day.
Yet even as I strive to do
          the things which bless and free,
I know the strength to do Your will
          is strength You give to me.

Help me to shun all wickedness,
          those paths which seem so wide--
a thousand days of worldly lusts
          cast holiness aside!
I'd rather take that narrow way
          which brings me to Your door.
My yearning heart would make its home
          with You, forevermore.

A M Tindall 12/3/81

(Does "A thousand days" take a singular or plural verb form?)
Does 3:6 need objects for "Bless and free" because they're left hanging the way they're used here?

Rev. at App. C, p. 349
ER p. 213

210

1984 form of st. 4:

> Keep me from paths of wickedness --
>> alluring, easy, wide --
> a life embracing worldly sins
>> casts holiness aside.
> I yearn to keep that narrow way
>> which brings me to Your door;
> I'd serve You there, and find my home
>> with You forevermore.

Erik Routley
929 Route 518, R. D. 1
Skillman, NJ 08558
Tel. (609) 921-7806

9 December 81

Dear Adrienne -

Very good to have your latest letter. I will tell you the story of BRIDEGROOM [p. 80]. In May 1968 my friend Peter Cutts was staying with us for a week-end. He's twenty years my junior and I have known him for about 25 years. He came to church with us in the morning - and I recall (it has nothing to do with the immediate story) that our organist was not well, and I persuaded him to stay home for the evening service, and let Peter play - which in the end he did. However, after lunch I presented him with the 'As the bridegroom' text, and remarked that I thought it a very pleasant one, and that it needed a decent tune. So he forthwith went to my piano and composed this one in about twenty minutes, and at once I knew it was a winner. Oddly enough I was at the time working on a hymn book which was never published because the diocese that had asked for it ran out of money: it would have appeared in that, but instead it appeared in <u>100 Hymns</u>

<u>for To-day</u>, and has gone from there into many others. He wrote it in G, it's usually published in F, but I remember that we agreed that G flat was the ideal key.

　　　　<u>The Pilgrim Hymnal</u>: the fact is that 'Pilgrim' is a kind of in-group code-word for American Congregationalism (or was when it existed). It refers to the Pilgrim Fathers who were Congregationalists, and has much to do with Boston, where of course the headquarters of the Congregationalists used to be. That's a title I envy, because, since most people don't know that Pilgrim is a synonym for Congregationalism, they've treated it as an ecumenical hymn book. I am still looking for such a title for our Reformed job: and of course those who weren't Congregationalists in the Mayflower were Dutch Reformed people. But I don't' think we can call it the Mayflower hymnal: people will think it's for the removal company.

　　　　Psalm 83 [p. 206] is one of your best things - not least because it's such a difficult psalm to get a message from. I am not sure which version of III 2 [sic: should be II 2] I prefer; both are effective.

　　　　I am a little less sure about 126 [p. 207], because the spirit of that psalm is (to me) that of deliverance. 'When the Lord brought us back out of captivity, it was like a dream!' - the unbelievable had happened, from which the people were supposed to learn that one should never give way wholly to despair. I think your version starts after they've got back home, as it were. But perhaps all it needs is a first stanza before what you have at the moment. I wouldn't know how to do it! There isn't a tune in that metre, though NORTHAMPTON (A&M 369) would conceivably fit if one took the first syllable of the last line into the second note of the slur at the end of the previous one, and divided it into two quarters: [example enlarged]

It's a rather attractive and very singable tune.

　　　　Psalm 123 [p. 208] is nice: but I notice that you had a problem with the opening stanza. Were you half-consciously thinking, 'Patient, loving, good and meek' is what I ought to be: but should I claim to be any of those things?' If so, I share your doubts. So 'Let my purpose' would be the better version of line 3 - it makes us say, 'I know this is what I ought to aim at.' I wonder anyhow about the word 'meek' nowadays. In older hymns it sometimes appears, and we always have to tell people that it mean's 'gentle' (if you haven't read 'Christian Maturity' by Daniel Jenkins - SCM Press 1976 - do so: his second chapter has a splendid passage on 'Blessed are the meek.'). I think it's a rather faded word now, but that may be over-sensitive. The metre is undoubtedly 8.7.8.7 and one would call it 8.7.8.7 Trochaic to distinguish it from the metre of 'The King of love', which is 8.7.8.7 Iambic.

137 [p. 209] is a fine poem - probably not a piece for communal singing, but then neither was the psalm. All I miss is what is to me its most precious line, 'If I forget thee, O Jerusalem, may my right hand forget her cunning' - which always seems to me an astonishing kind of vow to be made by a musician. As to contractions - I don't care for them mostly: I tolerate them in Isaac Watts, but prefer nowadays to avoid them. In III the last line, I personally prefer 'serenity' to 'security'. It is a most interesting metre, and might make a very effective solo.

In 84 [p. 210] I think your new last stanza is an improvement. 'A thousand' would take the plural verb as you have written it. I think I would put a dash after 'wickedness' and a semicolon or even a full stop after 'so wide' since the next couplet contains a quite different thought. I like 'I'd rather find that narrow way'. Yes, I think I share your doubt about 'the things which bless and free': I think 'Bless' is possible without an object, but 'free' much less so. Otherwise I have nothing to complain of.

You are quite right about 'Jerusalem': the old tradition is that Jesus, as a child, was brought to England by Joseph of Arimathea, who some say (without biblical warrant, of course) was a relation of his family, and a trader in tin: tin was the primary export of England in those days. (Strictly I should say Britain, because it wasn't England until about 600 AD). So a legend grew up that he stayed at a village called Priddy, which is in Somerset, near Glastonbury. Hence, 'And did those feet....' It's the sort of legend the carols deal in: one can believe it or not as one pleases. Some even say that Joseph of Arimathea himself died and was buried in Britain. Anyhow, Blake had it in mind when he wrote those lines: but he hardly suspected that they would become almost the English national anthem. Parry's tune is most remarkable, I think: one of the truly great memories [sic] of all time. I have seen the manuscript once: my friend John Wilson has it because Parry left it with Walford Davies, and Walford Davies was John Wilson's uncle. [John Wilson corrected this: Quoting his letter of 6 May, 1983: "May I ask you to make a note - on the original of Erik's letter of 9 December 1981 - that he is incorrect in saying that I showed him the manuscript of Parry's 'Jerusalem'? If I had this I should have presented it to the British

213

Museum ages ago! What I showed him was an early copy in someone else's handwriting. I should be sorry if a false rumor about this classic tune were started."]   It would be nice to be able to sing it here: but we must leave it in England, because it won't do to tamper with Blake. (The Canadian 1971 has a new text for the tune by R.B.Y. Scott, who is a good writer: but I don't think it will do).

The very best to you all for Christmas, and I hope it will not be too exhausting for you. There's always something there at the centre which no amount of trivia can altogether extinguish!

Yours ever,

December 7, 1981

Well, I guess I'm like the one who said he'd go to the vineyard and then didn't.... because I'm writing again...

But as I got to thinking back over psalm 137, the "Babylon" seemed preferable as a second verse, and the heaviness of the enclosed possible st. 1 certainly is justified by the psalm... isn't it? Anyway, I thought I'd send the whole thing along, even though it's undoubtedly too long to be good anyway.

And besides I wanted to play around with the carol enclosed, and that really decided sending 137, and this follows so closely on the heels of the letter in your hand it can almost be regarded as a P.S......

Should I generally be trying to keep psalms as short or shorter than the biblical form? One thing I try to do (like not bringing out the "tents" of wickedness) is to use the analogies that are more familiar. Yesterday during church when the "small dust of the balance" was read, I realized that unless that's explained it doesn't carry much significance these days....

Re the carol: and I use that term with some trepidation.... but anyway I wanted to see what you thought on various things:

Is that really too "free" to revise two little poems into one like this? Not that the last stanza is all that good in its present form, with the original unstressed syllables on the first instead of the second pulse....

Does the continuity of ideas seem okay? I may have been just so enamored of the idea that they could go together that I got carried away unnecessarily....

I caught some of the parallels in the tune setting....! But I figured that the unison "D" spots could be stylistically justifiable.... awfully static harmony at first, but I was kind of thinking of simplicity as typifying a carol (does it...?)

Would you rather I bothered someone locally about some more coaching in harmony, etc. rather than asking you by letter? I would like to end up someday feeling capable of coming up with a good hymn tune and a decent harmonization thereof....

And now I really do say Merry Christmas....! We leave the 24th for the cabin, and will have all our four daughters plus Jack's family along - so we'll have a super one - "extra" in my eyes, because I really didn't hope the two daughters from California would both be able to come....

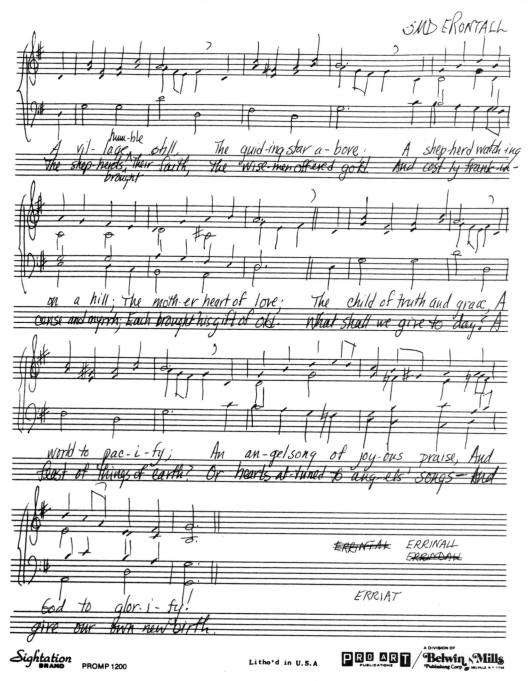

A vil-lage, on/ll, The guid-ing star a-bove: A shep-herd watch-ing
The shep-herds, their faith, the wise-men offered gold. And cost-ly frank-in-
brought

on a hill; The moth-er heart of love: The child of truth and grace, A
cense and myrrh; Each brought his gift of old. What shall we give to day? A

world to pac-i-fy; An an-gel song of joy-ous praise, And
feast of things of earth? Or hearts at-tuned to ang-els' songs— And

God to glor-i-fy! give our own new birth.

ERRINTAL   ERRINALL
ERRINTAL

ERRIAT

Sightation BRAND   PROMP 1200   Litho'd in U.S.A   PRO ART PUBLICATIONS / A DIVISION OF Belwin Mills Publishing Corp. MELVILLE N.Y 11746

[Note: No early versions of this melody and harmonization have been findable. This version incorporates Erik's corrections and harmonization.]

App. C. p. 363
ER p. 221

Psalm 137 (1st Setting) (Revised Version)

Must inhumanity and strife
  make mockery of peace?
Must innocency's sufferings
  continue and increase?
      Cruel adversity,
        injustice, revenge --
what can bring release?
Will lust and greed and hate go on?
  Will they never cease?

Sometimes it seems like Babylon --
  a hostile, rootless place.
Sometimes I feel I'll never rest
  secure in heavenly grace.
      Captive of ridicule,
        exhausted, maligned,
  I struggle to keep pace --
a joyless representative
  of the human race.

There must have been a nobelness   [sic typo for "nobleness"]
  when time was first begun,
when God proclaimed, "Let there be light!"
  ordaining stars and sun...
      giving His imaged child
        dominion and power --
He spoke, and it was done!
Can God's plan have futility
  with no victory won?

Dear God, I need to feel Your love
  embrace my world, and me.
I need awakening from this dream
  of sad despondency!
      Spirit is everything,
        the joy of my life!
  Your Son must help me see
through greatest trials, Your strength sustains
  my serenity.

Mortality has no effect
  upon Your perfect way,
and even when I doubt and fear,
  You listen when I pray.   (You hear me when...)
          Jesus has proved to me
          Your love and Your power;
  You never turn away!
You fill the darkest hours with light
  and eternal day.

So even when I'm overwhelmed,
  I'll turn from my despair;
I'll look within my heart of hearts
  to feel Your presence there.
          Patiently, faithfully
          I'll hold to this truth:
  Your love is everywhere!
No power can shake my faith in God,
  and He hears my prayer.

                    A M Tindall 12/7/81

ER p. 220

218

ERIK ROUTLEY
929 ROUTE 518, R. D. 1
SKILLMAN, N. J. 08558
TEL. (609) 921-7806

10 December 81

Dear Adrienne -

   I had just mailed my letter when the splendid parcel of good things arrived - which will certainly make Christmas that much [more] festive. Since our son from Australia is going to be with us at Christmas - and he has no problems about waistlines and what not - I am sure he will help us demolish them.

   This is actually the first time we've encountered in the U.S. what in England we regard as honest boiled sweets that taste of something apart from chemicals - I refer to the things with which the plastic container was heaped. We love those and welcome them avidly. And as you know we are addicted to the candy. So thank you very much: we shall eat your health at Christmas!

   May you have a very blessed one.

                    As ever -

December 10th

Well Hi again....

But this one really doesn't count because none of the enclosures requires anything,... and you may already know all about them and the problem is the early date (1966)...

So starting at the beginning - I just opened WORSHIP Nov. 81 and there you are again, so of course I read it right away... In discussing the David Perry Index you wish that someone would do the same for American Hymns...

219

I learned about Hymns and Tunes - An Index by Katharine Smith Diehl (Scarecrow Press, 1966) from Dale McCurdy during your class at Garrett... went over to the library where he said it was, saw it, called long distance to New Jersey to order one, and have used it especially when I reviewed the texts and tunes in the CS Hymnal, coordinating with my index cards. Enclosed are some Xeroxes showing what's in the book, in case you in fact don't know of it... it's a fat book, and I daresay a computer project. . . .

Two weeks till Christmas... surely I can leave you in peace for that little bit of time! Goodness knows I have lots of non-hymnic distractions right about now!

Best wishes as always,

[Hymns and Tunes, An Index has no ISBN, but is L. C. 66-13743. I enclosed photocopies of pages of the First Line Index, of the Tune names with tunes, indicated in *solfege*, etc. Interestingly enough, six of Erik's tunes are included in the index: CLIFF TOWN, ABINGDON, MILL BROW, SUTTON COURTENAY, VARNDEAN, and WYCH CROSS.]

Erik Routley
929 Route 518, R. D. 1
Skillman, NJ 08558
Tel. (609) 921-7806

11 December 81

Dear Adrienne -

Actually you'll have had my thoughts about Ps. 137 [p. 217] by now: I am not sure that your new version doesn't move rather farther away from the spirit of that psalm - which I think is a psalm of homesickness rather than a prayer for peace. (I was much entertained, by the way, by your NOBELness - a Freudian slip?) I am worried by the allying of 'adversity' with 'injustice and revenge', mainly because injustice and revenge are vicious, but adversity isn't. It gets much better as it goes on; but when you say 'It seems like Babylon', you are really in Babylon, which of course the Psalmist was. (You may have noticed how Abelard made use of that image in the full version of his 'O quanta qualia' - English Hymnal 465).

The carol [p. 216] is charming. If the originals were yours, I want to ask why 'A village', and 'A shepherd', but 'the star', 'the heart'? I don't think that the fact that one pair is human the other, presumably divine, really justifies the abandoning of the 'surprise' effect you'd get if you said 'a' each time. Try it. The use of two sentences without verbs just gets by, I think, though what I look for in the second half is something that says, if I can express it, 'It was almost unbelievable: that's why I left the verbs out: but it happened: so now we'll have one.' There's a slight 'crack' between the first and last halves still. But it's almost there. In the last line, since your typewriter got away from you (as mine constantly does) and it wrote 'and give own own new birth'; I'm not sure what you mean. If you intended 'and give our own...' I think I shall ask, ' our own what? Feast? Songs? Thought? Your doubts about that ending are perhaps well founded - and I wonder if the thing has strayed a bit because you've deserted the carol style in that stanza and gone all moralistic. I know the original 2 stanzas did, but when you run the two compositions together the opening is so ecstatic that one feels a bit let down when one finds one's being preached at after all.

There's a snag about the tune. I forget whether you have New Church Praise, but if you do, and turn to #54, you'll see that Peter Cutts wrote the first two phrases before you! I turned the sheet over and scribbled a conceivable amendment which will take it out of his territory. I think the harmony in the extended bar near the end is a bit elliptical: somehow it has to prepare the singer to hear those two eighth-notes coming in the melody; the singer will be much tempted to sing D-B-G-E - straight down in thirds - if warning isn't given to the ear. Unless you yourself want to alter those notes: it would of course be quite in order to come down in thirds though somebody else has done something rather like it. (I now remember: it's in an awful tune called LLOYD, which you won't know and mustn't ever see, but which was very popular a generation ago among English north-country nonconformists). I think, with the version as you have it, it's an F-natural that is needed to give the warning I speak of. Something like what I have scribbled. [See only version found, on p. 216, which incorporates Erik's harmonization.]

You will have a splendid Christmas with all your family! Enjoy it.

As ever -

221

January 25, 1982

Dear Dr. Routley:

And that reminds me of a question ... because I never want to address someone less formally than they desire, or inaccurately, either... a friend (D. Mus.) [Don Spies] referred to you as "Mr. Routley" and I corrected him, and he said that in academic circles (he teaches at a small college) it is accepted practice to skip the advanced degrees in addressing others when both hold the same degrees. Is that the way it is in your background too? England etc.? I've not heard of it before, but would like to think my friend wouldn't goof in an unnecessary way....

Well in any case it's been so long since pestering you! Evidence of the fact that I've broken stride, or something. What's enclosed basically doesn't thrill me either, but I haven't been able to get things going again the way I'd like. But two things enclosed, and a bunch of questions that I've been cogitating and knowing I'd like to get answered when you have the time (knowing your schedule in the past, you're prompter than one could ever anticipate, but please don't feel these are urgent - I've waited all this time to ask, after all!).

    The Christmas "Carol" [p. 216] is two poems, neither of them mine. I ran across them in two Christian Science Sentinels when I was looking for things I thought might be interesting as hymns (I keep hoping they'll get going on revising the 1932 hymnal).
    Now: if they're not my poems then I really shouldn't revise them, eh? Ideally one should have people write hymns for hymns and therefore carols for carols, and therefore no need for an outside person revising. But I was experimenting a bit. And seeing as the world isn't really short of Christmas carols, this is reaching too hard, I daresay....
    The tune: As usual I love your harmonization. It doesn't lie under my hands at the keyboard which I wish it did, but then being almost illiterate in piano left hand capabilities, a lot of things don't lie under my hands, and I need feet to help out.
    I had just recently gone through and played Peter Cutts' tunes in a few of the books / supplements I have, and had seen his tune, but had completely forgotten it. It's obvious I liked it, though my face is quite red as to be so sieve-headed to forget that the tune I'd "come up with" was mentally retained from acquaintance a couple of months before...
    The text: Perhaps the first half was all "A" with no "The"s in the author's original form, but it got edited. . . . That's one of the things I like

about articles I read by you - your style is inimitable, and is allowed to shine through so that I can virtually hear you speaking the article, as it were. Makes it all very alive, and the periodical it's in all the more broadly based in appearance....

I thought the last verse was reasonably clear - in fact completely clear to me, if only because the "right" answer seemed so obvious ... The original was:

> What shall we offer on Christmas Day?
> Feast of the things of earth?
> Or thought attuned to angels' songs --
> Gift of our own rebirth?

In revising it to fit (isn't it remarkable that I'll kick like the proverbial steer at editors messing with my prose, and then under the guise of "regular meter" mess up someone else's poetry! I think I'd better think about that ... and please go ahead and laugh, in view of your comments to me, because I've asked you about revising before, but I still seem to "help myself" freely...)... in revising it to fit the stress pattern I don't think I did enough to obscure the meaning....

Probably not worth worrying about, if the revising is too great anyway, though. I'll just have to take the tune and come up with a new text.... The original poems date from 1956 and 1955. The "preachiness" of the second really didn't bother me. Maybe it's because I consciously feel the need of remembering what Christmas is about, during the Christmas season when things are so busy in the non-sacred things.

Another unfinished item Psalm 126. As I reread it I think I'd rather redo it than add a st. 1, at which I was so unsuccessful in the past. I think when I first read it, it came to me as a confirming of God's always delivering from evil, whereas now the very beautiful sense of "Remember in this present trial that God delivered in the past, therefore realize He will continue to do so" is a very appealing awareness.

Thinking of this one and the Babylon one (enclosed plus the one you have) makes me realize that my efforts have taken on a direction not quite toward versifying what's in the psalms per se, but more what they seem to say to me, an "ordinary Christian in the 20th century." I can't relate too much to singing about living in Babylon, and even as a poetic reference it doesn't have deep meaning except as based in historical understanding of the exile experience of the Hebrews (Jews, Israelites, whatever the term best fitting for that time). I think that's how it drifted into a psalm of peace - the 20th century brink-of-war-ness (even though I do vaguely remember W.W.II shortages, etc. which is as close as the Midwest got to things in a small fry's eyes) would relate more to a yearning for freedom from fear of aggression, than to bondage

223

/ prison camps... particularly in people who weren't around in the 40s... younger than myself, and as insulated as I've been, etc...

So I think it's kind of a direction I've gone off in - what the psalms say to me as a Christian, in this day and age, in the face of the trials, situations, difficulties of now... and that's why some of them "miss" what the psalm <u>really</u> says. If you think I'd be doing better (learning more, etc.) to stick closely to the text I'd like to have you say so....

Psalm 123 I see what you mean about using "Let my purpose," to go with "Patient, loving, good, and meek." I was recalling Mary Baker Eddy's line (which is one of my favorites), "What we most need is the prayer of fervent desire for growth in grace, expressed in patience, meekness, love, and good deeds." (Science and Health p. 4). It fit in rather easily.... I'd be delighted to read Daniel Jenkins' "Christian Maturity" - is <u>SCM Press 1976</u> indicating a book or a periodical? Is Garrett likely to have it, or Seabury Western?

This is getting too long (so what else is new...) ... so on to the enclosed briefly . . .

Psalm 137-2 - sticks more closely, but still doesn't seem a communal psalm-to-sing... maybe I should define my basket more clearly for myself, before I go on working with these psalms, to see exactly what direction I should be aiming in my efforts; . . .

Psalm 101 - even knowing that David was working through his approach to administrative government (per Kidner) I've related to it as to how it would affect me, even though a non-king in the day-to-day world...

So glad you liked the hard candy! I've saved you out some more, which I'll drop in the mail. I thought of rushing you off the recipe, but then didn't know whether your wife loved making such stuff or not (it has to be easy if yours truly can do it with no difficulty!). Tell me which flavors you like best, and I'll do those next time I get inspired....

Many many best wishes, and thanks as always, for your patience with lots of questions and letters that are very wordy and convolute...

Ps. 137 - (2nd Setting) (1st Version)

I'll live in Babylon
oppressed by hate and cruel foes,
my hope for freedom gone,
I'll live condemned to alien scenes
while Zion's beauties fill my heart,
her deserts like a rose.

I'll put all joys aside,
the harps, the melodies, the song.
My foes will be defied --
I will not let them mock my faith!
My trust is in almighty God;
He will requite this wrong!

I'll give up every skill   (art)
my hand to work, my tongue to speak --
I would far rather kill   (part)
all hope, than look for mortal rest   (with hope....)
through yielding my Jerusalem,
through faith that is too weak.

God help me in this strife!
The sneers, the scorn, the captors' prod --
be now my only life!
I'll yield past comforts, spurn false hopes,
I'll give up every thought of peace,
but not my faith in God.   (sustained by faith in God.)

A M Tindall 1/13/82

Rev. p. 233, App. C p. 359
ER p. 213

from Psalm 101 (1st Version)

God, help me be Your perfect child --
       my heart is filled with loyalty!
Help keep my living undefiled,
       and strengthen all my constancy.

I'll keep my eyes from wicked things,
       I'll keep my feet from error's way;
unseen perverseness will not cling;
       I'll strive to listen and obey.

I will permit no slandering word --
       no egotism, no false pride.
Deceits and lies will not be heard,
       all wickedness I'll set aside.

My friends will be the faithful ones
       whose lives reflect Your truth and love.
Perfection, like the rays of suns,
       will guide their footsteps from above.

God, help me be Your perfect child
       who thinks and acts with Christly grace.
Help me, through life that's undefiled,
       make this a little better place.

               A M Tindall 1/21/82

Last couplet a problem slightly: could be
       Help keep my living undefiled,
       to make this world a better place..
but that sounds a bit egotistical; "a little better place" is kind of accepted jargon for humble
righteous desires .... I think ....

               oops contractions

Rev. p. 232; App. C p. 352
ER p. 228

[no letterhead]

29 January 82

Dear Adrienne -
        ...Very well, then, we'll have a little essay on protocol in address! Your friend was, I think, correct concerning American procedure. Colleagues who hold doctorates tend in this country to address each other, if they don't know each other, by 'Mr.'. I myself don't, but that's because I am English. Our older custom was for such colleagues who didn't know each other to write simply 'Dear Routley': but that's more or less disappeared, I think. It certainly sounds very odd now. I myself am less free with Christian names than some are, but I often find myself doing the wrong thing! On the whole I don't care to be addressed by my Christian name by people I've never seen, who are writing for the first time. And I am dreadfully old-fashioned about addressing people of a senior generation otherwise than formally: but then there are many fewer people alive senior to me than there used to be! I should address them otherwise only by their invitation.
        That said: anybody who sends me candy is entitled to address me as ERIK if they want to....
        Of course, when it comes to writing to an unknown lady, the difficulties are much more hazardous! Recently I heard from a person who signed 'Lynn Edwards'; since we have several masculine Lynns on our campus and several feminine ones too, what was I to do? I could only write back 'Dear Lynn Edwards; and address the envelope 'Lynn Edwards' without title. Since the lady turned out to be one of those married ladies who keeps her unmarried name this turned out to be right: but suppose she'd been a he...
        Actually I myself don't fuss about my own rights in these matters. The one thing that sends me right through the roof is being addressed in speech or writing as 'Reverend Routley'. That's appalling. That title is only written, never spoken (as my theological friend Daniel Jenkins says, like the name of God in Hebrew!). And when used it has to be written with the Christian name, or if that isn't known, the title (Mr.

or Dr.), never with the surname alone. What fun. Ministers are as difficult as modern ladies.

Pooh. Call me Erik.   NEVER Eric............

PSALM 137 [p. 225]. Good, and moving. Very imaginative. 'Part from hope...', I think, would be the best phrase, with 'art' in the earlier line. The deserts in st. 1 rather look as if they are Zion's; I think you want us to think of them as Babylon's. But the idea from Isa. 35 is delightful. 'While Zion's beauties in my heart make deserts like a rose....'? I should keep your order of stanzas: Babylon must come right at the beginning to set the scene. But I think it's one of your best.

PSALM 101 [p. 226]. I don't myself mind 'I'll': what's good enough for Watts is good enough for me. But I do have my doubts about 'egotism', especially as four syllables. Not being a psychiatrist I am not sure what it means, but if it means selfhood or selfishness, maybe it were better said that way. There's also an awkwardness in st. 4 - 'your child... who thinks' being in apposition with 'me': it's one of those cases where strict grammar requires something that sounds odd; I suspect that the proper person for the verb would be 'think' and that sounds crazy: how about 'to think...' - which is a legitimate consecutive clause - 'your perfect child, to think and act with Christly grace.' I am put off a bit by 'a little better place': I think it's got to be a little place or a better place, but not really, in this sort of writing, 'a little better'; it suggests a slightly obsequious modesty anyhow. If you want it better, don't settle for making it a little better! First and last I think I'd like you to think again about that stanza: but I see you have done, and your substitute couplet is much better. I don't go with humble righteous desires. Ponder, perhaps, on Nehemiah's superb outburst, 'Should such a man as I flee?' Not I think, arrogance: simply courage. Still, I think a reconstruction here will be useful because 'help keep' is a bit awkward.

SCM Press is a publisher - 36 Bloomsbury Street, London WC 1.

As for Christmas - exactly what is and what is not sacred? A nice question, I think.

Well, this business of tinkering with other people's stuff is, of course, often rather sordid. I know how you feel. I was asked recently by one of my best friends in England to attempt a piece expressing the spirit of Ps. 119 to go with the tune we usually know as Psalm 36/68 in the Genevan Psalter - that huge 12-line tune (English

Hymnal 544): he found out - I didn't know it - that it was originally written by Greiter for Psalm 119. I did it and he wants me to mess it about and I don't want to..... If you at any point think I am asking you to say what you don't mean, ignore me at once: or if I say 'you shouldn't be meaning that' and you think you should.

Warmest greetings!

February 16, 1982

Dear Erik......!

And I accept your kind invitation to write thus, because even though it feels a little self-conscious, I think I'll get used to it and it will help not feel so self-conscious about writing so often....

Anyway, I forwarded your comments to my friend... and how glad I am to know the ins and outs of using "Reverend"! I like to address people correctly, and the whole area of church titles is huge and difficult, as there is no clergy in a Christian Science church so it's all new and therefore not so easy to follow.....

There are several things I'd like to pursue from your last letter... very important first, though, is that I always am interested in any tinkering you feel moved to suggest in things I send you. That's why I'm such a pest.... I just want to understand why you suggest what you do... and if I don't understand, I'll ask. For example, Psalm 137. You say "The deserts in st.1 rather look as if they are Zion's; I think you want us to think of them as Babylon's. But the idea from Isa 35 is delightful. 'While Zion's beauties in my heart make deserts like a rose....'"?

I was thinking in this psalm of the singer's being unplacatable, if that's a word... but now that you mention it, didn't the Hebrews get a pretty decent treatment [during the exile] once things settled down? I seem to recall that they got their own section of town, their own housing which was not portrayed as bad; even Ezekiel could be consulted by the Jews when they wanted to, so there wasn't a very jail-like confinement forced on them.... Anyway, my intention was to show that the singer was relating only to the beauties of Zion in his heart, and screening out any outward vistas....

So if the latter is less good as a focus, would you explain to me so? Did Babylon have deserts around it, which would be "redeemed" through the inner awarenesses of Zion? I think of the whole area as arid...

Psalm 101 is revised. Maybe "For I would live life undefiled" is still too awkward.... a couple of other changes. I can see what you mean about obsequiousness... sometimes I acknowledge that my own lack of confidence doesn't jibe with really relying on God's strength and wisdom...

A couple of new ones. Psalm 96. I didn't worry much about rhyming... The threefold "sing" and "give" were mentioned in the commentary; I just noticed the "joy" one.... The last stanza seems necessary for content even though it doesn't fit the threefold pattern. But maybe that gets a little singsong anyway - too much so?

Psalm 70 another irregular meter, and I don't think I am too sold on it - feminine endings up against unstressed syllables in the following lines seem rather awkward rhythmically.... anyway what do you think? I've used "power" (st. 2) with 2 syllables; that's all right to have it either one or two, isn't it?

What an interesting area your rhetorical question brings to mind! "As for Christmas - exactly what is and what is not sacred?..." I can think of a lot of things that would masquerade as not sacred which needn't be seen so - kitchen work probably, even hostess work that is preparing for a caroling party; we give two carol parties of some size, and although it's a lot of work, people do seem to regard them as a wonderful reminder to focus on observing the season.... I think I would have to feel that television toy ads are not particularly sacred - how can you redeem those...? But then if one gives "secular" an inch, maybe it would claim to take over everything else, right into misinterpreting what's really going on in church activities and festivities. Twice in the past month I've had perfectly nice people imply that musicians in church "only do it for the money," which I, at least, could point out is not necessarily the case, and which they knew came from my first-hand experience....

For me to remember, though, is not to let the "secular" appearing activities overshadow higher motivations and inspirations, during the Christmas season especially, behind those same activities.

I've looked up EH 544 - what a nice tune! How does one respectfully and politely and extremely interestedly wonder whether one could see your text... could that possibly go with the salutation... to ask? Is there any other 119-based text?

I guess that's all for now - I seem to live at the church these days, preparing for the organ. Why I can't be efficiently accomplishing more while I'm there, I don't know - it would seem like an opportunity to continue with these psalms....

You know, I don't recall ever asking whether you would continue to critique these month after month - I think I just started.... anyway thanks as always!!!! Of course if I only get a couple off in a month, that's not too extensive a bother.... (I hope...)

Thank you again,

Psalm. 101 (Revised Version)

God, help me be Your perfect child --
  my heart is filled with loyalty!
For I would live life undefiled.
  God, strengthen all my constancy.

I'll keep my eyes from wicked things,
  I'll keep my feet from error's way.
Unseen perverseness will not cling;
  I'll strive to hear You and obey.

I will not heed a slandering word --
  no selfish seeking, no false pride --
deceits and lies will not be heard,
  all wickedness I'll set aside.

My friends will be the faithful ones
  whose lives reflect Your truth and love.
Perfection, like the rays of suns
  will guide their footsteps from above.

God, help me be Your perfect child,
  to think and act with Christly grace,
for I would live life undefiled
  to make this world a better place.

A M Tindall 2/15/82

Last verse lines 2 and 4 both starting with "to" leads thought toward expecting a parallel construction between them? One could change 3 to "with thoughts and acts (deeds) of Christly grace" to avoid that, if necessary...
  Or could start line 4 with "would make..."

App. C p. 352

Ps. 137 (2nd Setting) (Revised Version)   686886

I'll live in Babylon
     oppressed by hate and cruel foes,
my hope for freedom gone,
     I'll live condemned to alien scenes
     while Zion's beauties fill my heart,   (...in my heart)
her deserts like a rose.   (make deserts)

I'll put all joys aside,
     the harps, the melodies, the song.
My foes will be defied --
     I will not let them mock my faith!
     My trust is in almighty God --
He will requite this wrong!

I'll give up every art,
     my hand to work, my tongue to speak --
I would far rather part
     with hope, than look for mortal rest
     through yielding my Jerusalem,
through faith that is too weak.

God help me in this strife!
     the sneers, the scorn, the captors' prod --
be now my only life!
     I'll yield past comforts, spurn false hopes,
     I'll give up every thought of peace,
but not my faith in God.

                  A M Tindall 2/16/82

App. C p. 359

233

Psalm 96 (1st Version)

Sing, and sing and sing again!
Sing your praises to the Lord.
   Tell all people, friend and stranger, **
   He is God, all-wise Creator!
Praise His greatness, bless His name!
Sing, and sing and sing again!

Give, and give and give again!
Give due reverence to the Lord.
   See His majesty and glory,
   honor Him with strength and beauty,
bring an offering, bless His name.
Give, and give and give again!

Joy, and joy and joy again!
Echo joy unto the Lord.
   With the heavens, fields and forests,
   with the seas and all their fullness,
Praise His power, bless His name.
Joy, and joy and joy again!

Worship God our Judge again,
giving thanks unto the Lord.
   Know His true and righteous judging
   brings salvation with His guiding.
Holy lives will bless His name!
Worship God our Judge again!

      A M Tindall 2/8/82

**peoples, friends, strangers possible...

Rev. p. 244, App. C p. 351
ER p. 248

234

Psalm 70 (1st Version)

Help me God!
My need is urgent!
For my enemies are proud and strong,
and seeking to hurt me;
what they wish to do is wrong!
The danger fills me with fear; my need is great!
Help me now, O Lord my God, and do not wait!

Help me God!
Your strength can save me.
Let Your power silence evil's pride.
Let all who would hurt me
be confused and turned aside.
I turn to You in my poor and needy state.   (I look to You...)
Help me now, O Lord my God, and do not wait!

Help me, God,
to seek and praise You!
Let Your joy and gladness be my shield.
I love Your salvation more
than protections earth can yield.
I honor those who would magnify Your name; (And with all those...)
help me now, O Lord my God, to do the same.

A M Tindall 2/9/82

'_'
_'_'_
__'_'_'_'
_'__'_
__'_'_'
_'_'__'_'_'
__'_'_'_'

Rev. App. C p. 347
ER p. 237

Erik Routley
929 Route 518, R. D. 1
Skillman, NJ 08558
Tel. (609) 921-7806

22 February 82

Dear Adrienne -

As to the Hebrews, you are quite right. The Return from Babylon was accompanied by much wise and generous treatment from Cyrus and his successors (Iranians!); they always resented not being a sovereign state any more, but that raises a very curious matter. Myself, I love the Jews[;] wherever they are there's no gentile culture that they haven't enriched. But I can't stand the Israelis. Here we are, with all this business in the Middle East, which is really Israel and Edom continuing their historic strife. I don't know whether the Israelis will ever learn to grow up as a nation: but at present it still seems to have been a huge mistake to provide them with the context in which they could pursue their peculiarly virulent form of nationalism. Not being a nation (in that sense) they had time, over all these centuries, to be a distinctive influence which was what they were best at. If I wasn't a Christian I'd love to be a Jew, but if I wasn't an Englishman I wouldn't want to be an Israeli. The very fact that the Jews have always been picked on by tyrants like Hitler and the Russian mobs (not to mention the pogroms one hears of in the Apocrypha, and the Merchant of Venice) makes one admire them the more. But yes - Psalm 137 wasn't the end of the tale.

As for Psalm 119 - I will enclose a copy of what I did for John Wilson; we are in dispute at the moment over my favourite line in it (you know the feeling!). Actually in the Reformed Hymnal we probably shan't use this, but shall use two selections from Watts. There is one little section of his which is beautiful, and there's another possible gathering from among all the rest. There is also a Ps 119 cento in Songs of Zion (Woodward 1910) to carry the Genevan tune - #304. All one can do with that psalm is to gather up some of the leading ideas - but if one can, results can be good.

Sacred and secular. Ah - when 'money' comes in, people blackmail others unscrupulously. If somebody told me I do my job 'only for the money', my answer would be 'in what sense only?' Of course people have to live & there's nothing discreditable in being paid for what one does: if you aren't you're on social security so other people are paying anyhow. If somebody does something only for the money the implication is that they hate doing it & therefore they should be pitied,

236

not sneered at. (Paul said there was nothing wrong in paying preachers, though he had special reasons for not wanting to be paid). People should be more careful in their conversation: carelessness leads to unnecessary brutality. But I myself don't think that there's anything in itself discreditable about 'the secular.' I think it's a good idea to be medieval and say that there are just about seven things which are the origin of things going wrong, and that no pejorative emphasis should ever be given to anything else. It isn't the secular that's wrong but the greedy, lustful, avaricious, envious, indifferent, malicious, and proud. So at Christmas it isn't the fact that shops are open that's wrong: it's making money out of selling unnecessary and stupid things that's wrong. It isn't wrong to play 'O come all ye faithful' through the muzak system: it is wrong to render it with deliberate carelessness and spurious sentiment. It is, in your word, the motivations that one has to watch. And of course anybody who hopes to make a million in church music is, to a quite sinful degree, mistaken!

Your psalms are delightful. In Ps. 96 [p. 234] I prefer 'friend and stranger' every time: the singular is always more decisive and telling than the plural. In stanza 4 I think I might suggest keeping judge for line 3, so that the opening line can be a jubilant as that of the other stanzas (without necessarily taking the same form). I think the assonances in the middle lines are very skilful. There ought to be a good German tune in this metre. And Ps. 70 [p. 235], especially as a poem for reading, is good. I doubt if it's one for singing - the original psalm can't have been often sung except by a soloist, even though it does have a musical direction above it. But it is a sensitive version that you have made, with just the right lift at the end.

Well done!

as ever -

237

PSALM 119, cento. Erik Routley 1981   original version
Tune EH 544 (whose original association was Ps. 119 in German)

Grant this to me, Lord: let me live   17
and, living, keep your word, and give
    my life to gain its treasure.
Here but a stranger, let me trace   19
my path toward a resting place
    where ⌐ shall find pure pleasure.
Much kindness you have shown to me,   65
promise and pledge of joy to be;
    continue thus your blessing!
Wisdom that moulded all my life   73
guides me, in days so full of strife,   161
    gently my heart possessing.

Though we are creatures of a day,   Isa. 40.8
though heaven and earth may pass away,   Lk 21.33
    your word is deeper founded.   89
I see that all things have an end;   96
your statutes past all time extend,
    by breadth and length unbounded.
You speak, and all things come to be: Ps. 33.9
you speak, and Satan's legions flee,   Lk 11.20
    scattered by love's brave splendour;
you speak, and my forgiveness seal,   28, 154
you speak, and generous grace reveal,   156
    in precepts wise and tender.

Blessed are they who hunger sore   123
to see your righteousness once more   Mt. 5.6
    enthroned in hearts and nations.
Blessed the pure in heart, who seek   Mt. 5.8
to hear what God the Lord will speak   Ps.85.7
    in blissful contemplations.
Blessed be God who gives me light;   105
blessed the mercy and the might
    which all the day attend me.
Blessed the promises of grace   140
Blessed the laws that still embrace,
    enlighten, and defend me.

238

Ps. 119, E.R. Revised version 1982 in response to suggestions of John Wilson

God speaks, and all things come to be;
God speaks, and Satan's legions flee,
    scattered by love's brave splendour;
God speaks, and our forgiveness seals,
God speaks, and generous grace reveals
    in precepts wise and tender.
I see that all things have an end:
God's statutes past all time extend,
    by breadth and length unbounded.
Though we are creatures of a day,
though heaven and earth may pass away,
    God's word is deeper founded.

Grant this to me, Lord: let me live
and, living, keep your word, and give
    my life to gain its treasure.
Here but a stranger, let me trace
my path toward a resting place
    where I shall find pure pleasure.
Much kindness you have shown to me,
primise and pledge of joy to be;
    continue thus your blessing!
wisdom that moulded all my life
guide me, in days so full of strife,
    gently my heart possessing.

Bless'd are they all who hunger sore
to see God's righteousness once more
    enthroned in hearts and nations.
Bless'd are the pure in heart, who seek
to hear what God the Lord will speak
    in blissful contemplations.
Bless'd be our God, who gives us light;
bless'd be the mercy and the might
    which all the day attend us.
Bless'd be the promises of grace ,
bless'd be the laws that still embrace,
    enlighten, and defend us.

(The revision was in response to JW's information that in the original
the opening was objective rather than subjective: so the language here is
cast in a more public form. St 1 line 7 is the line which against all
comers I shall not change: it is one of my favourite texts in the KJV,
and was the subject of my presidential address to the Congregational Church
in 1970).

[N. B. In © Version, 1:7 revised to "Though all I see must have an end"]

239

Two centos of Psalm 119, Isaac Watts

I

Behold thy waiting servant, Lord,   X 1
  devoted to thy fear;
remember and confirm thy word,
  for all my hopes are there.

Thy mercies fill the earth, O Lord,   IX 1
  how good thy works appear!
open my eyes to read thy word
  and see thy wonder there.

'Tis like a sun, a heavenly light   IV 3
  that guides us all the day,
and through the dangers of the night
  a lamp to lead our way.

O that thy statutes every hour   XV 1
  may dwell within my mind;
thence I derive a quickening power,
  and daily peace I find.

O that the Lord would guide my ways   XI 1
  to keep his statutes still:
O that my God would grant me grace
  to know and do his will.

II

As Congregational Praise 225, with this final stanza substituted:

My faith and love, and every grace
  fall far below thy Word;
for perfect truth and righteousness
  dwell only with the Lord.

Note: Sts. 1, 2, 3 from CP 225: Add as st. 4 the st. quoted above as "II", to the following:

Lord, I have made Thy word my choice,
      My lasting heritage;
There shall my noblest powers rejoice,
      My warmest thoughts engage.

I'll read the histories of Thy love,
      And keep Thy laws in sight;
While through Thy promises I rove,
      With ever fresh delight.

'Tis a broad land of wealth unknown,
      Where springs of life arise,
Seeds of immortal bliss are sown,
      And hidden glory lies.

240

March 4, 1982

Dear Erik:

Amazing evidences of how small this world is sometimes... is the John Wilson of your Psalm 119 someone connected with Hope Publishing? I thought perhaps he was, when I heard that there is a John Wilson there....

Your letter came Friday, and in order to read it in a relaxed fashion as well as the first once-over, I took it with us to Wisconsin Saturday morning at 7:00 a. m.; we took an architect and his wife up there to see it, as we're hoping to build a house in 1983 and want it to "feel" like the relaxed feeling of the cabin.... In any case the architect is very active in his church, and I think now that I cull my memory, that he mentioned a John Wilson who lives in La Grange, and I thought the name sounded familiar... well maybe it's not the same one; I had sort of pegged your John Wilson as being in England....

You haven't asked for any comments on your 119, but how can I resist saying how much I like it?!!! I like the subjective opening - it really speaks to me... but the objective opening is nice too -- what a terrific first line! The enclosed fun/project [puzzle] had me delving into first lines a lot, and heightened my appreciation of them specifically.... St. 3 I can see the revising will go better into a words-only hymnal (even Gracia Grindal wouldn't be nervous...), although certainly your original has no difficulty at all with the music, does it.

Would you say just a little about your favorite line? Walter Carlson (the architect) thought it might mean "all things have a purpose" rather than a termination... but the line comes across a bit differently (to me) in the revision than it did in the original (probably because of turning the 1-2-3-4-5-6 into 4-5-6-1-2-3.) I've looked at several translations and commentaries tonight, and there does seem to be a lack of unanimity as to what's being said.... But the whole thing has such a marvelous feeling of breadth - like the tune... thank you so much for sharing it!!!!! I have to notice too that you have followed your own advice to stick close to scripture... I love the way the beatitudes fit in - the awareness of blessing in God's law through cherishing and obeying it...

The Watts I like cento II, and the substitution better than CP225. I think I like yours better than cento I; are you having two Watts versions so they can be used together because the meter is the same? In fact, I'm quite sure I like yours better; I like the breadth for so magnificently proportioned a psalm.... besides, is it too tactless to suggest that st. 1 and st. 2 of Watts are too similar with 3 of the 4 final words identical? Even the slant rhyme is the same... Of course one could move the two verses apart somehow... if it is of any importance...

Now that was all very brazen of me - to be offering comments when none was invited... will you forgive? Tell me if my opinions are off the beam, will you? Every instruction helps...

I will have to pursue Paul's comment about preachers being paid but not wanting to be paid himself (of course you might tell me where it is... ☺). I've felt that way often; I don't play in church for the money, . . . if I only did it for the money I'd probably never practice (thereby vastly increasing my hourly wage), and then I'd have less joy in playing (it's much harder to make mistakes than it is to play things right....), and would start a vicious circle of no enjoyment and therefore even moreso doing it only for the money.....

Enough! I love playing anyway, most of the time (if I've practiced enough, felt inspired selecting the music, etc.).

Another version of 96 enclosed; is this more what you meant? The first line [of stanza 4] is exactly like the others, even though you said it needn't necessarily have the same form. Praise seems to come into the psalm in adequate focus for this though, don't you think?

Psalm 24. God and floods don't rhyme, but then I didn't want to use trod or shod or plod or... I recall that the interpretation of the "seek thy face, O Jacob" which I preferred and which makes the best sense, is to suspect some sort of haplography (what a delicious word!) and mentally insert to "O God of Jacob." Does it seem okay this way? Certainly there's no bump in the meaning....

Psalm 3. Any meaning problems with the last stanza? With these which have weird stress patterns (like Psalm 70) I keep them absolutely regular so that they could be set for singing congregationally. With 70 you said that probably wouldn't happen .. was that because of the meaning? I really am glad when you like something though, but be sure to pin down negatives - I want to know you're not just being nice.....

I'm going to end on this page because I tax your reading time overmuch, I suspect. The other enclosure see if it's fun [crossword puzzle]... Jack suggested I send it along.... If it's not your thing don't bother, though... and apologies about some of the definitions!!!!! (Not all, though...) (One - you can guess

242

which - I had a hard time thinking of what possible definition to use, there are so many that would fit....) Thank you thank you as always,

Psalm 3 (Only Version)

When I cried to God with a fearful voice   4,5
      He heard me...
        out of His holy hill, He heard me,
and made me rejoice!
And my sleep is sweet, my life secure,
for the Lord's love is both strong and sure.

How increased the foes that surround me here,   1,2,3
      they mock me!
        Claiming that God is weak, they mock me,
they plague me with fear!   (they fill me....)
But the Lord's own glory is my shield --
through the Lord's power all my fear is healed.

I am not afraid of ten thousand foes!   6,7,8
      God saves me!
        Saved from the evil one!   God saves me!
My confidence grows.
For His blessing stands, my guard and guide;
I will trust Him, and be satisfied.

A M Tindall 3/4/82

Stress pattern:
'_'_'_-_'_'
_'_-
'_-_'_'_-
_'_-_'
_-_'_'_'_'
_-''_-_'_'

App. C p. 329
ER p. 248

243

Psalm 96 (Revised)

Sing, and sing and sing again!
Sing your praises to the Lord.
    Tell all people, friend and stranger,
    He is God, all-wise Creator!
Praise His greatness, bless His name!
Sing, and sing and sing again!

Give, and give and give again!
Give due reverence to the Lord.
    See His majesty and glory,
    honor Him with strength and beauty,
bring an offering, bless His name.
Give, and give and give again!

Joy, and joy and joy again!
Echo joy unto the Lord.
    With the heavens, fields and forests,
    with the seas and all their fullness,
Praise His power, bless His name.
Joy, and joy and joy again!

Praise, and praise and praise again,
giving thanks unto the Lord.
    Know His true and righteous judging
    brings salvation with His guiding.
Holy lives will bless His name!
Praise, and praise and praise again!

A M Tindall 3/4/82

'_'_'_'
'_'_'_'
'_'_'_'_
'_'_'_'_
'_'_'_'
'_'_'_'

App. C p. 351
ER p. 248

Psalm 24 (1st Version)

All the earth belongs to God!
He sets the world upon the floods.
Its fullness comes through his commands,
He claims the people of its lands.

Those found worthy of His place
must have clean hands, hearts filled with grace.
They speak the truth, shun worldly cares,
for blessings from the Lord are theirs.

Let us see our need, confess,
and seek His face, His righteousness.
Salvation is the gift He gives
through Jesus Christ, who died, and lives!

Lift the everlasting gates!
Enthroned is Love, abolished hates!
The King of glory enters in --
Love's power has vanquished death and sin!

A M Tindall 2/26/82

7888   '-'-'-'
        _'-'-'-'
        _'-'-'-'
        _'-'-'-'

App. C p. 334
ER p. 248

245

ACROSS   (KJV)
1. Christ Jesus _____ death's...
6. Of, pertaining to wings
10. _____ dark Gethsemene
14. "I knew a man in Christ above 14 years
_____, ...caught up___the third heaven..."
15. Part to play
16. ____ whose will is life and good
17. "O thou of little faith, wherefore
didst thou _____?"
18. "Consider the lilies, how they _____"
19. Entreat earnestly
20. Planned exit route
22. For thee, O _____ country
24. Mod parlance
26. Lifts up
27. "_____ daughter of Zion" (Zech2:10)
30. British 6686 6686
31. Stiff water
32. Beach (Span)
34. Paranoid monarch
38. Long pile rug
40. Sound the _____!
42. Composer
43. The _____ God goes forth to war
45. _____+S = sslsddtdrm
47. _____ every morning is the love
48. _____ thank we all our God
50. Rise up, O _____
52. "The leaves of the tree____the healing..."
55. "these waters____out toward the east..."(Ezk47:8)
56. Setting a wage scale again
58. "I rejoice in the Lord greatly, that now _____
your care of me hath flourished again...(Ph14:10)
62. & others
63. "See them down in ___ Square,/Dropping h's"
65. Printing meth.
66. Post WWII alliance
67. "Tiny _____with their eyes all aglow/..."
68. "_____into his courts with thanksgiving..."
69 With Ra, early Egyptian deity
70. Scottish island
71. Leaven

246

DOWN

1. Load on board
2. Excited
3. "Go _____ way; tell John..."
4. "If _____ our God...is able to deliver us from the burning fiery..."
5. "Thou hast enlarged my steps under me; so that my feet did _____."
6. Gold (Chem)
7. Holy, holy, holy, _____
8. Lily
9. "...great is your _____ in heaven."
10. 16th c. harmonizer
11. Monsters
12. White garments for public wearing in times of peace (Lat)
13. If you're giving Germans lots of alternatives, you'll need lots of entweders and lots of _____
21. Prefix: Pertaining to sacred rites or observances
23. "Be not _____ with thy mouth" (Eccl 5:2)
25. 19th c. translator
27. Rent, tear (Ger)
28 Romantic organ division
29. "I'll go home with bonny _____"
33. Heraldic borders
35. Then _____ the bells more loud and deep,/God is not dead...
36. Margarine
37. Maker of harpsichords
39. _____+ROYAL=sldfmrmdl,...
41. Table, altar (Lat)
44. "Lest thou dash thy _____against a stone..."
46. Erik
49. Probable location of nails
51. Catlike
52. Where Christians were martyred
53. Edge a hankie again
54. Muse of poetry
57. Cranny's partner
58. _____boy! (sl)
60. "...I don't know,/Because_____just my girl."
61. Wrongful act
64. Suffix, comb form

Solution p. 294

247

Erik Routley
929 Route 518, R. D. 1
Skillman, NJ 08558
Tel. (609) 921-7806

9 March 82

Dear Adrienne -

      Thanks for your last one. No, my John Wilson isn't at Hope Publishing. Actually I have known four John Wilsons here and there (and the Hope Publishing one is not among them). This JW is my master in all things hymnological - a most worthy and delightful fellow, now 77. He appears in hymnals as the composer of, e.g. LAUDS, and arranger of other things in <u>Westminster Praise</u>; and nowadays no reputable hymnal editor goes to work without consulting him. He is indeed in England - he spent all his working life as a schoolmaster, for 17 years being director or music at Charterhouse, a very well known English school.

      Oh no your architect is being too clever about Ps. 119.96; it means exactly what it says - all things come to an end. Not God's commandment. The enclosed tract [<u>Into a Broad Land</u> by ER] may serve to make it obscurer to you.

      No, I am not offering my Psalm 119 to our committee - at least I don't think so: for the Reformed church that tune goes with P. 68 and another member of the committee has done a good version of that, so I think if I offered mine to carry that tune it would confuse things. But of course the ampler meter of the old German tune makes it possible to get more in than Watts could in CM. I shouldn't expect people to sing both versions of Watts consecutively: they are alternatives. I appreciate very much what you say about mine, though. I am not a facile hymn writer at all: my first text was written when I was 49, but that is now a long time ago!

      Your new 96 [p. 244] is splendid. So is Psalm 3 [p. 243] - a fascinating metre which I am sure could attract a good tune. In Psalm 24 [p. 245] I suppose one might quibble about 'hates': for if love is singular why is hate plural? (There might possibly be a theological answer to that but it slightly bugs me). Otherwise, very serviceable. You are now producing some very good things - the style is more natural & singable, and you seem to be really into your stride. I am very happy with these.

      Paul on preachers' pay - I Cor. 9 3 -14, where he is at pains to say that although he has his own reasons for making his living in other ways, in the ordinary way people should expect to contribute to the maintenance of apostles (ministers). Fair enough. If anybody says of anybody else 'They do it for the money' there's always a rather nasty undertone; I am rather abrupt with people who talk like that.

You ask whether there's any obscurity in the last stanza of Ps. 3: not to me. it seems pellucidly clear.

As ever, -

[re pamphlet]
I notice I use the word <u>polarize</u> in its technical sense; it doesn't properly mean 'to place in opposition': it is a word opticians use when making a certain kind of spectacles. Rays of light come toward the eye from all angles, and this, when they are intense, produces dazzle: so they make polarized spectacles ("Polaroids") which flatten out the rays and present them to the eye from a single direction. I am not sure whether in the USA the word is used in this sense but that is what is used to mean in Britain.

I also notice, not having looked at this for 12 years or so, that I use forms of speech & writing to which nowadays in the USA objection might be made on the grounds of implied sexism. I learned so to corrupt my style & rhythm as to accommodate these demands only when I came to the USA in 1975. I don't know whether in your case apology is needed!

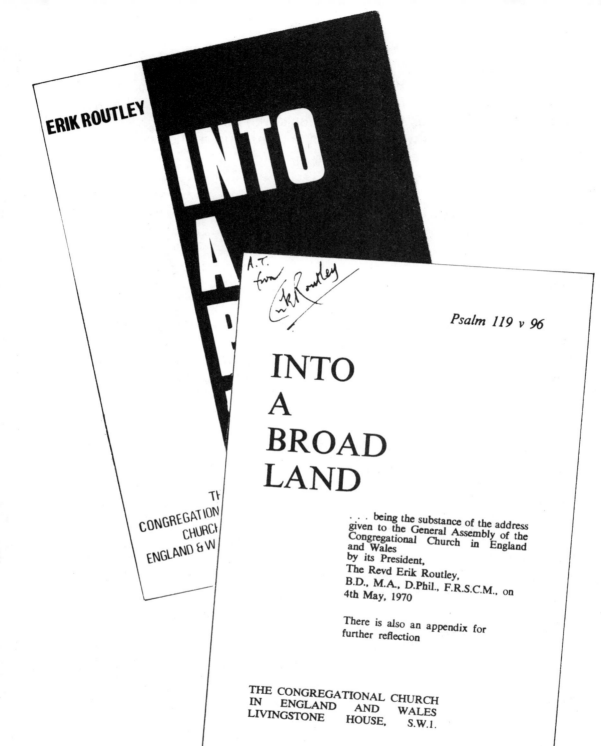

ERIK ROUTLEY

INTO
A
B...

TH...
CONGREGATION...
CHURCH...
ENGLAND & W...

Psalm 119 v 96

INTO
A
BROAD
LAND

. . . being the substance of the address
given to the General Assembly of the
Congregational Church in England
and Wales
by its President,
The Revd Erik Routley,
B.D., M.A., D.Phil., F.R.S.C.M., on
4th May, 1970

There is also an appendix for
further reflection

THE CONGREGATIONAL CHURCH
IN   ENGLAND   AND   WALES
LIVINGSTONE   HOUSE,   S.W.1.

April 12, 1982

Dear Erik:

It's been so long! Happy day after Easter.....

Writing two psalms has been on my list of things to do so many days that I can't even recall how many ... and enclosed are two versions of one psalm. I wonder if it would help my developing sense of taste (for lack of a better term) to "verbalize" what I think of my own efforts ... I don't want to discourage you about them before you read them, but I think I shall do so this time, and if it bothers you, please tell me?

The CM version I did first... and don't like much.... Some of the lines seem contrived purely for the sake of rhyme. Maybe it's just the wrong meter for this psalm's content. The whole thing comes off rather ordinary and non-buoyant, if you know what I mean.... I like part of st. 2 - about the tomb, though...

The irregular version I think shows more vitalness, even though the irregularity of the rhythm tends to be a tich disruptive sometimes. It seems a little short, although I couldn't think of an additional st. (1 1/2?) to insert, so left it. And that shortness tends to perhaps make things come at you without preparation, unless you know the psalm well enough to recognize the basis of a line.... If you know the last verse of the psalm you can make sense of the last line, but probably not if you don't....

Another thing about the irregular meters -- which I just pick out of the air, more or less, taking the way the first stanza comes and then matching the rest to it -- my original aim was to versify psalms so they could be sung, but I still think some of these meters present more challenge to a congregation than is perhaps worthwhile for writing a tune....

Also enclosed is a solo setting of my Psalm 133 - I'd appreciate any comments and suggestions you might have, including whether you find it appealing? I enjoyed doing it - a very simple concept actually, inspired by the birthday of a lovely soprano voice I know.... [Note: the final version is included here instead of an earlier manuscript; this version incorporates some of Erik's suggestions.]

I enjoyed your Into a Broad Land and it wasn't too much "obscurer" although I did find it easier to read in the morning than late at night.... The end reminds

251

me of the Drummond "Greatest Thing in the World" and I can see that your sense of the line [in Ps. 119] is parallel with what he's talking about for I Cor. 13. The end of temporal things being immanent [sic] I can understand very comfortably in that sense - and I can feel comfortable with the line in that context. I think that if you (and you didn't ask, but you won't mind if I comment with a small suggestion.... will you?), if you went back to your original sequence of lines for the second half of your revised first st., then it would be clearer for the singer to identify with what you are in fact saying. As your present revised st. is, "God speaks" starts all four thoughts, immediately followed by "I see that all things have an end:.." and the thing that nudged me was the implication that the ending applied to the things spoken by God. If you restore "Though we are creatures of a day..." preceding "I know that all things..." the ending applies to creatures of a day, to the material heaven and earth, if you see what I mean?... and your contrast with God's statutes being eternal is more clearly supported.

I still love the text and its fitting with the tune. Even though I can see what you mean about that tune also having Psalm 68 for your Reformed hymnal. Are you therefore following a general policy of using each tune with only one text? It's an area that I'm not at all clear on at this time, although I do know that tunes are used for more than one text (at least some tunes - not the obvious only-one-text ones like NICAEA, etc.) in current hymnals in the U.S. But perhaps in the 80's that multiple usage is being set aside.... I'm looking forward to seeing and getting this new hymnal you're doing, when it's available!!!

Thank you so much for your Into a Broad Land by the way! I shall be pleased to have it, and there is indeed much to ponder in it. I can see that you intend me to keep it, and feel quite pleased and grateful... how kind you are!

Would you tell me a bit about a theological question? Don't tax yourself endlessly with it, even though I daresay one could write forever on the subject and not reach an ending....

I have always thought that some denominations had a doctrinally defined clarity that the Trinity - Father, Son, Holy Ghost "separately" identifiable - is their belief, while others (Catholic particularly) state that Jesus is God come to earth, thereby making Mary the Mother of God (in Catholic prayers....? I think I recall that). In today's ecumenism I am feeling less and less clear about this general area. My own sense of things, and understanding the statements in the New Testament (such as "I and my Father are one", "My Father is greater than I", "I go unto the Father," etc.) is a oneness of quality between the two, but a

252

definable identity to each that is <u>not</u> a oneness of <u>quantity</u>... can you see what I mean? My fundamentalist friend explained that they believe Jesus is God come to earth, and that although they can't "explain" the statements implying two identities as Father <u>and</u> as Son, that the explanations will come as we grow in our understanding.

I recall in the Introduction to the New Testament course that I took at Garrett, the professor said that John I "In the beginning was the Word ... And the Word was made flesh" had within the Greek some usage that implied <u>not </u>that the Word was <u>exhausted</u> when made flesh, thereby leaving a vacancy where the Word had been. But that doesn't seem clear to me, the non Greek-reading person looking at the Interlinear Greek-English New Testament, where the word for "Word" is identical on the page ... even though the professor's comments fit quite well with my own "oneness of quality though not quantity" feeling about it.

I would be grateful for anything you might say about this, but please don't take more of your time that you should ... I am right, aren't I, that it's a vast area?

I wonder if I would have figured out your polarized usage? I have Polaroid sunglasses - of a shape and style very specially comfortable to me, and I am familiar with that meaning, even though I guess in prose one would more readily associate with the "opposite sides" meaning. But then your usage just <u>couldn't</u> have meant opposite sides, ...

It's about time to make some hard candy again (my soloist thinks) and why don't you just mention say four flavors you like best? She just <u>couldn't</u> consume all 16 pounds one ends up with...!!

Thank you as always... your letters are special not just in being your inimitable self, and your endlessly patient help with texts (and the <u>et ceteras</u> this time...), but in the fantastic contrast they offer interest-wise with the prodigious quantity of stuff that comes through the mail slot these days! I even wrote the postmaster telling him junk mail couldn't possibly be paying its way and why don't they raise the rates (that might at least discourage some of it!!!).

Did I ever mention to you that these little checks I enclose I do declare on income tax? I suppose that means that you should too - is that too much of a nuisance? I could tell you how much to declare... what a bothersome squandering of potential (a waste of the time spent figuring) is all this income taxing! Would that there were a simpler way to do things.... . . .

Do you really not mind my pestering you? I hope it's not too bad. Please be frank about the enclosures - okay?

Psalm 56 (CMD Version)

O God, You are my heavenly strength,
      You save from earthly foes!
They would oppress, destroy my life --
      each day their threatening grows.
In times when fear is great and strong,
      You only have my trust.
I'll praise Your word, I'll feel Your power,
      and scorn earth's powers as dust.

I feel the malice and the hate
      that lurk in evil's gloom.
But sin has not the power to fight
      the power that rends a tomb!
O God, whose name is Truth and Love,
      Your Son dries every tear,
and every life is healed of sin,
      and every life held dear.

In times when fear is great and strong,
      You only have my trust.
I praise Your word, I feel its power
      and scorn earth's powers as dust.
Your love delivers me from death,
      Your promise, too, is heard --
the hates of earth must bow at last,
      obedient to Your word.

A M Tindall 4/8/82

CMD

ER p. 264

254

Psalm 56 (1st Version)

God, I trust myself to Your mercy!
For earth teems with enemies plotting my death:
every day they lurk, they threaten, oppress,
watching my footsteps, and counting my breath.

God, I know You care for the righteous,
and surely You save from an enemy thrust!
Hate must fall, and love will win through Your word --
Love is my fortress, my hope, and my trust.

God, I feel the power of Your promise --
it lives in the life of Christ Jesus, Your Son.
Every shadow death would cast is eclipsed --
light is Your law! My pathway is won.

A M Tindall 4/9/82

Meter:
'_'_'__'_
_'__'__'__'
__'_'_'__'
'__'_'__'

App. C p. 343
ER p. 264

Psalm 133

Psalm 133,
Paraphrase ADRIENNE TINDALL

ADRIENNE TINDALL

good and how pleas - ant it is_____ when the chil - dren of God_____
_____ dwell to - geth - er in love____ and un - i - ty!_____

ER p. 260

258

ER p. 260

Erik Routley
929 Route 518, R. D. 1
Skillman, NJ 08558
Tel. (609) 921-7806

15 April 82

Dear Adrienne -

Many thanks for your letter. Most interesting.

Your setting of Psalm 133 [pp. 256-259] is very delightful in almost all ways. I have one major comment and one minor one. The minor one [incorporated in the version included] is that in the coda, four measures before the end, your A flat ought to be a G#, and the following G should be naturalled. The G# is part of the key of A which is relevant: the A-flat would be part of the key of E-flat which isn't.

The one thing I have doubts about is the modulation to E major. What I long for is a modulation to F - that whole passage being transposed up half a tone and the modulations adjusted to match. I think that the key a whole step above the home key is the one to which composers using your idiom most rarely attempt to go. Mind you, I was relieved to find that you did return to the home key; many compositions nowadays start in one key and move up to the whole step above and stay there: and were I a choirmaster I wouldn't perform any of them; no reputable composer using this vocabulary ever did it. You have better sense, of course. All the same, I have a hunch that an episode in the key one step up is rare, and that there are important musical reasons for its being so. You look at a Beethoven movement in A major: he may skip about all over the place but the one key he won't visit is B major. Or at any rate - if he used only two keys (as you do) the other one absolutely certainly wouldn't be B major. I don't think there are any passages in the opening movement of the Hammerklavier (B-flat) in C major, - there aren't any in F either but that's for a quite special reason. Apart from those it goes all over the place. I expect that at once half a dozen pieces by people from Bach to Brahms will occur to you that form exceptions to this rule - but at the moment none has occurred to me.

The trouble is nowadays that so much music is written in a vocabulary to which this doesn't apply, that it seems legitimate to make such transitions even in the vocabulary to which it does. Obviously what

I have said doesn't apply to Schoenberg, to John Cage (heaven knows what does) or even to Vaughan Williams; and I often find composers feeling that the things they [Schoenberg, Cage, VW] do, in their vocabularies, they had better do themselves. But it's better not to if you're writing in the same vocabulary that's been in use for close on 300 years. Mind you, there's plenty of music to be written in that language, and there's nothing discreditable about using it. The great thing it has is limitless possibilities for tonal contrasts; but I do think that people avoid D major - E major - D major for just the same reason that if you wear contrasting colours there are some contrasts you never wear. (I am insecure here of course! But I doubt if pink and orange do well together most of the time).

I have jotted down a possible link to show that it is possible but you'd better not take too much notice of it. Otherwise the piece is charming. [The link was evidently forgotten on the desk...]

Oh well, whew, about the Trinity. As briefly as I can put it, I think that orthodox Christian doctrine amounts to this.

(1) It's always been clear to people of the Jewish/Christian tradition that God is really beyond human understanding. And yet that as far as we can understand him, we must try. That's paradox #1.

(2) The Jewish people of the OT found it impossible to think of God otherwise than as a person: so they called him everything they could think of - Father, Savior, Leader, Husband - but they were never allowed to draw a picture of him (second commandment). Paradox #2.

(3) The same people were inclined, at times, to think of God as revealing himself in more than one way. Proverbs 8 is the most impressive attempt to get that through: there is Something there (Wisdom, it's called) which was 'in the beginning with God', having a part in the creation of everything. Not the same as God but in all things equal to him - being there before anything else was. Paradox #3.

(4) That prepared the way for the doctrine of the Trinity, but still there is a big jump. That Doctrine is not specifically proclaimed in the New Testament: in one place in the Gospels we are given a pattern for it, and here and there in the Epistles it's assumed. The Gospel passage is John 14.15,

> If you love me...
> I will pray the Father
> and he will send the Spirit.

That way round, you notice - and it's human experience. The first thing we really feel we know is Jesus; to a child, God's somewhere out there are we're glad he is: but Jesus is somebody we catch hold of. Knowing

261

him we learn a good deal about God. Then comes the Spirit. (More in a moment)

. The Epistles assume the doctrine in such passages as the last verse of II Corinthians - 'The grace of the Lord Jesus Christ, the love of God, the fellowship of the Holy Spirit' - same order again because (again) that's how it actually comes to us in time.

(5) Now the teaching of Jesus as recorded in John 14-16 has this also. 'If you have seen me you have seen the Father' - and nobody ever did before. Then (16.7), 'It is necessary for you that I leave you: otherwise the Spirit won't come.' The action is that shape. The coming of the Spirit depends on what Jesus does: the existence of Jesus depends on the existence of the Father - but still we see Jesus first, go 'back' to the Father, and go 'forwards' to the Spirit.

(6) Now all this responds in another way to human experience - as Augustine works it out. Augustine says that in all human creative activity there's (a) the idea (b) the working out and (c) the communication. The timeless inspiration - Mozart hearing a whole opera of his in a fraction of a second: the laborious working out of it: and, given all that, it's still not really operational until somebody has understood, received and enjoyed it.

If you haven't read Dorothy L. Sayer's 'The Mind of the Maker', do so soon: it works all this out in terms of artistic creation and is quite fascinating in the way it shows that incomplete activity at any of the three points shows up at once in the completed work: for example - here are three unsuccessful works or art (bad sermons if you like): (a) the one that is well worked out and delivered with lots of rhetoric but has no real idea behind it; (b) the one that has a fine idea and a good delivery but is entirely muddled because it wasn't worked out; (c) the one that has a good idea, well worked out, and is yet a complete bore. (It is great fun doing that with hymn tunes).

(7) Now what we say about the Trinity is that God reveals himself in those three modes: the Creator who is before everything; the human being who worked it all out, establishing the relation between the Godhead and humanity; and the Energy who is to be found in every person who not only believes but acts on the belief. That functions in the history of the church as given in the NT with great clarity. The disciples were unable to do anything so long as they only believed in Jesus and in his Father: something had to happen to them to transform them from helpless human beings to people who turned the world upside down. 'Only he can do it' had to be replaced by 'But we can!'

(8) However - nothing is more dangerous than to think we've grasped the lot when we've mastered a formula. For example: once this had been more or less codified by the church's earliest thinkers,

there was always the danger of saying 'Oh, I see. There are three of them. God creates. Jesus redeems. The Holy Spirit sanctifies.' As if there were a heavenly staff of three who divided the needful work between them. No, said the church: that is 'Dividing the Substance.' (Thus the Athanasian Creed.) No, the whole Godhead is involved in all activities of God even if the way we see it - because of our limited vision - is tending to make us attribute this to God, that to Jesus, the other to the Spirit. Another paradox.

(9) But again, people might say, 'Oh well, there's really no difference is there?' This at once gets you into mental difficulty because Jesus obviously is in a sense different from God. He who said 'I and my Father are one' did not say 'I and my Father are the same.' To say 'we are one' means 'in one sense we are one, but in another we are two.' I do not myself think that the expression 'Jesus is God' is helpful and I never use it. It is always liable to be interpreted too simply. We might end by worshipping him in the way he didn't want. 'Why do you call me good? Only my Father is good,' he once said. His mission was always directed towards setting right our relation with the Father - that is with absolutely everything: our tendency to say (as some almost do) that so long as we pay Jesus due honour, nothing much else matters, is what leads to so much too-intense and too-humanistic religion. Anyhow - saying 'There's no real difference' is what the church called Dividing the Substance (Athanasian creed again).

(10) All that is all very well: but from our own point of view there's one principle we must never lose sight of. It's fatal to work too hard on this. There is a very real sense in which Luther is right to oppose faith to works. Every time we work too hard, something in the machinery slips - or it's like an electric fuse breaking an overloaded circuit. Strive too hard and it will elude you. Personally I never saw anything better on this that what [C. S.] Lewis said - and I expect you know this, in 'Beyond Personality.'

He says (I paraphrase him), imagine you are a creature that knows only two dimensions - forwards and sideways, nothing about 'up'. Imagine somebody trying to describe to such a creature a cube. Such a person might say 'It is six squares but one body (or unit)', and the creature would probably say, oh yes, six squares laid side by side in some pattern. No, not that. There's the third dimension (height) to be taken into account. Ah, says the creature, you mean six squares (which have no height) laid 'on top of' one another (since you can[,] there is an 'on top of' dimension). No again.

There I think we have it. Three and One implies a dimension, or way of existing, we can only take on trust: we can't even imagine it.

The great thing about the doctrine of the Trinity is that in so many other, and intelligible, ways, it works. See above.

Your specific question about 'In the beginning was the Word' got the right answer from the instructor. We say - in our dimensions - if he's here he can't be there, can he? If the Word came to earth then he wasn't in heaven. Wrong - because there's nothing in that world against the Word being 'in two places at once': both 'place' and 'time' - which both appear in that phrase - are things which mean something to us - indeed without which we can't think at all: they don't mean anything in the eternal world.

The one thing that comforts me in the Doctrine of the Trinity is that it was the result of the Christians out-thinking all the rest of the world: there is nothing like it in Greek thought, and only a groping after it in the Hebrew world. It's simply the best minds of the time grappling with mystery - and in the end insisting that mystery is what it finally is.

PSALM 56 [pp. 254, 255]. I should keep the version in the unusual metre and forget the DCM one - I think your assessment is quite right. Is your use of 'enemy' as an adjective all right? Yes, I see from Webster that it is. 'Enemy action' of course. I see nothing here to quarrel with. Irregular metres, by the way, are metres in which stanzas are not exactly the same, so yours aren't irregular - they are only unusual and, as such, very welcome. Of course if your psalms are to be sung they will have to wait for tunes which will make the metres of the unusual ones friendly to singers: but that's happened before and will happen again, given time. And thank you for your remarks about my Ps 119 piece: I've now passed it for publication in the British Methodist hymnal so I think it'll have to stay as it is, but your points are well taken.

You needn't figure out the total of the checks: I have it on record and it's far too generous anyhow. I am at the moment very sensitive about tax; I changed my tax agent this year, not being quite satisfied with the previous one. The result is that the new one has calculated that I owe so many back taxes as to have very nearly cleaned out all I had saved! This really is an astounding country - such fun to live in, but don't you have to work hard to keep above water? We actually are quite frugal at home - during this last winter we made a great reduction in heating bills, only heating above 55 when somebody was known to be calling on us! I recall with such pleasure Alistair Cooke telling us about poor President Nixon when all the fuss was on. The taxes he paid in 1972 amounted to $714. But somebody caught up with that, of course. Be assured, we are painfully honourable about all this. Was there something somewhere about rewards in heaven? Your own kindness, is, I assure you, most warmly appreciated, and also your thoughtfulness in advising me about your own declaration. It's a most legitimate professional expense at your end!

I trust you have not been made to feel ill by the blue type. My black cassette ran out back there & I'm immobilized by a strained leg muscle, and my wife wasn't at home for me to holler at her & ask her to go to the store! It's getting better. Nuisance, though.

Warmest greetings as always,

yours ever,

May 13, 1982

Dear Erik:

Well, apologies first!!!!! Because when I reread my last letter to you a few days after I sent it, I was very very offended by the tone of voice that could (even though it was not to be) have been read into my comments about your Psalm 119. How very telling that it did not get in your way too much.... . . .

Your views of the solo setting are appreciated. I too share your feelings about a piece starting and ending in the same key, and am not too happy with pieces dropping me off somewhere away from "home...." I would be interested to see your suggested modulations (did you forget to enclose them?) even though to use them would necessitate transposing the piece, as it goes high enough for performance with the E Major... I admit I just "heard" the E Major key, as I was playing the D Major parts, and then forced the modulation into it. Coming home again did itself a bit; I've gotten to be a very non-rules lazy dabbler in composition (a rusty talent that wasn't used all that much in college, anyway...). Never thought analytically about the relationship being consistently avoided... My soloist likes the piece, so maybe it will get sung someday...

I've reread your letter several times, and what a helpful capsulization of the Trinity! Have not been able to locate the Athanasian Creed, except brief mention of it in an encyclopedia (under Nicene, I think it was...). I can see what it's aiming at, I think, though...

You know, I have noticed that mention of Jesus was first in the Epistles' "listing" of the Trinity, and often wondered about it. The reason should have come to me, because several years ago I realized very clearly that Jesus' life and teachings and healing work were the keystone in making God and God's love relevant and believable; without Jesus how could anyone prove the other? Well, in any case it's just as well your letter is in blue because then I can pick it out readily from the file, and I know I'll be able to take in more of what you've said than I've done so far... it's very helpful, understandable (inasmuch as it <u>can</u> be understood, that is), even from a vantage point at a little different point along the chasm....

I don't know the "Beyond Personality" source, but I did read a novel little book by some nineteenth century writer, which I think was entitled "Flatland." It was, of course, a two-dimensional world, with very imaginative adaptations of our own life patterns to the restrictions of two dimensions. For example (don't tell the ERA uptighters!) women were only straight lines (one dimension), and, in order to be seen by "people" approaching them from front or back, they had to "undulate" or wave themselves back and forth, so that their fellow beings did not <u>impale</u> themselves on a woman, (who would look merely like a point). Women and girls continued as lines through generations, sons had one additional side, when compared to their fathers. The "hero" of the book was, I believe, a square, and he had two pentagon sons. A creature from another world entered his life, trying to tell him of a third dimension, but the "hero" resisted valiantly because the governing body of Flatland would take anyone who claimed there was a third dimension, and incarcerate him in a mental institution for something like "treasonable lunacy". . . . There was an exploration of the incredible difficulty of trying to tell someone about a third dimension, when that someone has no grasp on the concept and no vocabulary to accommodate the concept... There was a brief discussion of Lineland, which caused its occupants difficulty as no one could pass anyone else... and

Pointland was just mentioned, maybe as an impossibility - how could more than one person exist after all?

Tell me what you think of <u>this</u> analogy, which I thought was fun, in relating to what one could call the "dimension of Spirit..." or the "Fourth" dimension (that number being arbitrary; I daresay science and physics have taken us far beyond four in theory...):

Last winter I went for a snowmobile ride with my husband one morning, just before we left the cabin. It was cold (15° below zero!), and since snowmobiling isn't my thing, I was thinking of what I could get out of the ride that would be interesting and of value to me.... The landscape was beautiful - pure white snow because it never melts in the winter up there, brilliantly blue sky, muted tans and earth tones of the weeds which stuck through the snow which sparkled in the sunlight, uninhabited and trackless expanses, with just the snowmobile trail through the middle. And it occurred to me that if someone from another planet, say, who had never seen a summer landscape there, came and took at face value what he saw, he would have a time-place view of things which would entirely exclude summer's greens and animal life, but would be complete, and still completely beautiful in its way, with 15° below zero temperatures, snows, frozen lakes, etc. And that the addition of the "dimension" of warmer temperatures would take the same time-place situation and completely change it.

Adding the dimension of Spirit, or of the Kingdom of Heaven, or of divine Love's activity to what we think of as life in our time-place, would be just as dramatic. Now I know one must not push analogies (parable-like) too far, and sometimes the greatest lesson is where an analogy breaks down.... In this case of course one can't assume that divine Love is inactive in our time-place world, nor that the Kingdom of Heaven is remote or removed,... but it seems to parallel the paradoxes, which need the added dimension of spiritual understanding, because they are "unexplainable" to us at this point... can you sense what I'm trying to say? (It was a beautiful ride, once I was thinking of such interesting things!)

Enclosed please find ... and I shall comment on them, again, to see if you agree with my present evaluations...

Psalm 52. It doesn't seem to bother me that there are no rhymes, even though I generally find complete lack of rhyme disappointing. Maybe God rhymes with God enough to carry it through... other than that it seems okay to me...

"From Psalm 53" goes further afield and perhaps not rightly? The first line appealed to me just because of itself, and I "took off" from the general sense of the psalm. "The parents or the youth?" may be a problem... I suppose it should be "youths" anyway... the line does fit with the "generation to generation" sense the Hebrews had. I didn't like the "older ones" which I had first, although I didn't mean to exclude bachelors and single ladies when I used "parents"! . . .

I am really rather depressed about your tax expert. Jack's accountant does our tax form, and I would have to study it for weeks to understand it even a smally reasonable amount.... If only one could feel that the money were being well spent! But the government does many vexatious things, I fear, and inefficiently at that. It is of course rendering unto Caesar, but even Caesar would never have dreamed of taking so much, would he have? Not except from the slaves.... . . . Hope you're back on both feet, and I can't even guess how your King's English would pronounce 'holler' let alone visualize you doing so, and I got all this on three pages... manymanythanks as always....!

[See psalms on pages 276 and 277, following the 6/2/82 letter.]

June 2, 1982

Dear Erik:

I'm sending off a quick note because if my last one went astray I shall then be able to send you its inclusions again, and if your last one went astray... well, I guess the same inclusions are the ones I'm interested in....

If you've not had time to answer that's perfectly all right! Certainly this length of time would be nothing for me to let go, and the same is appropriate for you when you're busy. But seeing as you usually answer amazingly promptly, I'm going ahead.

Psalm 96-2 I am of course competing with one of my own, which as I recall wasn't all that bad. But what do you think of this one?

Psalm 13 again has an unusual stress pattern, carried through all verses. In both of these I've repeated the ends of the verses in each verse (stanza, I guess, right...) Does it seem too much, too boring and repetitive?

The fudge store has opened up again up north.... so far I've spared you, but if you have any preference you may as well so state.....

Enjoyed your article on God's gender... I very much agree that what the minister can and should say, within his free form prose expressing, is not necessarily what one should expect a congregation to sing, within the historic quoted hymns of not necessarily contemporary expression.... (I must add that a Christian Science congregation would not be too bothered by the expandings in this area though - they already have "O Love, our Mother ever near" and "O Father-Mother God, Whose plan/ Has given dominion unto man" (man generically, and so understood...)). I would suspect that the so-called average church-goer would still strongly resist anything but God the Father as an appellation, with of course Lord.... Tell me, is there a kind of deliberate non-clarity about whether "Lord" refers to Jesus or God, based in the oneness of the two?

Now I shall close because you will then be properly amazed at a one-pager.... Thank you thank you as always...and wishing you a joyful summer-starting-up! Giving any workshops in the northern Midwest?

Adrienne

Psalm 96 - (2nd Setting) (1st Version)

Where can we find new songs for God?
What songs can hope to express His greatness?
        His greatness ... or our love?
Glory is His, and the beauty of holiness:
show forth His salvation today, and tomorrow,
        and tomorrow, and forever!
Sing new songs of His greatness!
Sing new songs of our love.

Tell all the world that God shall reign!
His honor, majesty, strength and beauty
        all power, everywhere!
Give up our hearts and our lives to serving Him   (your...your?)
Show forth His salvation today and tomorrow   (Reflect His perfection)
        and tomorrow, and forever!
Sing new songs of His greatness!
Sing new songs of our love.

Let all the heavens and earth rejoice!
Sing grateful praise to the God who made them --
        all-knowing, loving God!
Joy is our heritage, based in His kindliness,
His grace is our blessing today and tomorrow,
        and tomorrow, and forever!
Sing new songs of His greatness!
Sing new songs of our love.

A M Tindall 5/82

'_-'-'
-'-'_-'-
_'-'
'--'--'--'--   Does "kindliness" sound kind of "undeific"?
-'--'_-'--'-
_-'-'-
'-'_-'-
'-'_-'

ER p. 273

270

Psalm 13 (1st Version)

Would You forget me, God, forever?   1,2,5,6
Would You always hide Your face?
Will I never feel Your comfort?
Will I never mirror forth Your love and grace?
       I trust Your mercy,
       my heart will rejoice,
       Your salvation is my song forever!
       Dear Lord, hear my voice.

I fear my enemies' prevailing,   3,4,5,6
will I sleep the sleep of death?
God, deliver me from evil!
Be my strength, my wisdom, refuge, life, and breath!
       I trust Your mercy,
       my heart will rejoice,
       Your salvation is my song forever!
       Dear Lord, hear my voice.

O loving Father, when Your Son came
with his healing love and power,
he was proving that Your mercy
is a shield to us in every testing hour.
       I trust Your mercy,
       my heart will rejoice!
       Your salvation is my song forever!
       Dear Lord, hear my voice.

A M. Tindall 5/82

```
---'-'-'-
--'-'-'
--'-'-'-
--'-'-'-'-'
-'-'-
-'--'
--'-'-'-'-
-'"-'
```

App. C p. 331
ER p. 273

271

Erik Routley
929 Route 518, R. D. 1
Skillman, NJ 08558
Tel. (609) 921-7806

26 June 82

Dear Adrienne -

Oh dear, oh dear..... We are, at last, the victims of our temperamental mails. It is true that we have been on vacation, but before we left, in a frantic last-minute rush, I did write to you – to thank you, among other things, for the excellent candies you so kindly sent. I am so grateful to you for sending again Psalms 13 and 96. I am afraid our home is so small that I can't file letters, and your previous one has gone - so I can't recall what it asked and what I said. I do apologize, and hasten to thank you for this one.

Well, actually, this one arrived while we were away. We snatched (as we had to) the chance of taking 2 weeks off, and what we did was to spend 14 days driving to San Francisco, where I had a workshop. We had an unbelievable time - our route took us through southern Colorado, Northern Arizona, Southern Utah and Nevada - so as you deduce, we visited the canyons - Grand Canyon, Bryce, Cedar Breaks, Zion Park, not to mention Mesa Verde and Sequoia National Park. In SFO my wife's ways and mine parted: she took the car on to Irvine, south of LA, where some dear friends of ours live: and she's driving back with one of them, to arrive July 2. I got back on the 20th by plane, and had to plunge at once into a summer session week which involved 30 hours of teaching, rescuing the backyard from the incompetent treatment of the Almighty, in whose hands we left it, and writing 52 letters in answer to the accumulated mail. Now it is Saturday, and my first free day. Vacations have to be good to be worth it, but this one was.

I am glad you are with me on the Gender of God. The thing that bugs me about these high-toned scholars is that they forget how ordinary people talk, and how to talk to ordinary people. I think every theologian ought to be a parish minister! (Sour grapes: I have been the latter but not the former).

In Psalm 96 [p. 270] you ask whether 'your' and 'our': I think strictly we have to say something like 'Give we our hearts' or give up your hearts': the problem is the first-person imperative, normally expressed as 'let us give....' For my ear, 'Give we' is perfectly euphonious and I like it: but I think the 'we' has to be in; it can be 'understood' through the rest of the stanza. Otherwise it has to be 'your' with the same provision. What a very nice meter this turns out to be. 'Kindliness' is perfectly appropriate. 'For me, kind Jesus, was thy incarnation' (Bridges). it's a splendid word - don't apologize for it. As for 'reflect his perfection' - it's just as good as 'show forth his salvation', and it simply depends on which you want to say - they are very different expressions. The 'show forth' one is, of course, nearer to the language of the psalm.

I think Ps 13 [p. 271] is very effective too: it's a good idea to bind it together with a refrain-section. I have no comment except praise for this one.

As for that wicked stuff you send from Wisconsin, we love it. It does terrible things to my figure and nothing at all to my wife's, which is unfair but I can live with it! Again I do apologize for your not getting my earlier reply: our correspondence is frequent enough for the law of averages to take its toll. One has to be content with one letter in about twenty to go stray. Why, I ask myself, cannot the post office provide the kind of service we get from Bell telephone? The latter never fails to astonish me - the former finds me resigned and defeated!

As ever -

July 22, 1982

Dear Erik:

There's nothing new in this letter, except the joyous although somewhat
breathless announcement that I have become a mother-of-the-bride! And
Jackie, my eldest, who introduced her fiancé to us over July 4th weekend, is
calling forth my most efficient efforts, as the wedding is to be October 2. I
cannot complain as she is 25 and the step seems AOK - they have much in
common in many ways, and he is a superlatively nice person - imagine my
getting a son-in-law who wants to sing hymns in the evening! He also poses
readily, and encourages my daughter to do also, for the many pictures I feel like
taking....

The rest is a repeat of the letter whose answer was lost...

Psalm 52 no rhymes, but it didn't bother me, even though a completely
non-rhyming poem usually bothers me quite a bit in the regular patterns of a
potential "hymn."

Psalm 53 as I reread it I think I'll play around with it a bit - its present form
seems a little disappointing in several spots.

I shall take my little books up north with me next week and make a project
again of doing several texts. I seem to get out of the stride if I put them aside
for too long, and even though the present distraction [Jackie's wedding] is
significant and must be attended to by myself and no one else, I still don't want
to lose the thread completely! . . .

I have now taken a week to try to revise 53, not succeeding, and to add
something new to the letter, also not succeeding... and we head north tomorrow
so there is a certain zoolike quality in my life today, with everything going
which way... but I shall get this in the mail and then, knowing your fantastic

promptness (always assuming you have a moment, please never burden yourself), . . .

Hope your schooling for summer is going excellently and that the weather is being reasonably cool ... a young friend of mine here is applying to WCC for I think graduate work - I wonder if she'll get in? - but in any case she came out there for entrance exams and was very impressed at how great everything is - I've told her to take one of your courses early if she gets in - that way she'll be able to take as many as possible once she discovers what a ball it is!

Thank you as always - I cannot really indicate to you how much your kindness means to me... well I can give you a little insight perhaps by telling you that Psalm 133 "How good and how pleasant it is" Jackie and Doug liked so much that they would like it sung at their wedding - it will be as a duet. I still like the piece pretty much, and it makes me grateful to participate in that way... and it started with a psalm version written to send to you...!

Psalm 52 (1st Version)

I will praise You forever, God!   8,9
I will trust Your mercy,
        rejoice in Your love.
I will be like an olive tree,
        verdant, fruitful,
deep-rooted, forever secure in the house of God!

And the wicked shall perish, God!   1-5
In devising mischief,
        they cause their own fall.
Their deceits are condemning them --
        evil, lying, --
all sin is cast out by the goodness and power of God!

Let us worship the Lord, our strength,   6,7,9
witness evil's downfall,
        and laugh in our awe!
Let the hearts of the faithful be
        steadfast, holy,
forever rejoicing, and praising the name of God!

                A M Tindall 5/3/82

--'--'-'
--'-'-
-'--'
--'--'--
'-'-
-'--'--'--'-'

App. C p. 341
ER p. 279

from Psalm 53 (1st Version)

God looked down from heaven   2,5,6
            upon the children of earth.
Did any feel His love,
            or know His mighty worth?
Did any see how foes were conquered
            by His sword of truth?
Did any sing salvation's song?
            The parents? Or the youth?

God looked down from heaven
            upon the foolish and slow;
He even sent His Son
            to teach them how to go.
He called them back from fears and evil
            with His law of love;
Gave each the freedom found in Truth,
            protecting from above.

God looks down from heaven
            upon His children today.
And do we feel His love?
            And choose His narrow way?   **
Come! Find protection through earth's trials -
            Truth shall still prevail!
He puts His message in each heart:
            My love will never fail.   (God's love...)

A M Tindall 5/3/82

**   Draw near Him when we pray?

'-'-'   (Is this too "pat"? Are the "and"s okay in 3:4-5?)
-'-'--'
-'-'-'
-'-'-'
-'-'-'-
'-'-'
-'-'-'
-'-'-'

Rev. in App. C, p. 342
ER p. 278

277

Erik Routley
929 Route 518, R. D. 1
Skillman, NJ 08558
Tel. (609) 921-7806

4 August 82

Dear Adrienne -

Thank you so much for your letter which came in yesterday, with Psalms 52 and 53. I hope this reply won't go astray. Let me first thank you for some <u>most</u> tasty things which came a month or more ago and which I am afraid I may never have written about. We have been having a monumental summer one way and another and Summer Session (now almost over) has never been so busy or exhausting: and I have in several cases been unsure whether correspondence has been dealt with or not. Anyhow - the parcel contained the things we enjoy most, and it was lovely to have it.

Your psalms. Yes, both have great character though neither may yet have reached its final form. Ps 53 [p. 277] is a tremendous utterance in the original, and of course what you've done is to take one idea out of it - which is a perfectly legitimate thing to do. You don't seem satisfied with it, and possibly that's because you wonder what's happened to that momentous opening, 'The fool said in his heart: there is no God'. I also value, myself, 'then were they in great fear where no fear was' (v. 5) - and I was sorry when the scholars got at it & said that that was a mistranslation! (NEB has; 'they were in dire alarm when God scattered them.') And that marvellous finish: 'Israel would rejoice, and Jacob would be right glad.' When in your footnote you wonder if it's too 'pat', I think perhaps you are conscious of the big scale of the original. I don't at all mind your version but I expect that in the end, like Watts, you'll probably make another to go with it and include some of these other notions. Possibly also in the last line of the existing version you might think 'My love will never fail' slightly unexpected. I really did expect 'His love.....'

278

With 52 [p. 276] I feel you did quite right in extracting the main positive idea: it's not one of the psalmist's best efforts really! I like it very much; I am much impressed by 'let us laugh in our awe' which is just the sort of thing a hymnal committee would turn down because of its unusualness - but it has a splendid counterpoint in it. I would take your alternative version for the opening of st. 3. It's a very interesting meter, awaiting an effective tune.

So I should keep 52 as it is, but ruminate on another 53 to put alongside the present one. You are making interesting experiments with meter - but your question about being 'singsong' is revealing. The meter of 53 possibly lacks breathing points. A couplet like

Did any see how foes were conquered by his sword of truth -

which has to be sung continuously like that - demands 14 syllables without a caesura (breathing spot); 'Praise to the Lord, the Almighty' does that, but uses a triple rhythm that makes it all dance along very well; yours uses a duple rhythm (accent every second beat, not every third) which makes it perhaps a bit monotonous. St. 2 really works out at (in your notation) -'-'-'-'- - -'-' (lines 5-6) which might be quite difficult to set or sing. But it's a small point and I am really only interpreting what I think is in your mind & may well be mistaken.

Talking of breathing spots - they're what I've been short of. Summer session coincided with the final work on the ms of the hymnal, which yesterday I took to New York to be Xeroxed for the committee - almost 700 pages of ms and typing, plus two indexes completed. It's nice that it's progressed so quickly but it's filled up a lot of leisure. Then I have, to my amazement (and it may be evidence of national degeneracy) three composing commissions waiting to be seen to - one has been done but the other two are nagging. Nice of people to think of it. One of the remaining ones is an ordinary anthem and I think I can handle it: the other is for a children's choir and I'm terrified of it but it's for the college & I must do it somehow. But I have nothing to complain of - we had a splendid vacation - 2 weeks for me with my wife travelling to San Francisco by road via those deserts and canyons, not excluding Death Valley: nearly 4 weeks for her because she ended up with a friend in LA with whom she made the return journey. And my 2-piano sonata (1981) gets its first - no doubt also last - performance tomorrow. Next week I have to preach 4 sermons at Massanetta Springs, Virginia -

an amiably crazy place where the piety does me no harm because I
don't inhale. When we're back into regular work I may get a little more
time to be a decent correspondent.

I will duly send this to your Box 632 and hope for a change
of mind in the Post Office.

As ever -

ψ 53: the ands are OK, I think
/ And they come, and filled with the ships ...
Lk 5·7

[missing AT letter, which evidently mentioned sitting by the fire at the cabin,
reading through a hymnal, asking about anthems, ... undoubtedly warned that
candy was on the way, but must not have included any psalm versions]

Erik Routley
929 Route 518, R. D. 1
Skillman, NJ 08558
Tel. (609) 921-7806

20 August 82

Dear Adrienne -

Another parcel of sinfully good fudge &c yesterday - how generous you are: and in this particular case, how unusually timely: for we have with us for a few days one of my wife's nephews and his new (delightful) wife: and to-morrow his sister, her husband, and 2 young ruffians aged 1-1/2 and 5, will descend on us. That will help entertain them!

I am not surprised to learn that you have needed a fire. To us it presents itself as the most blissfully cool summer we've so far had in the US. We're at August 20 and have had only one thunderstorm, instead of the usual dozen, and we actually haven't even installed the air-conditioners, making do very well with fans. I don't know if the universe is running down, or whether this means that in '83 we shall get a real shocker, but we're thankful for this, especially as semester begins on Sunday (22nd) and continues until a day or two before Christmas.

It seems odd to have the hymnal out of the house after these two years in which it's been growing up. It will be back soon, and the committee may have second thoughts about lots of things which I'll then have to re-copy. But basically I think it's not bad. I did, of course, pass on at an early stage what your publisher told me about selling a words-only edition, and that's why we are so glad we're going to have one. Oh yes, one can profitably read-through a hymnal that is arranged on the Church Year, as far as that goes: but there's no hymnal that gives more than about a quarter of its length to the church year. The thing to do is to read through a hymnal backwards and see how long it takes to get to anything useful or interesting! So often the junk material is sent down to the far end. (Not with the Episcopals, though). Doing it our way makes it more difficult for the junk to get in at all. We have some. One of our committee, resignedly accepting a real evangelical horror for the sake of Iowa, sighed & said, 'Well, I suppose there must be one worst hymn in the book'.

You don't want to know about my anthems. Not really. Here are one or two for you to discard. This confounded thing for 600 children, brass band and heaven knows what else, has been a great

281

worry but I think it's just about coming straight now. I was pleased with the 2-piano sonata. I am getting a tape, I think, but I doubt if it will ever be heard again. They played it from a professionally-copied manuscript - I couldn't ask them to read it from my writing. It's ages since I had anything professionally copied and I was duly rocked back by the price - which was about three weeks' wages.

Again, thank you so much for the goodies, which are the kind we like best of all.

Enjoy the rest of your time in the north -

as ever,

[Anthems enclosed:
Draw Nigh, O Lord (Flammer A-5909)
By Gracious Powers (Hinshaw HMC 165)
The Prayer of Manasseh (Hinshaw HMC 241)
Sing We Triumphant Hymns of Praise (Hinshaw HMC 275)
Lift Up Your Heads, Rejoice (Agape ER 1922*)
Two for Pentecost (Hinshaw HMC 267)
Come, O Thou Traveler Unknown (Agape ER 1920*)
* Erik Routley Choral Series]

October 21, 1982

Dear Erik:

It's been so long since I've pestered you! And I've wanted to write, not only to get back into the psalming, but to perhaps hear how the hymnal is going, the composing or whatever, ... I saw your anthem listed in the Diapason - for the affair there at WCC?

The wedding was beautiful. I shall include a picture of my daughter, which picture I took (myself!) and that makes it even more special to me... you may admire and then dispose of it as I've ordered enlargements etc. of my favorites.

Enclosed please find as usual... Psalm 4 gets too repetitive in its first form, so I thought through a possible second form today [probably the one included; no other version found]. Psalm 6 I may try a tune someday as it borders on the impossible...?? Obviously one can't sing 20 syllables, no matter how the text presented itself to me.... Is it theologically a nono to refer to Jesus as God's "mercy"? It seemed to me he certainly exemplifies it.... One could also say "My heart takes courage, steadfast in Your love" if that's all right syntactically; that seems to be what my little commentary suggests David ended up with...

This is brief because I haven't even taken the chance to review the last letter or two to see where we are, but it's 4:25 and my daughter's last hockey game starts in 5 minutes, directly after which we leave for a weekend in Wisconsin - the first since August, due to the wedding busyness - am I ever ready to sit by the fire!!!

Best wishes, and thank you as always,

Psalm 4 (1st Version)

Hear me when I call, O God of righteousness,
strengthening me when I am in distress,

                have mercy; hear my prayer.

I will not be turned from God by worldly jeers,
vanities and riches have no lures;

                have mercy, hear my prayer.

God has set aside the righteous for Himself.
He is listening to each call for help.

                His mercy hears my prayer.

Stand in awe of God! Hold thought above all sin;
let your heart feel God's own peace within;

                His mercy hears your prayer.

Never tremble in the face of doubt or fear:
God's own smile lights up the darkness here!

                His mercy hears each prayer.

Offer sacrifices through your righteousness.
Wait, and hope, and trust; His love will bless

                with mercy, hearing prayer.

God has put the greatest gladness in my heart --
greater than the joys earth can impart;

                His mercy answers prayer.

Sweet and peaceful is my sleep; I am secure --
God Himself has made my safety sure.

                I know He hears my prayer.

                A M Tindall 10/20/82

'_'_'_'_'

'_'_'_'

_'_'_'

284

Psalm 6 (1st Version)

O Lord, dear Lord, rebuke me not
      with all the anger and reproach
      that I deserve --
            Have mercy!
I cannot of myself deserve Your grace,
            Have mercy on me, Lord!

My will is drained away
      by woe and guilt which plague me,
      undermining strength and nerve --
            Have mercy!
How can I ever hope to see Your face?
            Have mercy on me, Lord!

Within this vale of tears
      I find no hope, no joy, no peace,
      no sign of victory won -
            Have mercy!
And can Your blessing reach from heaven above?
            Have mercy on me, Lord!

Yet even as I pray,
      You give your answer in the life
      and loving of Your Son --
            Your mercy!
My heart takes courage, resting in Your love,
            Your mercy to me, Lord!

            A M Tindall 10/21/82

Stress pattern will certainly challenge setting to music!

The rhyme pattern probably doesn't show up unless this is formatted as two stanzas... and at this point "loving" and "love" in the last stanza might be stronger if not a repetition of the word?
      Is it logical and acceptable to refer to "Your Son" as "Your mercy" ?

_'_'_'_'_'_'_'_'_'
_'_
_'_'_'_'
_'_'_'

285

Margaret Routley
Route 518, R. D. 1
Skillman, NJ 08558

Nov 23 '82

Dear Mrs. Tindall,

I am very sorry to have to tell you that Erik died in his sleep on October 8. . . .

Yours sincerely,

Margaret Routley

Appendix A
THE LETTERS

Items enclosed with the letters are, in general, indicated. A few discussions indicated.

TINDALL	ROUTLEY
7-7-79 God's Power and Love / MEAD'S BRIER	
	7-9-79
8-1-79 Watts' 10 commandments God's Power and Love / MEAD'S BRIER	
	8-4-79
8-26-79	
	9-1-79
11-12-79 "All who love and serve" typo?	
	11-21-79
12-10-79 Let your light so shine What is this lovely fragrance? 10 commandments	
	12-15-79
12-12-79	
	12-19-79 (postcard)
12-26-79	
	12-29-79
	1-24-80 (postcard)
1-29-80 "All who love and serve" suggestion	
	2-4-80

3-11-80
10 commandments / WYCH CROSS?

3-14-80

6-6-80
[postcard]

6-30-80
Psalm 16

7-5-80
SOUTH CERNEY

7-12-80

7-18-80

(AT letter missing)

7-21-80

8-14-80
"Thank you!" / JENNEL

8-19-80
ER harmonization JENNEL

9-2-80
"Thank you!" / JENNEL

9-5-80

(AT letter missing)
Dear God, I would be holy

9-19-80

10-21-80
Dear God, I would be holy
Brookfield program (incl. BRIDEGROOM)

10-29-80

11-14-80
Montgomery hymn

11-19-80

12-1-80
(Dunaway Christmas 1970)

12-4-80

12-18-80
Dunaway Christmas 1970

(1-9-81 Missing)

1-31-81
Dunaway Servant

2-7-81

2-17-81
Psalm 34

2-20-81

2-23-81
Psalm 8

2-28-81

3-2-81
Psalm 51
SERVITOR

3-14-81

3-20-81
Psalm 51

3-21-81

3-24-81

4-4-81

4-5-81
Psalm 139
Chosen Vessel

4-9-81
OLD 137TH

4-14-81
Psalm 16 st. 1

4-23-81

5-19-81
Psalm 131
Psalm 133
Hymn program with 6 "new" & "very new" examples

6-7-81 (handwritten)

7-1-81
Psalm 42
Psalm 130
Psalm 131
POLLSTIN for Psalm 133

7-6-81

7-27-81
Psalm 42

8-7-81
Psalm 84
Psalm 139
"70 x 7"

8-11-81
Psalm 45

8-19-81
Psalm 15
Psalm 26
Psalm 65

7-31-81

8-25-81

9-4-81
Psalm 26
Psalm 47
Psalm 61-1
Psalm 65
Two tunes for Ps 65

9-12-81
"all of"

9-23-81
Psalm 121
ER tapes

10-1-81
JSB leading tone
melodic skips
KAPHAR
sin, error
hymnal
ER tapes

10-20-81
Psalm 61-2
(Psalm 84)
Psalm 147

10-26-81
"SOMETHING LIKE THIS"
WARWICK

11-10-81
Psalm 47
Psalm 83
Psalm 93
Psalm 127

11-17-81
LAC DU FLAMBEAU

12-3-81
Psalm 83
Psalm 84
Psalm 123
Psalm 126
Psalm 137-1

12-7-81
Ps 137-1
2 poems as a carol

12-9-81

12-10-81
(Diehl book)

12-11-81

1-25-82
Psalm 137-2
Psalm 101

1-29-82
Protocol

2-16-82
Psalm 137-2
Psalm 101
Psalm 96
Psalm 70

2-22-82
Psalm 119 2 versions
Watts 2 centos

3-4-82
Psalm 3
Psalm 24
Psalm 96
Crossword Puzzle

3-9-82
"Into a Broad Land"

4-12-82
Psalm 56 (two versions)
Psalm 133 (Solo version)

4-15-82
Discussion of the Trinity

5-13-82

293

6-2-82
Psalm 13
Psalm 96

6-22-82

7-22-82
Psalm 52
Psalm 53

8-4-82

8-20-82
copies of anthems

[AT letter missing]

10-21-82
Psalm 4
Psalm 6

11-23-82

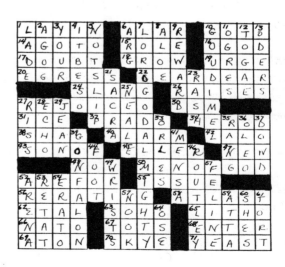

Appendix B

Quotes from Notes - Garrett & Appleton and some Garrett Handouts

from Notes at Garrett

Be aware of what it's like in the pew. Don't be like the minister who was trying to cater to the congregation, and was surprised that what he was calling for was not being well received -- "You're supposed to be loving it!" He was <u>assuming</u> what the people wanted, and then giving it to them.

A parable of worship:
Worship is like a Friday evening party.

Step 1 - Mirror - for "Schmücke dich" - dressing one's self up: "just as you are" won't quite do.
Step 2 - Ringing the Doorbell - A certain "liturgy" for the host and the guest - normal gracious procedures.
Step 3 - A "cautious" entrance to the party - a listening to "what's the rhythm of this party?"

After these three steps, for the rest of the evening, others become more fascinating - and you do, too. You are more "you" than you were -- through good conversation (lively, humorous, serious, energetic, etc.). You're interesting because of other people.

There's something to eat and drink (otherwise the evening is just a seminar).

There's a liturgy of leaving. And on the way home, saying to each other "That was a good one."

This parallels public worship.

The "host" has more work to do than just during the party (preparing, cleaning, etc.), so that people can come in and feel at home. That's what a liturgist does also. When people feel at home, it's because someone has taken care of the details. Informality can be embarrassing and unkind, works only in family. One must have a formality which doesn't show.

Musicians have to get the people to do the <u>right thing</u>: make the right thing the most fun. To get people to feel at home - get people to do what's right naturally, because you know it's right and are hired to know. Make the right most delightful. Make people <u>more themselves</u> than when they came in.

[But we all need that "schmücke dich" effort:] You can't get anywhere if you think you're good enough "just as you are."

The subject of worship is the Glory of God.

"Tyrannical worship" gives the spirit no exercise and avoids the pain of exercise. Today we always say it should be pleasant; in church they must have what they like. In actuality, people don't know what they want.

The Ethics of the Gospel means it is possible for duty and delight to be the same thing: what you want is what you need: this is what I'd like to do -- I must and I can.

Worship is organizing people; crowd control; party planning. Remember the right thing can be good. Say this: we are going to enjoy this, even if it is a little hard at first.

Relationship of pastor and musician - they are both artists, therefore have a common ground. The artist is the person who communicates that which makes other people grow.

<u>Communication</u>

At level 1. Information, when just simple facts, does not involve artistic communication. When you pass the coke can, you don't release it until the other has a firm grasp.

[Level 2: Artistic included]: However, when you're throwing someone a Frisbee, it is rude to bring it up and hand it to the person. There is satisfaction in catching it - in reaching for it. That is communication at level 2.

Poetry says in a few words what prose would take pages to picture.

Like a Frisbee thrown, poetry must be written, read, and then heard. We're all after that. We're learning the mechanics of the service, the history, the symbolism, as well as what it's really about. The Lord is throwing the Frisbee. We [as the ones running the service] shouldn't go put it into their hands.

Worship of God (humanly speaking) is designed to deliver GROWTH. We spend all this time [in our daily lives] being pulled down by the devil from clean objective thinking. Worship releases the tension of being pulled out of shape, and snaps us back into the right shape. A hope of the preacher is that someone will go out and right a bad situation; or do something comparable, and feel it is possible because he has come back into shape. That's what the aesthetic side of worship is involved in. See Luke - don't rejoice that the devils fall, but rather rejoice because your names are written in heaven.

ER is worried about the "extinction" of hymn singing - in a church service, singing one hymn "before anything's happened," and one "after it's all over" is NOT ENOUGH. Hymns should let the congregation say "Yes, Wow!", <u>during</u> what's going on. Get hymn singing back (without knocking the choir). Get the choir interested in worship, and thence to smaller activities (responsibilities during the service).

A poor hymn "vocabulary" is a natural result of minimized hymn use. Poor choice of hymns also results. Can one get rid of the "Processional"? This shouldn't just be a musical way of getting the choir in and out which coincides with congregational singing. Robing is supposed to be for anonymity; let the choir enter during the Prelude, and exit during the Postlude. This would permit a short hymn to be a good first hymn choice , if the text is just right for the service that day.

Use hymns in the service as *precision* tools - cannot be too precise in these matters. Take as much trouble as possible.

[Recognize your] channel of worship -- for instance, in cathedrals in Europe - 77 feet above the floor, will be a carved face in a dark corner - a carved detail, even though the one who carved it knew that not one out of 1,000 would see - it's the carver's [channel of worship, his] part of the arresting beauty. Don't be any less motivated, even if you don't know what the results of your labors will be [or who will see / appreciate it].

A hymnbook is a big bag of tools. There is a tendency to let them get very large, because we won't throw away enough. [Keep a NOWAY list of hymns, when using the book.]

The Five Movements of a Full Service

Approach (always)
Conversation
Offering
Communion
Withdrawal (always).

All five can be celebrated with music. In a large, prosperous church, the choral music is apt to be what's used for the three middle movements (plus Doxology, etc.) It is an abuse of the Gloria Patri to sing it all the time as the only response....

One must send the people out whistling (it is unkind not to)... bearing in mind the unreality in which they're living all week, and the reality they're being introduced to in church.

For example - one section of the tool kit (hymnal) - the Praise section - relates to **1. the Approach**. - knock at the door. You are in a special place doing a special thing (the bridge between the street and the interior). [Hymn:] which war-horse is the right one? People find out the direction of the service from there.
    A. Thanks for having us (Praise)
    B. Confession - I'm not here deserving to be...

2. Conversation - Reading / preaching, thoroughly credal. Celebrates Scripture and doctrine. (hymn or choral for music). Reflect the general direction of scripture, or OT to NT "here is the Lord." The Bible initiates the worship.

3. Offering - the Answer. There is an offertory even if a collection is not taken. Also includes concerns of the church and prayers for others. Climax is the laying on the altar of people's commitment. Symbolizes church living on the bounty of the people. You can have an offering anthem of commitment, concern, or a hymn that shows Christian concern, intercession.

4. Communion (ER likes going to the rail). A rather long gap. Word has done all it can -- now action and few words. Silence here is okay. (Congregation doesn't sing very well at this point; better for the choir. Use a hymn like Schmücke dich.) Don't try to fill up the time - leave plenty of silence - and all one can hear is feet -- the "most godly sound" -- "Let all mortal flesh keep silence..." a short hymn by the choir with just the right words. Or "The bread of life, for all men[!] broken".

5. Withdrawal A good "Thank you!" on the spot. Cheerful, affirmative, simple -- and "get busy" [feel]. "Ye servants of God Your master proclaim" sums it up. You want people to leave with hope. Can use "Father eternal, Ruler of creation", although it beats one over the head at spots.

There are certain activities, without which it is not worship:
> Bible in all its drama: Old and New Testaments. It isn't necessary always
>> to talk about the Bible [sermon], unless it's a long [full] service.
> Prayer (public)
> Praise (including music).

It will be helpful to congregation to know these five movements are happening, and when.

If you are in trouble and go to a party, the host has to be especially compassionate.

Gloria should be used only after a sung psalm.

Doxology isn't the only way to celebrate the offering.

"Holy, holy, holy" is a marvelous hymn - though desperately overworked. Usually slugged out with strong beats, or slow marched for the choir. It should be sung once a year, on Trinity Sunday. It's a good opener - based on Exodus 33. But not for closing; one can't finish a service with a hymn that doesn't mention Christ. (Plays it very slow and heavy, with an absolutely regular rhythm.) Brass sounds good with it. It is out of romantic hymnody; don't blunt it by overuse.

In hymn texts, "up" and "down" is an image shortened for "different." Could have said hell is on the left and heaven on the right. Don't worry about "sky" -- it's easier just to accept the imagery, just "above and better."

Some hymns are fine and deliver a message easily. Others need to be a genuine response to something [*i.e.*, relevance to preceding Scripture], in order to get their message across.

"The King shall come when morning dawns" set to ST. STEPHEN. Deals with the second coming (Book, *The Stammerer's Tongue* by Head. Prayers for non-erudite Christians, children in the faith.), *i.e.*, Lord, I don't understand much about the second coming, but if it's you who's coming, I don't mind.
    This hymn shows the second coming is not so fierce. And no one will find the music difficult. When one's had enough of overripe, obese hymn tunes, ones like this are cleansing.

If you are putting a text in the bulletin, use the correct indentation. *English Hymnal* the best for proper alignment.

Writing a hymn (text):

It is cleverness to get a lot said with minimum fuss.

When you write a hymn, it would be wise to have the Bible open - the hymn is going to be better if it touches Scripture.

When King James Version was the only translation used, a small phrase would strike [ring] a bell. The mind of Scripture is still there, even with the many translations being used these days.

William Cowper and Robert Bridges are the only first ranking poets who also wrote hymn texts. Note the use of big and small words.

All hymns require some sort of originality. They can't be just a rehash.

J. S. Bach wouldn't have understood the term "church musician". He didn't put on a church face to write for it.

Sullivan / "Onward Christian soldiers" slightly pompous bombast (appropriate for church, perhaps...).

Writing a hymn tune:

Start with the melody of a hymn tune; it should be okay even if never harmonized.

If you come back to the home key in the middle of a hymn tune, you risk anticipating the end of the tune. You must listen to what's in the mind of an unmusical singer (VW did).

Composers who haven't been to church write clever things that won't be sung.

Stepwise melodic movement usually = relaxation, leaps = energy. Put them together [interestingly].

AUSTRIA (Haydn) - "He knew what he was doing" Compass of melody 8ve plus 4th. Folksong architecture -- goes somewhere and gets someplace.

Brother James is a bore.

Repeating words [phrases] is tiresome.

With long tunes, repetition is extremely helpful.

ST. DENIO - last line is not quite the same - clever.

ECUMENICAL PRAISE - "Come, Thou Holy Spirit" (Latin 12th, Trans. Caswall), set to GOLDEN SEQUENCE -- only the composer and Alec Wyton can play it.

[Viewpoint] from [the] pew-point: What makes hymns live? Good value... Will make things more fun, edifying for all (not just the musicians).

Increase the hymn vocabulary. "Though painful at present, 'twill not last for long." (John Newton)

We're all a little bit corrupted by commercialism. Restrain the desire for immediate delivery of satisfaction through pleasure. 17 year olds today (born i.e. in 1966 or thereabouts) are some of the worst in this failing.

Some hymns instinctively are in unison (traditionally first and last stanzas?) "Emphatic unanimity".
        Von Herfer - says theologically this is right (ER says that is a very German attitude).

To write a descant, the soprano, the descant, and the bass line (regular or new) must be good three-part harmony. See examples in *Festival Praise* - but these required recomposition of the tune [*i.e.*, the harmonization of the hymn tune?]

If a descant for choir sopranos (on the organ, called a varied accompaniment), be careful about balance. Hymn must be so familiar that the descant won't throw the congregation.

Don't introduce hymns with mixtures! They obscure the tune in block harmony. Use 8', 4', 2', (1') flues. Add mixtures later.

Don't you dare leave the congregation out of the music!!!

Problem: How to get them started (i.e., giving out). Why play all of "Onward Christian soldiers" as intro? Or AUSTRIA - it's disproportionate to play the whole thing. Sometimes one can play the first and last phrases, but omit the middle.

Allow time for the congregation to "find hymn 501 with gloves on and glasses off." If you're worried about not enough time - a few seconds' silence is okay. (If the hymn number is not announced, don't jump in so fast).

Don't have "hitchups" between stanzas -- modulating up. These come from commercialism.

People are singing faster [these days] because of acoustics. Big stone churches [used to have long sound decay]. People are also singing faster because of a pushing sense in America - people are so busy! It seems really strange to give things time. (The saying, "The weakest go to the wall" comes from cathedral times -- being able to sit on the stone ledge [the pilaster] around the ornamental colums set in the cathedral wall. There were no seats for the people in those days; the congregation stood. But tired people could sit on the ledge.)

Who should choose the hymns? The minister, then submitted to the musician for approval. (This presupposes that the minister knows how to choose hymns! A thorough hymnology course should be required for all ministers.) You can't announce the subject, or you would be frustrating the Holy Spirit "...as if the Holy Spirit were the spirit of disorder -- when actually he is the spirit of order." [*i.e.*, the Holy Spirit will see that people get the subject....]

Amens -- really something in liturgy [which] makes all end the same way -- bad! English have dropped the amens. ER refuses to play them except for alumni. If you must have it, play it in the hymn's rhythm.

They were tagged on originally - tractarian churchmen in the 1830s - translating Latin hymns and the amens on them -- because not everyone sang the hymn, so everyone sang the amen.

The artist isn't concerned with avoiding doing [something] wrong; rather, he concerns himself with packing communication in.

Texts: A good one has good statement and good argument for that which you feel the people and you believe, or people should hope to believe. You can't say it contains "what everybody believes." People are at different stages in a miles long procession. Therefore, don't eliminate a hymn that goes farther than the people have gotten - but SKIP ones that drag them back. Concentrate on the pilgrimage image. It's bad if anyone encourages us to stop, to stay where we are, or to back up.

History [is a factor]: some hymns with a point to make may not be relevant now.

* A great hymn must be able to be used constantly.

Still, [a hymn] must not encourage people to do and act [on their own], not [recognizing that they must also] leave everything to God, [and] Jesus.

********* A good hymn should make you say, "That's what I meant! But it's said better than I could say it."

Question yourself: Is this something I don't believe and people shouldn't believe? Then don't use the hymn. OR, Is this something I just don't understand, but hope to? Go ahead and use.

It is sad that people have been taught that if they don't like something, it's "wrong."

We need to be challengingly critical in looking at the words.

Occasionally a fine text is murdered by the tune.

Hymn services, festivals - sharing hymnody.
This age is kind of waiting for them.

To recover interest:
How to teach new hymns? Informal (non-sanctuary).
Can be a bore - avoid being too long (60-75 minutes ideal).

Cultivate your own <u>articulacy</u>.
Associate each hymn with two kinds of comments:
      1. Brief on author
      2. [*Ex tempore*:]
            Here's a fine tune
            There's the climax - prepare for it.
              (ex. LOBE DEN HERREN, 3rd verse)
      (3. Practical - in the bulletin - who sings at what point)

Therefore, 7 to 8 minutes for each hymn. (singing - about 3 minutes for the hymn itself).

Don't use more than nine hymns or the people tire.

2. Vary as much as possible - not too loud all the time, and not in a row either.
      Theme which connects the selections
            Radiating from a center, or
            Sort of a journey.

Possible themes for hymn programs:

1. Examples related to the Liturgical year
2. Examples of American hymnody
3. Wesley - must be sensitive to juxtaposing. Not too "heavies" together.
4. Watts - "There is a land of pure delight", "Give me the wings of faith", etc.
5. 20th century social concerns, etc. Like other centuries? Different?
6. <u>Not</u> by composer - too demanding of him for a whole evening.
7. Lectionary for the week..
8. by Subject - Providence, Creation, etc.
Any Biblical subjects [as a basis for a hymn program] must be extremely well known.

Don't always have the people standing. Say only three times in eight hymns. Make people realize hymns are their response.

[If you] omit and amend hymn stanzas - be sure to have very good reason, and not just running out of time. [And] Watch out... Example - first and last stanza?? "In the cross of Christ I glory" (first and last sts. are identical).

[A class closer:]
"All right that's it for today. Bless your hearts, I don't know how you stand it!"

The 20th century jungle - finding a path.
"This confounded 20th century." At about 9:30 there's a "contemporary" service, and at 11:00 a "traditional" service. This divides the congregation.

Contemporary service: no collar, no tie, imprecise language, nothing lasting said; bulletins say things like "Time to get together," "Time to sing - you choose," "Time for a little humor."

Work to maintain and cultivate the following:
Self respect - Skip the informal blather. Don't say "informal" -- like saying "I'm going to make a joke." It just means no one has taken trouble. "Formal" doesn't exclude humor, non-dulness, etc.
Reason
Quietness - in church. Somehow the 20th century "dare not be silent." [Perhaps] gabbiness is making the young go to transcendental meditation?
Precision - not stiff, though.

It is damnable to object to the word "man"; it is perfectly normal to use it meaning humankind (although ER does not like "Rise up, O men of God").

Isa. 29. Unpunctuality is a sign of appalling imprecision.

Altering texts? Charles Wesley's are not exactly as he wrote them (he accepted change). Words have changed meanings since texts were written:
"Bowels" has changed (not an anatomical use). Substitute "mercy" in the text.
WORMS.
"Rock of Ages" has "eyestrings crack", [changed to] eyes will close"

If you edit a text - <u>SHOW VERY GOOD CAUSE WHY</u>...... Watts' text "...for such a worm as I?" In Watts' time, worm [equivalent to] bug, louse. Changed line to 'To sinners such as I?"

<u>ALWAYS CONSULT THE AUTHOR'S ORIGINAL TEXT</u>.
English Hymnal is easily the hymnal as close to original texts as you can get. Consult author's works for texts not in a hymnal; "we need more respect for the original!"

from Notes at Appleton

Music - isn't "sacred music", rather, "music used for a sacred purpose" -- the same raw material.

There is no reason why church music should lack excellence, integrity. But it must still be practical. The "limitation" of having a "non-musical" congregation -- regard the limitation as fun, not as frustration. [merely a challenge...] Music is there waiting for all the kinds of people coming in: it is tolerant, kind, exact, considerate.

Parallel -- the minister may know the Bible in Greek. But it's unwise to talk Greek to his congregation....

If there's a low level of taste, the musician must decide how much compromise is necessary, and still be loyal to his vision... Bad taste is immoral and subversive. As church lurches through history, one sees less and less modesty, precision, respect for privacy.

There's an "Abominably philistine attitude in seminaries toward music."

The duty of the musician is to be able to express high standards in non-musical terms. Simplicity, subtlety, reason all relate to greatness.

Music relaxes and sharpens the mind. If one has no experience of music whatsoever, one isn't educated.

A Bach fugue - a monumental right that explodes into music!

How much of a Christian do you think you ought to be in order to take a job? Do you have no positive disbeliefs? Then don't worry [take the job].

The church is in a position to take a commanding lead [in musical taste-forming], if the music is something to reach up to. Don't work down to lowest tastes. (This takes more time.) <u>Don't treat church as a concert hall</u>, though. Musical worship is music made for the un-musical people. Keep [including] folk type music, etc., that's appropriate for that situation.

Keep judgment and joy together - don't separate them.
Don't remove mystery.

Distinguished, chaste simplicity always wins out. In all ages.

Paraphrasing an English bishop: A steam train driver has a Christian duty to do his job well (and not study Scripture while he's doing it!).

Ministers should develop a sense of humor about themselves, and be serious only about truth.

Theology and music can both provide delight -- can they ever meet each other? They must find a common ground of infinite vision, and bring that vision into the channel of the people groping to be more like God meant them to be -- and happier!

Selected Hand-outs from Garrett

MONDAY June 18		4.15-5.15 today only A Parable of Worship ①	
TUESDAY 19	The Structure of Worship ②	Music and Worship — some problems ③	
WEDNESDAY 20	HYMNS — DISCOVERY AND REVIVAL How to enjoy and ④ respect the classic ⑤ hymns of the church ⑥		
THURSDAY 21	THE ART OF THE HYMN WRITER AND COMPOSER ①&②true How hymns and tunes are made: with an ⑦ experiment in class composition ⑨		
FRIDAY 22	THE INTERPRETATION OF HYMNS Hints for organist, director, worship leader ⑩	QUESTIONS ⑪	
MONDAY 25	JUDGMENT — What is a good hymn? ⑫	⑬	
TUESDAY 26	PSALMS — how to use them and sing them. Plainsong: anglican chant: Antiphonal ⑭	⑮	
WEDNESDAY 27	Special services using hymns and other music ⑯	⑰	
THURSDAY 28	The 20th Century Jungle: recovery of purpose and ⑱ direction ⑲		Discussion of Projects ⑳
FRIDAY 29	QUESTIONS ㉑		

PROJECTS
① Composition of a hymn text
② Composition of a hymn tune
③ Setting out a Bulletin with full order of service (with or without Communion) for the Sunday after Ascension Day
④ Devising a service using hymns and readings, with prayers but no sermon, upon any subject of your choice which is appropriate to Christian Doctrine.

Present one of these at Session ⑳: Explain it and be prepared to answer questions about it.

Tindall

HYMNOLOGY — Books

Reynolds and Price - A Joyful Song, Holt-Rinehart & Winston, NYC, 1978
  Revision of W.J. Reynolds 'A Survey of Christian Hymnody' 1953. About 250pp. Music exx.

M. Patrick and J.R. Sydnor - The Story of the Church's Song, Westminster Press c.1962
  Revision by an American authority of a very good short book. Out of print.

A.E. Bailey - The Gospel in Hymns, c.1950. Widely read: recommended with reservations.

L.F. Benson - The English Hymn, c.1915. About 600 pages, the acknowledged standard
  work, up to its date. Should be in libraries.

H.W. Foote - Three Centuries of American Hymnody, 1940. Very sound and exhaustive

E. Routley - Hymns and Human Life, 1952, 1958 : out of print but may be in Libraries
  The English-Speaking Hymnal Guide, Liturgical Press 1979 ($29.50): notes on
    origins of 888 hymn texts and on their authors.
  A Panorama of Christian Hymnody, as above 1979. Historical essays + 593 text examples
  [The Music of Christian Hymns, to be published in uniform format with above,
    is at present in preparation]

Note: all the above except the bracketed one are about texts. the bracketed one will
  be the only history of the tunes in print.

Much useful information can be assembled from the Companions to hymnals: these deal
with tunes as well as words but of course only with those in the hymnal each refers to.
  Companion to Methodist Hymnal, Young, Lovelace, Gealy, Abingdon c.1970.
  Hymnal (1940) Companion (Episcopal) — Church Hymnal Corp, NYC 1949
  Companion to Baptist Hymnal, by WJ Reynolds — Broadman 1975
  Companion to Hymns for Christian Worship (Disciples/Baptists) by A. Wake. Judson 1970
  Dictionary - Handbook to Hymns of the Living Church, by D. Hustad, Hope, 1977
  Guide to the Pilgrim Hymnal, by A. Ronander and E. Porter: UCC Press, 1966

More details about these and British Companions on the next 2 pages.

The Hymn Society (T. Smith, Secretary) Wittenberg University, Springfield, Ohio, 45501

The Royal School of Church Music, Addington Palace, Croydon, England, CR9 5AD

The Hymn Society of Gt Britain and Ireland (quarterly journal) — enquiries to the
  RSCM as above

SOME HYMNALS WORTH POSSESSING : with British hymnals always order FULL MUSIC EDITION

	TITLE	DATE	CHURCH	PUBLISHER	COMPANION ?
USA	Hymns for Colleges and Schools	1956	campus	YALE Univ. Press	Biog. Index included
	Harvard Univ. Hymnal	1964	campus	HARVARD U. P.	" " "
	Hymnal 1940	1943	Episcopal	Church Hymnal Corp, NYC	yes
	Pilgrim Hymnal	1958	Congl. - UCC	UCC, Philadelphia	yes
	UCC Hymnal	1974	UCC	UCC, Philadelphia	yes no
	Hymns for Christian Worship	1970	Baptist / Disciples	Judson / Bethany	yes
	Lutheran Book of Worship	1978	Lutheran	Concordia / Augsburg	possibly coming
	Worship II	1975	R C	G I A	no
Canada	Hymnal of the United and Episcopal Churches	1971	UC and Episc C. of Canada	Distributed, pub. depts of these churches	IF SUCH HOLY SONG, from Dr S. Osborne, 705 Mason St, OSHAWA, Ontario
International	Cantate Domino	1974, 1980	Ecumenical	Words and melody — World Council of Churches Dept of Publications, P.O. Box 66 : 1211 GENEVA 20 Switzerland Full music - due early 1980 Oxford University Press 37 Dover St., London W1.	no
English and Australian	With One Voice	1977, 1979	Uniting Churches of Australia including R.C.	Collins, 187 Piccadilly, London W1	coming shortly · author Wesley Milgate
US Supplts	More Hymns and Spiritual Songs (paperback '77) (81)	1971, 1977	Episcopal	Walton Music Corp, NYC	no
	Hymns - III (150)	1979	Episcopal	Church Hymnal Corp, NYC	no.
	Westminster Praise (60)	1976	campus	Hinshaw	yes
	Ecumenical Praise (117)	1977 paper 1978	Ecumenical	Agape, 350 S. Main Place, Carol Stream, Ill., 60187	no.

311

BRITISH HYMNALS worth looking at. * means 'Supplement to the above'

					companion?
Methodist Hymn Book	(984)	1933	Methodist	Epworth Press, 27 Marylebone Rd London NW1	The Meth. H.B. Illustrated 1934 The Music of the Meth. H.B 1936
* Hymns and Songs †	(104)	1969	Methodist	"	Short Handbook to Hys & Sngs
Hymns Ancient and Modern †	(636)	1950	Ch. of Eng.	Wm Clowes, 31 Newgate, BECCLES, Suffolk	Historical Companion to H. A&M (Very large) by M. Frost, 1961
* 100 Hymns for Today	(100)	1969	Ch of Eng	" "	no
* More Hymns for today (?)	(?100)	1979	"	" " "	no
English Hymnal ††	(656)	1933	"	Oxford U.P.	no
* English Praise	(120)	1975	"	"	no
Anglican Hymn book †	(640)	1965	"	Tyndale Press	no
BBC Hymn Book †	(542)	1951	Ecumenical	Oxford U.P.	no
Songs of Praise, Enlarged †	(703)	1931	Ecumenical	Oxford U.P.	Songs of Praise Discussed, 1936
Cambridge Hymnal	(130)	1967	Educational	Cambridge U.P. 200 Euston Rd, London NW1	no
Congregational Praise	(778)	1951	Congregational	United Reformed Church Publications 86 Tavistock Place, London WC1H 9RT	Companion to C.P 1953 (O.P)
* New Church Praise †	(109)	1975	URC	St Andrew Press 121 George St. Edinburgh, Scotland	no
Church Hymnary, 3rd edition ††	(695)	1973	Ch of Scotland (Presbyterian)	St Andrews Press	Handbook to C.H.3 by J. Barkley. 1979
Baptist Hymn Book	(777)	1962	Baptist	Psalms and Hymns Trust 4 Southampton Row, London WC1	Companion to B HB 1962
Hymns for Church and School	(306)	1964	Educational	Unwin Co, Old Woking, Surrey	no
New Catholic Hymnal †	(305)	1971	RC	Faber Music, 38 Russell Square, London WC1	no
Praise the Lord †	(334)	1972	RC	Geoffrey Chapman, 35 Red Lion Square W.1 or Collins, 167 Piccadilly	no

Those most interesting musically are marked † or (specially good) ††
Note also:
16 Hymns for use as Anthems (16) 1978 EXCELLENT about $4.00 Royal School of Church Music Addington Palace, Croydon, CR9 5AD
Ed. John Wilson

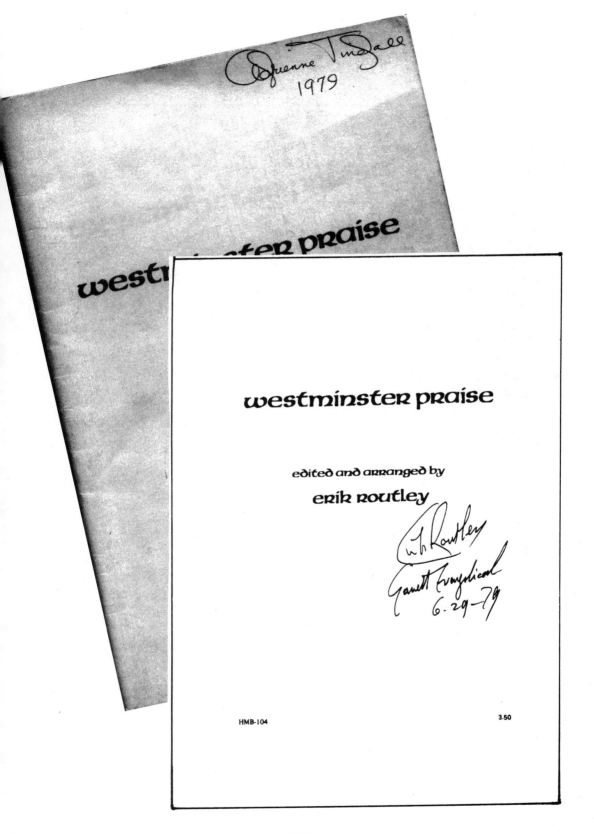

westminster praise

edited and arranged by

erik routley

HMB-104

3.50

PANGE LINGUA — translation of Latin hymn written about 575 A.D. Stanzas selected for Palm Sunday service. For full version (10 stanzas) see *Panorama* 156 or (different version) English Hymnal 95-6.

ALL
(f)

Pontifex?
harmonious?

1 Sing, my tongue, how glorious battle
glorious victory became,
and above the Cross, his trophy,
tell the triumph and the fame;
tell how he, the world's Redeemer,
by his death for us o'ercame.
                   man

2. Thirty years fulfilled among us,
perfect life in low estate, —
born for this, and self-surrendered,
to his Passion dedicate,
on the Cross the Lamb is lifted,
for his people dedicate.
                   immolate

WOMEN

3 God in pity saw us fallen,
                   mom
shamed and sunk in misery,
when we fell on death by tasting
        he
fruit of the forbidden tree;
then another tree was chosen
which the world from death should free

MEN

4 Faithful Cross, above all other
one and only noble tree,
none in foliage, none in blossom,
none in fruit thy peer may be:
sweetest wood and sweetest iron,
sweetest weight is hung on thee!

ALL
(P)

ALL
ff

5 Unto God be praise and glory,
to the Father and the Son,
to the Holy Spirit, honour
now and evermore be done:
praise and glory in the highest,
while the timeless ages run.

TUNE PICARDY
324

Translation
composite
1925, 1927
based on
J. M. Neale
1851

314

Alternative setting of doxology for 'Sing, my tongue...'

au E.R. 1960

PICARDY Voices in unison

Un-to God be praise and glo-ry, to the Father and the Son,

ORGAN

to th'e-ter-nal Spi-rit, ho-nor now and e-ver-more be done:

Praise and glo-ry in the high-est while the timeless a-ges run.

© Eric Routley

AMEN after Hymns

(1) AMEN has two functions. In literature it is asseverative, meaning 'indeed', as in 'Verily, verily I say unto you' in the Gospels. In liturgy it is an answer which you make to what somebody else has said — meaning, 'yes, I want to be a part of that.'

(2) Therefore it should be said by the congregation after a prayer said by the celebrant. It is quite legitimately used by some evangelical traditions to express support of or agreement with passages in a sermon. The use of it by any speaker to reply to what he or she has said, or sung, is a misuse.

(3) Strictly there is no need for it after a prayer communally said, but this misuse doesn't do much damage. But its use after hymns has the fatal effect of causing every hymn to end with the same cadence, so it adds aesthetic ugliness to behavioral incorrectness.

How did it ever come about?

The practice was unknown to Luther, Calvin, Isaac Watts, Charles Wesley, or any hymn-writer in any language except Latin down to about 1857. In Methodism in England none of the 3 Methodist hymnals with music — 1876, 1904, 1933 uses it invariably, though it is more frequent in 1933 than in the other two.

It came into use because it always appears in the texts of medieval Latin office hymns when they are set with plainsong music. Why?

(a) These hymns always ended with a doxology to the Trinity, and the inclusion of this was the result of a serious anti-Trinitarian controversy in the 4th century, when Latin hymnody began. So AMEN had a touch of defiance about it: but also

(b) In liturgical use no hymn was sung through by everyone present: all hymns were sung by monastic choirs only, antiphonally, and the only thing everyone sang together was AMEN.

It was when in England, under the influence of the Oxford Movement, scholars revived and translated this medieval hymnody, (hitherto unknown in English) that they came on those final Amens; believing that medieval practice was the right guide for everything in the modern church, they then attached Amens to all hymns. The first book to do this appeared in 1857: the first to make all Amens uniform musically was the very successful and influential Hymns Ancient and Modern, 1861. Both were anglican. Non-anglican books later adopted the practice.

By about 1920 anglicans saw where they had gone wrong and began dropping it. Later the non-anglicans followed suit, and now in G.B. one very rarely hears it except in Scotland.

Therefore the use of Amen after congregational hymns is an episcopal mistake long ago repaired by the episcopals in the country where it began. It is unhistorical, unmusical, and unliturgical — and the best thing to do is to drop it as soon as we can. Its perpetuation is purely sentimental, and one of many things we do because we think we always did, whose real history few people seem to be aware of.

P.S. Some modern composers compose an AMEN into their tunes so that the music remains unfinished if Amen is omitted. In such cases, and these only, it has to be retained but it is regrettable that these composers were not warned by church custom that they are perpetuating a most tiresome error.

Read II Cor. 1 for the source of AMEN in Christian worship.

316

Handout text / tune in ER ms:

"Come, let us to the Lord our God"

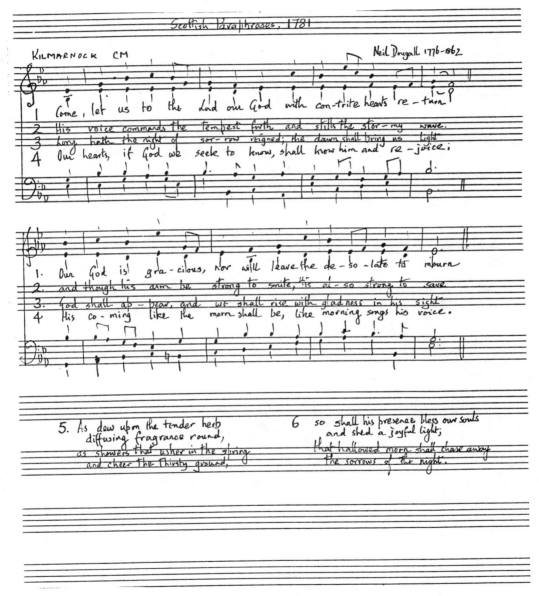

Scottish Paraphrases, 1781

KILMARNOCK CM · Neil Dougall 1776-1862

1 Come, let us to the Lord our God with con-trite hearts re-turn!
2 His voice commands the tempest forth, and stills the stor-my wave.
3 Long hath the night of sor-row reigned; the dawn shall bring us light
4 Our hearts, if God we seek to know, shall know him and re-joice;

1. Our God is gra-cious, nor will leave the de-so-late to mourn
2. and though his arm be strong to smite, 'tis al-so strong to save.
3. God shall ap-pear, and we shall rise with gladness in his sight.
4. His co-ming like the morn shall be, like morning sings his voice.

5. As dew upon the tender herb
diffusing fragrance round,
as showers that usher in the spring
and cheer the thirsty ground,

6 so shall his presence bless our souls
and shed a joyful light;
that hallowed morn shall chase away
the sorrows of the night.

317

Handout text / tune in ER ms

"Jerusalem the golden"

318

Readings and Music for (Palm Sunday)   Can be reduced to hymn service
PROCESS

NOTE: A full order, with hymns and choral music, titled Behold, Your King, can be obtained from the Publications Dept, Royal School of Church Music, Addington Palace, CROYDON, England, CR9 5AD. This is a simplification of it. *readings same.*

Readings of Carols but — not for Christmas — Been used. Can be compressed & ceremonious & can also reduce

PROCESSIONAL HYMN: Draw nigh to Thy Jerusalem, O Lord
The only practicable tune in MH is 236, ELLERS   *these*

Bidding Prayer — from the publication above — + Lord's Prayer

HYMN: Sing, my tongue, the glorious battle   tune PICARDY 324   *54 songs in there*
(b) Praise to the Holiest, omit st 4, xerox 471   *servant Is. references*
(c) 76, At the name of Jesus   *all gospels*

READING I   The Beginning of the Gospel   Isa. 48.1-4   St Mark 1.1-11
Here an appropriate anthem: or move the preceding hymn to this place

READING II   The Temptation   *Speak to exiles* Ezekiel 3.4-8, 14   St Matthew 4.1-11 *Temptation* *spiral consciousness of* tune MH 295 *temptation*

HYMN: (a) Shepherd divine, ms tune or tune   *recaps teachings Sermons*
(b) 284, Lord Jesus, think on me   Isaiah 58.4-8   St Matthew 5.1-12 *Beatitude*
or 430, Never further than thy cross   *Christian Characters*

READING III   The Teaching

HYMN: (a) O thou not made with hands, xerox 464   *Peter's Confession. shape of life*
(b) Jesus Lord we look to thee, 309 *Now paraphrase* Isa. 42.1-4   St Mark 8.27-31 *people*
or an anthem or carol (e.g. 'Now quit your care', OBC   *begin to see danger of...*

READING IV   The Messiah

HYMN: 355, Lord Christ, when first thou cam'st to men Isa. 50.4-7 St Mark 10.32-4 *walk to Jerusalem dark heavy*
or an anthem, e.g. 'Come, my Way', Westminster 36, Fest. Pr. 11.

READING V   The Way

HYMN: 427, Alone thou goest forth   Zec. 9.9   St John 12.12-15, 23-32 *shortest Palm Sunday*
or an anthem, e.g. 'Vox ultima crucis' by W.H.Harris (O.U.P.) *Behold your king*   *dark prayer "Save me from..."*

READING VI   The Judgment

* HYMN: 425, Ride on!   Isa. 53.3-6 (11-12) St John 16.25-33 *longest best known servant Song*
(with the card 'Tomorrow shall be my dancing day', OBC or Holst's setting (Stainer & Bell/Galaxy))   *How end? - Can't go on to Cruc. Easter "I have overcome the world"*

All remain standing
READING VII   The Victory

HYMN: 458, The head that once was crowned with thorns   *stand full organ — solid — don't make it trivial*
Collect for Palm Sunday
The Blessing

RECESSIONAL HYMN   424, All glory, laud and honor
_____

A hymn should be sung at the beginning and those marked * should be sung in any case. Use the Recessional only if you have a processional. Elsewhere anthems or other choral pieces can be substituted. If a carol is sung after VI, still do not omit 425.

Don't have Sermon, or informal prayer (for Pete's sake!!)

RSCM — Service published (listed)

Notice the note in the upper right hand corner: Erik undoubtedly wrote this tune at the time. Loder Hall is a dorm / cafeteria / bookstore building on the Garrett campus, also name of Garrett's president....

Invented for place in Nebraska

A Hymn-sequence on The Prodigal Son   St Luke 15. 11-32
which can be used on its own or fitted into a normal service.

as a service

'Son, thou art ever with me, and all that I have is thine' — v.31   (opening hymn)
    55 Praise to the Lord, the Almighty
          "Hast thou not seen
'He wasted his substance' — v.13   See 500 Panorama   (near prayer of) confession
                     ecology
    484 O God of earth and altar — society, gone wrong   Here read the whole story

'I will arise and go to my Father' — v.18 — Wasn't moment of repentance. (ER)
Be obvious   112 Sinners, turn, why will ye die?
Come let us to the (or, Come let us to the Lord our God)
Lord thy God (Scottish tune)
'When he was yet a great way off, his father saw him....' — v.20
             grace of God
    93 Come thou fount of every blessing — Good tune though bad harmonization

Sing these in a sequence, separated by 2-minute expositions

"replace Sermon."

if time is short omit one of these
'Bring forth the best robe .....' v.22
    127 Jesus thy blood and righteousness
'Music and dancing...' v. 25
    303 Jerusalem the golden — but use appended text
'Let us eat and be merry' — v.23
    314 For the bread that thou hast broken
          (or 318)

'The elder brother ..... was angry' — v.28 shame to us who seem content
    481 O Holy City, seen of John — omit st.2

Concerns, Offertory, Intercessions : but 481 before Intercessions

'He was lost, and is found'
    458 The head that once was crowned with thorns.

Closing Hymn
keep service reasonably economical

"as a Calvinist — our repentance of no significance whatever, except for the grace of God."

A hymn-sequence on the Good Samaritan   St Luke 10.25-37

'What shall I do to inherit eternal life?' — v. 25
     130   What shall I do my God to love

near 'Thou shalt love the Lord thy God ....'   v. 27   celebrate
confession   LM   Hark, my soul, it is the Lord   (Panorama 92)   2 commands
        Tune 309 or 311   absolutely   see sheets passed
        pleasant   beautiful   out

'Who is my neighbor?'   —   v. 29
     204   Where cross the crowded ways   — omit st. 3!

'He fell among thieves' — v. 30
     200   The voice of God is calling — useful contrast to

'They passed by on the other side' - v. 31
     481   O Holy city, — maybe a better one

'A certain Samaritan'   — v. 33
     183   begin at st. 2. 'Help us to help each other'

'He brought him to an inn'   — v. 34
     292   Christ for the world we sing

'Go and do likewise' - v. 37
excellent as   Jesus my Lord, how rich thy grace
offertory

Conclusion —
good   470   God of grace and God of glory.
to go out   50 yrs ago Riverside — minister
to.   said would come if church
      built in poorer section —
      it will witness among poor

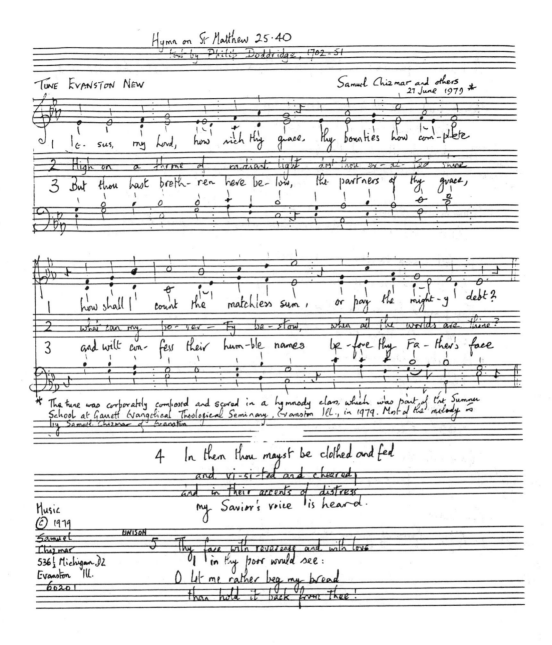

Hymn on St Matthew 25.40
text by Philip Doddridge, 1702-51

TUNE EVANSTON NEW

Samuel Chizmar and others
27 June 1979 *

1 Je- sus, my Lord, how rich thy grace, thy bounties how com-plete
2 High on a throne of radiant light dost thou ex- al- ted shine
3 But thou hast breth- ren here be- low, the partners of thy grace,

1 how shall I count the matchless sum, or pay the might- y debt?
2 what can my po- ver- ty be- stow, when all the worlds are thine?
3 and wilt con- fess their hum-ble names be- fore thy Fa- ther's face

* The tune was corporately composed and scored in a hymnody class, which was part of the Summer
School at Garrett Evangelical Theological Seminary, Evanston Ill., in 1979. Most of the melody is
by Samuel Chizmar of Evanston.

4   In them thou mayst be clothed and fed
     and vi-si-ted and cheered;
     and in their accents of distress
     my Savior's voice is heard.

Music
© 1979
Samuel
Chizmar
536½ Michigan D2
Evanston Ill.
60201

UNISON

5   Thy face with reverence and with love
     in thy poor would see:
     O let me rather beg my bread
     than hold it back from Thee!

8 a	From the deep·ness of the o·ceans						
7 b	To the reach of out·er space						
8 c	I will wit·ness God's all-pow·er						
7 b	Hold·ing strong its stead·y pace.					
6 d	No might but His sus·tains						
6 d	His law for·ev·er reigns						
12 b	No less·er force, no mor·tal power u·surps His place				

Tak·ing wings of bril·liant morn·ings,
Find·ing farth·est shores of sea(s),
Ev·en vale of
~~tiers of hell and death~~ ly shad·ows
Will not hide His love from me!
His ev·er-present ~~shows~~
~~That~~ Love ~~the ev·er~~ su·preme·ly flows,
And holds man·kind in its em·brace e·ter·nal·ly.
A stedd·fast power to help man·kind

From the love of our Re·deem·er (the Mes·si·ah)
And the heal·ing proofs he gave,
From his min·is·try's in·struc·tion
And re·demp·tion from the grave, —
The Fa·ther's love is proved,
~~The~~ sting of death re·moved.
The power of God is law, to heal and bless and save.

In the Christ·li·ness of mer·cy com·pas·sion.
In the no·blest deeds of man
In each act of lov·ing-kind·ness
I can feel God's ho·ly plan.
His ev·er wise con·trol
Stands fast while a·ges roll,
~~the~~ heav·n·ly ~~kingdom~~ se·cure with·in His span.

Lawrence University Conservatory of Music invites you to its annual

CHURCH
MUSIC
SEMINAR

ERIK ROUTLEY
Guest Lecturer
May 10 and 11, 1979
Come share the wit and wisdom of this internationally acclaimed church music scholar.

Thursday, May 10, 2:50 p.m. — Free
Lawrence Memorial Chapel
Discussion: Dr. Routley and participants
The Ministry of Music Today — The Dilemma of Excellence"

Friday, May 11, 9:50 a.m. — Free
Room 146, Music-Drama Center
Discussion: Dr. Routley
Music Ministry and the School Musician

Friday, May 11, 6:15 p.m. - $5.35 per person
Dinner with Dr. Routley (Please complete and return the attached card if you plan to attend.)
Gold Room, Jason Downer Commons

Friday, May 11, 8:00 p.m. — Free
Harper Hall, Music-Drama Center
Lecture by Dr. Routley
Good Taste in Hymnody

Erik Routley is professor of church music and director of chapel at Westminster Choir College in Princeton, New Jersey. In 1943, he was ordained a minister in the Congregational Church of England and Wales, and was president of that church in 1970-71. (Since 1972, the Congregational Church has been part of the United Reformed Church in England and Wales.)

Mr. Routley received his M.A., B.D., and D.Phil. degrees from Oxford University. He visited the U.S. 10 times on lecture tours before coming here to live in 1975.

Mr. Routley is the author of 32 books, including *A Short History of English Church Music* (1977), *Church Music and the Christian Faith* (1978), and *Music Leadership in the Church* (1966).

Since 1965, Mr. Routley has been a Fellow and a Member of Council of the Royal School of Church Music in England. He has been a Fellow of Westminster Choir College since 1971.

In Dec. 1982, Margaret Routley wrote: "There's a large file of your Psalm versions in the study. What would you like me to do with them?..." Would Erik have encouraged a collection at some later date? "The Spirit of the Psalms"? Did he save everything? Comment on some? *Why* didn't I ask for them?

The Encounter continues....

Appendix C

Psalms / Hymns Interlined

328 - from Exodus 20	When God demanded Israel's flight	WYCH CROSS
329 - from Psalm 3	When I cried to God with a fearful voice	RIDGEVILLE
330 - from Psalm 8	O Lord, our Lord, how excellent is Thy name	
	When I look up to the heavens	MARTHA
331 - Psalm 13	Would You forget me, God, forever?	LOVELACE 13
332 - Psalm 15	Lord, those who seek Your holy hill	LOVELACE 15
333 - Psalm 16	My inheritance is from the Lord	SOUTH CERNEY
334 - from Psalm 24	All the earth belongs to God!	EVERLASTING GATES
335 - Psalm 26	Each day, O Lord, I try to do	LOVELACE 26
336 - from Psalm 34	I will forever bless the Lord	MY SONG
337 - from Psalm 42	My soul is longing for my God!	THIRSTING DEER
338 - from Psalm 45	Father, bless this wedding	LOVELACE 45
339 - Psalm 47	Clap your hands, all you people of God	LOVELACE 47
340 - from Psalm 51	O Lord my God, I look to You	METTAWA
341 - from Psalm 52	I will praise You forever, God!	LOVELACE 52
342 - from Pslam 53	God looked down from heaven	LOVELACE 53
343 - from Psalm 56	God, I trust myself to Your mercy!	ST. MARY'S ROAD
344 - from Psalm 61	From the ends of the earth will I cry to God	SHELTERING WINGS
345 - from Psalm 65	You crown the year with goodness, Lord	LOVELACE 65
346 - (from Psalm 65)		LAKE FOREST MEADOWS
346 - (from Psalm 65)		VERNON HILLS
347 - Psalm 70	Help me, God! My need is urgent!	LOVELACE 70
348 - from Psalm 83	Speak to me, God!	WELLSHIRE
349 - from Psalm 84	How lovely are Your dwellings, Lord	ST. ASAPH
350 - Psalm 93	The Lord our Father reigns	LOVELACE 93
351 - Psalm 96	Sing, and sing, and sing again!	LOVELACE 96
352 - Psalm 101	God, help me be Your perfect child	LOVELACE 101
353 - from Psalm 121	My help is from the Lord most high	MEADOWOODS LANE
354 - Psalm 123	Heavenly God, hear my petition	LOVELACE 123
355 - from Psalm 126	Why should freedom be a dream	LIBERTYVILLE
356 - from Psalm 127	God must build the house	ORREN
357 - from Psalm 131	Lord, let me be a child	KINDLICHKEIT
358 - Psalm 133	How good and how pleasant it is	POLLSTIN
359 - Psalm 137	I'll live in Babylon	LOVELACE 137
360 - from Psalm 139	Search me, O God, and know my heart	NO HIDING PLACE
361 - from Psalm 139	Search me, O God, and know my heart	OLD 137th
362 - from Psalm 147	Let praise to God fill the music of earth	LAC DU FLAMBEAU
363 - Christmas Carol	A village humble, still	AIRIKAR
364 - Christmas 1970	It could be Bethlehem	DUNAWAY
365 - French Carol	What is this lovely fragrance?	QUELLE EST CETTE
366 - from Matt.5:xx-xx	Let your light so shine each day	GLENCAYNIG
367 - The Servant	The greatest man that walked this earth	SERVITOR
368 - O God I grieve	O God, I grieve within me	HIGHLY DEVOTIONAL
369 - Thank You!	Thank You, Father-Mother	JENNEL
370 - God's Power and Love	From the depths of ocean trenches	MEAD'S BRIER

from Exodus 20
Adrienne M. Tindall, 1979, sts. 1, 4, 5
Isaac Watts, 1715, sts. 2, 3, alt.

WYCH CROSS 88.88.88.
Erik Routley, 1947

1. When God de-mand-ed Is-rael's flight from Phar-aoh's land of pain and
2. "You shall have no more gods than me, be-fore no i-dol bow your
3. "When you o-bey this ho-ly pact you will not do a mur-derous
4. Lord, I would lead a right-eous life with in-ner peace through out-ward
5. O-be-dience to these ten com-mands still fos-ters peace in earth-ly

night, He shield-ed them up-on their way and gave them
knee. Take not the name of God in vain, nor dare the
act. You will ab-stain from sen-sual deed, nor steal, though
strife. I would be just, and hum-ble too, with mer-cy
lands. Fi-del-i-ty to God a-bove, and ac-tions

laws they should o-bey. The list-ening ear of
sab-bath day pro-fane. Give to your par-ents
you may be in need. Give true re-ports of
guid-ing all I do. I must re-ly on
prov-ing kind-ly love, will bless the hu-man

Mo-ses heard _____ in-struc-tion in God's ho-ly word.
hon-or due _____ so that long life will come to you.
hap-pen-ings, _____ and cov-et not your neigh-bor's things."
Christ-ly grace _____ to give Your laws their prop-er place.
fam-i-ly _____ and wit-ness heav-en's har-mo-ny.

328

from Psalm 3

Adrienne M. Tindall, 1982

RIDGEVILLE 10.3 9 5. 99.

Jack C. Goode, 1989

1. When I cried to God with a trem-bling voice He heard me!
Out of His ho-ly hill He heard me, and
made me re-joice! And my sleep is sweet, my
life se-cure, for the Lord's love is both strong and ___ sure.

2. How in-creased the foes that sur-round me here. They mock me!
Claim-ing that God is weak, they mock me; they
fill me with fear! But the Lord's own glo-ry
is my shield, – through the Lord's power all my fear is ___ stilled.

3. I am not a-fraid of ten thou-sand foes! God saves me!
Saved from the e-vil one! God saves me! My
con-fi-dence grows, for His bless-ing is my
guard and guide; I will trust Him, and be sat-is-fied.

from Psalm 8
Adrienne M. Tindall, 1981

MARTHA 11 4. 11 4. with Refrain
Adrienne M. Tindall, 1981

Refrain (beginning and end)

O Lord, our Lord, how ex-cel-lent is Thy _ name in all the _ earth! And _ high-er than the high-est stars of heaven Thy glor - ious worth!

Stanzas

1. When I look up to the heavens, the moon and stars, the end - less sky, I am hum-bled and as - ton - ished in my heart, for what am I?
2. Yet with Your own power You've given un - to us all an - gel - ic heights, and Your glo - ry and great hon - or make a crown each wears by right.
3. If Your will gives us do - min - ion's care for life found in this place, for the power that gives the earth, and earth it - self, must feel God's will o - beyed.
4. I am hum - bled and as - ton - ished in my heart, but un - a - fraid, ev - ery crea - ture of the task gives wis - dom, too: God's will o - beyed.

PSALM 13
Adrienne M. Tindall, 1982

LOVELACE 13   9 7.8 11. 5 5.10 5.
Austin C. Lovelace, 1997

1. Would You for-get me, God, for-ev - er? Would You al - ways
2. I fear my en - e - mies' pre - vail - ing, will I sleep the
3. O lov - ing Fa - ther, when Your Son came with his heal - ing

hide Your face? Will I nev - er feel Your com - fort? Will I nev - er
sleep of death? God, de - liv - er me from e - vil! Be my strength, my
love and power, he was prov - ing that Your mer - cy is a shield to

mir - ror forth Your love and grace? I trust Your mer - cy, my
wis - dom, ref - uge, life, and breath! I trust Your mer - cy, my
us in ev - ery test - ing hour. I trust Your mer - cy, my

heart will re - joice, Your sal - va - tion is my song for -

ev - er! Dear Lord, hear my voice.

Psalm 15
Adrienne M. Tindall, 1981

LOVELACE 15 LM
Austin C. Lovelace, 1997

1. Lord, those who seek Your ho - ly hill with
2. Their steps are stead - y, in the right. Their
3. Their tongues ac - cept Your love's con - trol, their
4. They hon - or those who feel an awe of

right-eous-ness de - ser - ving praise have al - ways lis - tened for Your
right-eous works will nev - er cease. The truth of God in - spires their
acts are for their neigh-bor's good. Their friend-ships have a beau - tied
God and His al - might - y power. Their vows, like gems with-out a

will to be their guide through all life's ways.
sight and moves their hearts to words of peace.
whole, for - giv - ing faults in broth - er - hood.
flaw, stay strong in ev - ery test - ing hour.

5. They are not careful of their worth,
   nor take from those of humbleness.
   Their godlike ways enrich the earth,
   true witness of the God they bless.

6. Unaided, Lord, I cannot live
   in paths so pure, and never roam!
   And yet, before I've asked, You give
   the Christ, to bring me safely home.

332

Psalm 16
Adrienne M. Tindall, 1980

SOUTH CERNEY 98.88.88.
William H. Hadow, 1906

1. My in-her-i-tance is from the Lord: no world-ly wealth can
2. I have set the Lord be-fore my face, and He has held me
3. God is show-ing me the path of life; my steps de-pend up-

win my praise. True rich-es bless me in His word; His
safe, se-cure. His own right hand be-stows me grace, His
on His care. No hell of tur-moil, pain, or strife can

coun-sel guides me through life's ways. If earth's con-fu-sions
love makes my po-si-tion sure. My heart is glad, my
harm; His love is ev-ery-where. The pleas-ures He be-

bring a night, His heaven-ly law re-stores the light.
joy is free, I glo-ry in His care for me.
stows are mine; I trust my-self to God's de-sign.

from Psalm 24
Adrienne M. Tindall, 1982

EVERLASTING GATES 78.88.
Austin C. Lovelace, 1989

1. All the earth be - longs to God!
2. Those found wor - thy of His place
3. Let us see our need, con - fess,
4. Lift the ev - er - last - ing gates!

He sets the world up - on the floods.
must have clean hands, hearts filled with grace.
and seek His face, His right - eous - ness.
En - throned is Love, a - bol - ished, hates!

Its ful - ness comes through His com - mands,
must speak the truth, shun world - ly cares,
Sal - va - tion is the gift He gives
The King of glo - ry en - ters in –

He claims all peo - ples of its lands.
that bless - ings from the Lord be theirs.
through Je - sus Christ, who died and lives!
Love's power has van - quished death and sin.

Psalm 26
Adrienne M. Tindall, 1981

LOVELACE 26 CM
Austin C. Lovelace, 1997

1. Each day, O Lord, I try to do what's
2. Your lov - ing - kind - ness shields my path, Your
3. I will not give an ear to lies, I'll
4. I'll wash my hands in in - no - cence and

good and clean and right. I walk in my in -
truth lights up the way, to show me what is
shun hy - poc - ri - sy. The sub - tle snares of
lift my thought with prayer, ap - proach Your al - tar,

teg - ri - ty, but Yours must be the might.
right and wrong, to guide me when I stray.
wick - ed - ness will gain no hold on me.
feel Your love, and know Your pres - ence there.

5. Thanksgiving moves my voice to sing
   the joy that's in my heart!
   I'd tell the world of wondrous works
   and blessings You impart.

6. I'll love the honor of Your house;
   its perfectness is pure.
   My heart escapes from sin unstained,
   unmoved by sin's allure.

7. Redeem me, Lord, for Your great love
   and mercy fill all space.
   I walk in my integrity,
   relying on Your grace.

from Psalm 34
Adrienne M. Tindall, 1981

MY SONG CMD
Jack C. Goode, 1988

1. I will for-ev-er bless the Lord, His praise shall be my song. My heart is filled with con-fi-dence that He will save from wrong. To-geth-er let us praise His name and glo-ry in His power; it is His hand de-liv-ering us in ev-ery test-ing hour.

2. O taste and see that God is good, our trust is al-ways blessed. Let faith-ful hearts ac-know-ledge awe, and in that awe find rest. Let all who hope for length of life, with days peace-filled and bright, keep words and ac-tions heav-en-ly and feel the Lord's de-light!

3. There is no sin in right-eous-ness for God is ev-ery-where. The hard-est steps a-long the way are not be-yond His care. So let us call up-on the Lord and hum-bly ask His aid; His love re-deems, His power re-stores. Trust Him: be not a-fraid!

Alt. Tune ELLACOMBE

from Psalm 42
Adrienne M. Tindall, 1981

THIRSTING DEER CMD
Austin C. Lovelace, 1989

1. My soul is long-ing for my God! When shall I see His face? Like
2. "Where is your God?" Must doubt-ing fears de-stroy my strength and peace? God
3. Why should I lose my hope to gloom? Why do I strug-gle so? God's
4. So will my soul be anx-ious now? And will it be dis-mayed? With

thirst-ing deer by wa-ter-brooks, I need His love and grace. The
is my Pres-ence, and my Rock, His lov-ing does not cease! No
good-ness is a foun-tain-head which will for-ev-er flow! I've
Love for-ev-er hold-ing me, I can-not be a-fraid! My

tears that fall in night-time hours have mocked my con-stant prayer — to
en-e-my can shake my faith by words of sub-tle-ness: "Where
seen in all the days gone by His sav-ing love is shown in
heaven-ly Fa-ther sent His Son that I be saved and healed. I

know God's pres-ence with me here, to feel His lov-ing care.
is your God?" My heart of hearts knows God at hand to bless.
acts of power and might, to save the ones He calls His own.
am re-deemed from earth-ly fears by heav-en's love, re-vealed.

337

1. Fa - ther, bless this wed - - ding,
2. Help them to be loy - - al
3. Kind - ness, joy, com - pass - - ion,
4. Christ, the per - fect Bride - - groom,

may the bless-ing nev-er cease! Let bride and groom ex -
to the home that they will share, to let their love and
hu - man qual - i - ties of grace, are God - or - dained, and
church, be - lov - èd as a Bride, help bride and groom live

press Your love – love filled with strength and peace.
hap - pi - ness bless all who en - ter there.
God - sus - tained: let these be giv - en place.
life as one that God be glor - i - fied!

338

Psalm 47
Adrienne M. Tindall, 1981

LOVELACE 47 95. 10 7.
Austin C. Lovelace, 1997

1. Clap your hands all you peo - ples of God,
2. Hear His trum - pets, the power of His call;
3. God the Lord is the King of the earth;
4. Praise His name, all the ends of the earth,

clap, and shout with song! For
wit - - ness, and pay heed! We
praise, and un - der - stand! His
praise, and praise a - gain! We

God most high is ex - al - ted on
each in - her - it God's pro - mise of
ho - li - ness is a won - der - ful
are His peo - ple, in - her - it - ing

earth; no en - e - mies tri - umph long!
old as A - bra - ham's liv - ing seed.
throne! He rules o - ver ev - ery land.
good; all bless - ings come from His hand.

from Psalm 51
Adrienne M. Tindall, 1981

METTAWA 87.87.D.
Adrienne M. Tindall, 1988

1. O Lord my God, I look to You and to Your lov-ing-kind-ness, for deep-ly do I feel my faults, — the way-ward-ness, the blind-ness. Let flood-tides of Your gra-cious-ness for-give this heart that's pray-ing! Let in-ward truths in-struct my sight, let wis-dom guide o-bey-ing.

2. Cre-ate in me a heart that's clean, re-new-ing my right spir-it, and, lov-ing Fa-ther, keep me close, to know Your word, to hear it. Your hands will wash to pur-i-ty, will blot out wrong and sin-ning. Re-store to me Your glad-dening joy in Christ, my new be-gin-ning.

3. Lord, o-pen now my lips to speak Your words of rev-e-la-tion, to sing Your praise in all the earth, a wit-ness to sal-va-tion. The sac-ri-fi-ces You de-sire are meek-ness and con-tri-tion. I of-fer these with all my heart! O Lord, hear my pe-ti-tion.

from Psalm 52
Adrienne M. Tindall, 1982

LOVELACE 52 865.84.13.
Austin C. Lovelace, 1997

1. I will praise You for - ev - er, God! I will trust Your
2. But the wick - ed shall per - ish, God! In de - vis - ing
3. Let us wor - ship the Lord, our strength, wit - ness e - vil's

mer - cy, re - joice in Your love. I will be like an
mis - chief, they cause their own fall. Their de - ceits are con -
down - fall, and laugh in our awe! Let the hearts of the

ol - ive tree, ver - dant, fruit - ful, deep - root - ed, for -
demn - ing them - e - vil, ly - ing,— all sin is cast
faith - ful be stead - fast, ho - ly, for - ev - er re -

ev - er se - cure in the house of God!
out by the good - ness and power of God!
joic - ing, and prais - ing the name of God!

341

1. God looked down from heav - en up - on the chil-dren of earth. Did
2. God looked down from heav - en up - on the fool-ish and slow; He
3. God looks down from heav - en up - on His chil-dren to - day. And

an - y feel His love, or know His might-y worth? Did
e - ven sent His Son to teach them how to go. He
do we feel His love? And choose His nar - row way? Come!

an - y see how foes were con-quered by His sword of truth? Did
called them back from fears and e - vil with the law of Love; gave
Find pro - tec - tion through earth's tri - als — Truth shall still pre - vail! He

an - y sing sal - va - tion's song? The par - ents? Or the youth?
each the free - dom found in Truth, pro - tect - ing from a - bove.
puts His mess - age in each heart: His love will nev - er fail.

from Psalm 56
Adrienne M. Tindall, 1981

ST. MARY'S ROAD 9 11. 10 10. Irr.
Adrienne M. Tindall, 1987

1. God, I trust my-self to Your mer-cy! For earth teems with en-e-mies
2. God, I know You care for the right-eous; and sure-ly You save from an

plot-ting my death! Ev-ery day they lurk, they threat-en, op-press,
en-e-my thrust! Hate must fall, and Love will win through Your Word —

watch-ing my foot-steps, and count-ing my breath.
Love is my for-tress, my hope and my trust.

3. God, I feel the power of Your

pro-mise — it lives in the life of Christ Je-sus, Your Son. Ev-ery shad-ow death would

cast is e-clipsed — light is Your law! My path-way is won.

343

from Psalm 61
Adrienne M. Tindall, 1981

SHELTERING WINGS 11 6. 10 6.
Austin C. Lovelace, 1989

1. From the ends of the earth will I cry to God —
2. When the en - e - my's power o - ver - whelms my heart
3. And my life is pro - longed, and Your power and grace
4. All my vows have been heard in the heights of heaven:

O lis - ten to my prayer! For
with dan - ger ev - ery - where, You
in - spire an in - ner peace. Your
what joy this know - ledge brings! I'd

You are my shel - ter, my shield, my tower; I
lead to the rock that will guard my life, and
mer - cy and truth ev - er bless my days, Your
live in Your dwell - ings for - ev - er - more, be -

st. 4

need Your love and care.
keep me safe - ly there.
lov - ing will not cease.
neath Your shel - tering wings.

from Psalm 65
Adrienne M. Tindall, 1981

LOVELACE 65 86.84.D.
Austin C. Lovelace, 1997

1. You crown the year with good-ness, Lord! A-bun-dance is Your way. Your
2. Your life-be-stow-ing streams flow free with bless-ings for the earth, the
3. Your strength holds moun-tains on their base, com-mands the seas to peace, – the
4. Sal-va-tion's right-eous-ness is Yours, and Yours all em-i-nence. Each

mag-ni-tudes of grace af-ford all good each day. The
grains and grass-es form a sea of love - ly worth. Each
war-rings of the hu-man race must al - so cease. In-
act of love and pow-er stirs my con - fi-dence. All

pas-tures, clothed with flocks of sheep, the val-leys green with corn, shout,
ten-der shoot is in Your care, is warmed by gen-tle rain, the
jus-ti-ces will not pre-vail, wrong-do-ings will not stain; for
praise must rise un-to the Lord, all vows o-bey his will. All

joy-ous for the watch You keep through night and morn.
sun-light, shin-ing ev-ery-where, brings forth good grain.
Your great love will nev-er fail to cleanse a-gain.
hopes must wait up-on His word, and flesh be still.

from Psalm 65
Adrienne M. Tindall, 1981

LAKE FOREST MEADOWS 86.84.
Adrienne M. Tindall, 1981

You crown the year with good-ness, Lord, a - bun-dance is Your way. Your

mag - ni - tudes of grace af - ford all good _____ each day.

from Psalm 65
Adrienne M. Tindall, 1981

VERNON HILLS 86.84.D.
Adrienne M. Tindall, 1981

You crown the year with good-ness, Lord, a - bun-dance is Your way. Your

mag - ni - tudes of grace af - ford all good ___ each day. The

pas - tures, clothed with flocks of sheep, the val - leys green with corn, shout,

joy - ous for the watch You keep through night _____ and morn.

346

Psalm 70
Adrienne M. Tindall, 1982

LOVELACE 70 6.5.967.11.11.
Austin C. Lovelace, 1997

1. Help me, God! Help me, God! My need is ur-gent! For my en-e-mies are proud and strong, and seek - ing to hurt me; what they wish to do is wrong! The dan - ger fills me with fear; my need is great! Help me now, O Lord my God, and do not wait!

2. Help me, God! Help me, God! Your strength can save me. Let Your pow-er si - lence e - vil's pride. Let all who would hurt me be con - fused and turned a - side. I turn to You in my poor and need-y state. Help me now, O Lord my God, and do not wait!

3. Help me, God! Help me, God! to seek and praise You! Let Your joy and glad-ness be my shield. Your love keeps me sa - fer than pro - tec - tions earth can yield. I hon - or those who would mag - ni - fy Your name; help me now, O Lord my God, to do the same.

last stanza

347

from Psalm 83
vers. Adrienne M. Tindall, 1981

WELLSHIRE 4.10 88.4.
Austin C. Lovelace, 1985

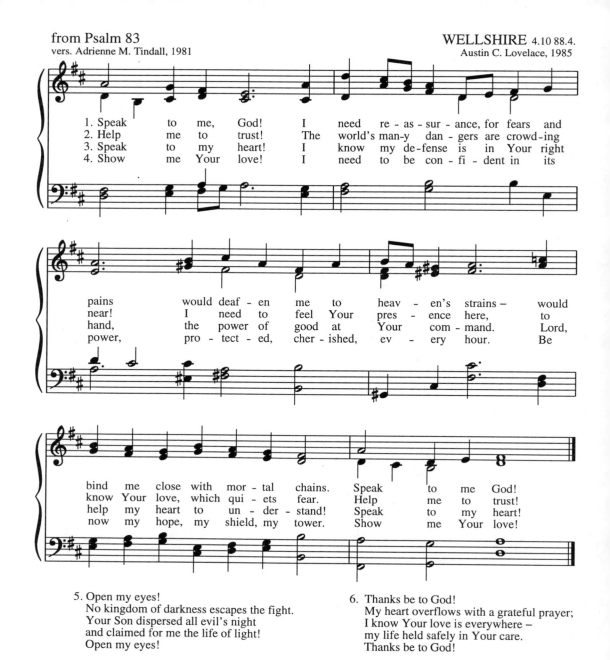

1. Speak to me, God! I need re-as-sur-ance, for fears and
2. Help me to trust! The world's man-y dan-gers are crowd-ing
3. Speak to my heart! I know my de-fense is in Your right
4. Show me Your love! I need to be con-fi-dent in its

pains would deaf-en me to heav-en's strains — would
near! I need to feel Your pres-ence here, to
hand, the power of good at Your com-mand. Lord,
power, pro-tect-ed, cher-ished, ev-ery hour. Be

bind me close with mor-tal chains. Speak to me God!
know Your love, which qui-ets fear. Help me to trust!
help my heart to un-der-stand! Speak to my heart!
now my hope, my shield, my tower. Show me Your love!

5. Open my eyes!
   No kingdom of darkness escapes the fight.
   Your Son dispersed all evil's night
   and claimed for me the life of light!
   Open my eyes!

6. Thanks be to God!
   My heart overflows with a grateful prayer;
   I know Your love is everywhere —
   my life held safely in Your care.
   Thanks be to God!

from Psalm 84
Adrienne M. Tindall, 1981, 1984

ST. ASAPH CMD
attr. Giovanni Giornovichi, c. 1790

1. How love-ly are Your dwell-ings, Lord, courts ech-o-ing with praise! My
2. And hap-py are the ones who know their strength is from the Lord; they
3. Lord, strength-en me and hear my prayer, a-noint me with Your grace; in-
4. Keep me from paths of wick-ed-ness — al-lur-ing, eas-y, wide — a

heart is long-ing to be there to sing each joy-ous phrase. The
tri-umph as they hold them-selves o-be-dient to Your Word. Your
spire my thoughts and acts to prove Your love in ev-ery place. Yet,
life em-brac-ing world-ly sins casts ho-li-ness a-side. I

spar-row finds her-self a house, the swal-low finds a nest; ___ Your
Son will guide their pil-grim-age, Your love will show the way ___ with
e-ven as I strive to do what You would have me do, ___ I
yearn to keep that nar-row way which brings me to Your door; ___ I'd

al-tars wel-come each of them and sweet-ly are they blessed!
showers of bless-ings, joy, and life, and rain-bows, ev-ery day!
know the strength that comes to me is strength I have from You.
serve You there, and find my home with You for-ev-er more.

Psalm 93
Adrienne M. Tindall, 1981

LOVELACE 93 686.886.
Austin C. Lovelace, 1997

1. The Lord, our Fa - ther, reigns! He clothes Him - self with
2. The floods of cha - os fail! The floods have lift - ed
3. Earth's laws are set a - side! Re - surg - ing powers of
4. The Is - rael - ites were saved. And as they fled from
5. Christ proved to us God's will. He told us of our
6. The laws of earth still bow. As we are faith - ful,

ma - jes - ty, He clothes Him - self with might. The
up their voice, have lift - ed up their roar. Their
birth and life must own a pri - mal Cause. Ac -
Phar - aoh's hordes the wa - ters rolled a - way. God
Fa - ther's love, he walked up - on the sea. The
just, and good, o - bey - ing God each hour, do -

u - ni - verse and all its worlds must stand or move as
waves will pound and fade a - way, the winds will shriek but
cept - ed pat - terns of the world, its grav - i - ty, its
sent them meat, gave dews as bread, be - came for them the
sick were healed, the dead were raised, the hun - gering seek - ers
min - ion is God's gift to us, all na - ture's for - ces

He or - dains; as He com - mands is right.
not pre - vail: God reigns for - ev - er - more.
times and tides, must bow to heav'n - ly laws.
Guide they craved with fire and clouds each day.
ate their fill and heard the truth that saves.
yield - ing now to His be - nig - nant power.

350

Psalm 96
Adrienne M. Tindall, 1982

LOVELACE 96 77.88.77.
Austin C. Lovelace, 1997

1. Sing, and sing and sing a - gain! Sing your prais - es
2. Give, and give and give a - gain! Give due rev - erence
3. Joy, and joy and joy a - gain! Ech - o joy un -
4. Praise, and praise and praise a - gain, giv - ing thanks un -

to the Lord. Tell all peo - ple, friend and stran - ger,
to the Lord. See His ma - jes - ty and glo - ry,
to the Lord. With the heav - ens, fields and for - ests,
to the Lord. Know His true and right - eous judg - ing

He is God, all - wise Cre - a - tor! Praise His great - ness,
hon - or Him with strength and beau - ty, bring an off - 'ring,
with the seas in all their ful - ness, praise His pow - er,
brings sal - va - tion with His guid - ing. Ho - ly lives will

bless His name! Sing, and sing and sing a - gain!
bless His name. Give, and give and give a - gain!
bless His name. Joy, and joy and joy a - gain!
bless His name! Praise, and praise and praise a - gain!

351

Psalm 101

Adrienne M. Tindall, 1982

LOVELACE 101 LM

Austin C. Lovelace, 1997

1. God, help me be Your per - fect child – my heart is filled with loy - al - ty! For I would live life un - de - filed. God, strength - en all my con - stan - cy.

2. I'll keep my eyes from wick - ed things, I'll keep my feet from er - ror's way. Un - seen per - verse - ness will not cling; I'll strive to hear You and o - bey.

3. I will not heed a slan - dering word – no sel - fish seek - ing, no false pride – de - ceits and lies will not be heard, all wick - ed - ness I'll set a - side.

4. My friends will be the faith - ful ones whose lives re - flect Your truth and love. Per - fec - tion, like the rays of suns, will guide their foot - steps from a - bove.

5. God, help me be Your per - fect child, who thinks and acts with Christ - ly grace, for I would live life un - de - filed to make this world a bet - ter place.

from Psalm 121
Adrienne M. Tindall, 1981

MEADOWOODS LANE LM
Adrienne M. Tindall, 1989

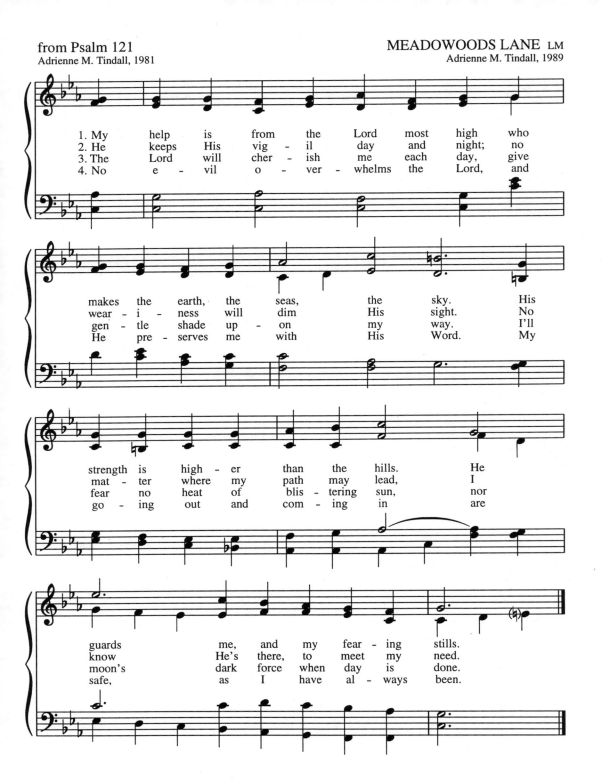

1. My help is from the Lord most high who
2. He keeps His vig - il day and night; no
3. The Lord will cher - ish me each day, give
4. No e - vil o - ver - whelms the Lord, and

makes the earth, the seas, the sky. His
wear - i - ness will dim His sight. No
gen - tle shade up - on my way. I'll
He pre - serves me with His Word. My

strength is high - er than the hills. He
mat - ter where my path may lead, I
fear no heat of blis - tering sun, nor
go - ing out and com - ing in are

guards me, and my fear - ing stills.
know He's there, to meet my need.
moon's dark force when day is done.
safe, as I have al - ways been.

Psalm 123
Adrienne M. Tindall, 1981

LOVELACE 123 87.87.
Austin C. Lovelace, 1997

1. Heav'n - ly God, hear my pe - ti - tion:
2. Let me sense Your slight - est ges - ture,
3. When con - tempt and scorn would mock me,
4. For he dem - on - strates Your mer - cy,

growth in grace is what I seek,
let me hear Your still - est voice,
hate and e - vil bar my way,
and his prom - is - es are true.

let my pur - pose be to serve You,
let me yield my all to Spir - it!
let me lean on my Re - deem - er,
You have claimed me for Your king - dom!

last stanza

pa - tient, lov - ing, good, and meek.
Let o - be - dience be my choice.
make his love my strength and stay.
I walk ev - ery step with You.

354

from Psalm 126
Adrienne M. Tindall, 1981

LIBERTYVILLE 77.79.
Jack C. Goode, 1988

1. Why should free - dom be a dream,
2. Laugh all peo - ples! Shout for joy!
3. Stop your weep - ing, lift your hearts!
4. Join the har - vest of the Christ;

free - dom which the Lord or - dains?
God ends our cap - tiv - i - ty!
Prec - ious seed is ours to sow.
bring your sheaves in - to his store.

Claim your free - dom as His child;
Sing His prais - es! Show your love;
Tears can nur - ture ten - der seeds;
Prove his glo - ry in your lives!

God's own power is break - ing all our chains!
as His chil - dren we are al - ways free.
God Him - self will cause the seed to grow.
Claim our God as King for - ev - er - more!

from Psalm 127
Adrienne M. Tindall, 1981

ORREN 56.86.
Adrienne M. Tindall, 1988

1. God must build the house or else we work in vain. His love and truth must move our hands, that la - bor's works re - main.
2. If we strive a - lone, our task is nev - er done. We work and rest, safe in the love of Him who sent His Son.
3. Rest - ing in God's love, – how sweet will be our sleep! Our watch - ing shows us God is here, that we are in His keep.
4. Chil - dren of the house, en - trust - ed to our care, God's gifts! Be wel - comed and sus - tained with lov - ing - kind - ness here.
5. House be - comes a home, se - cure as for - tress towers as hearts are shar - ing Christ - ly love and bless - ing fills the hours.

from Psalm 131
Adrienne M. Tindall, 1981

KINDLICHKEIT 66.66.D.
Adrienne M. Tindall, 1988

1. Lord, let me be a child who knows hu-mil-i-ty, who
2. Lord, let me be a child un-moved by e-vil's way, o-
3. Lord, I would be Your child — see Fa-ther-hood a-bove, see

seeks and trusts Your plan, and fol-lows stead-fast-ly. Let
be-dient to Your laws, re-joic-ing in Your day. Let
in Christ Je-sus' life an el-der broth-er's love. Lord,

ev-ery ray of light re-veal Your light of truth seen
trust-ing love be mine, as felt for par-ents' arms, to
I would be Your child who trusts Your con-stan-cy! Your

in sim-pli-ci-ty, — seen as with eyes of youth.
know that You are close and save from all that harms.
lov-ing-kind-ness-es are mine e-ter-nal-ly.

from Psalm 133
Adrienne M. Tindall, 1981

POLLSTIN 8.6.10.
Adrienne M. Tindall, 1982

1. How good and how pleas-ant it is _____ when the
2. How good and how pleas-ant it is... _____ like the
3. How good and how pleas-ant it is... _____ like the
4. How good and how pleas-ant it is _____ when each

chil - dren of God _____ dwell to - geth - er in
sweet morn - ing dews _____ when they kiss ev - ery
oint - ment of grace _____ which a - bun - dant - ly
heart o - pens wide _____ to em - brace all the

love and u - ni - ty! _____
flow - er ten - der - ly. _____
pours its love - li - ness! _____
world in Christ - li - ness! _____

Note: On the organ, where the soprano F-sharp (the third of the chord) continues to sound at full volume, the third is not "needed" in the tenor. Play as written. However, on the piano , the soprano F-sharp does *not* continue to sound at full volume. Consider adding an F-sharp in the tenor; this will preclude the sound of striking an open fifth.

Psalm 137
Adrienne M. Tindall, 1982

LOVELACE 137 68.6.886.
Austin C. Lovelace, 1997

1. I'll live in Bab-y-lon op-pressed by hate and cru-el foes, my hope for free-dom gone; I'll live con-demned to a-lien scenes while Zi-on's beau-ties fill my heart, her des-erts like a rose.
2. I'll put all joys a-side, the harps, the mel-o-dies, the song. My foes will be de-fied— I will not let them mock my faith! My trust is in al-might-y God— He will re-quite this wrong!
3. I'll give up ev'-ery art, my hand to work, my tongue to speak— I would far ra-ther part with hope, than look for mor-tal rest through yield-ing my Je-ru-sa-lem, through faith that is too weak.
4. God help me in this strife! the sneers, the scorn, the cap-tors' prod— be now my on-ly life! I'll yield past com-forts, spurn false hopes, I'll give up ev-ery thought of peace, but not my faith in God!

from Psalm 139
Adrienne M. Tindall, 1981

NO HIDING PLACE CMD
Austin C. Lovelace, 1989

1. Search me, O God, and know my heart, try me and know my thought,
2. Where could I ev - er hide from You? Where could I flee a - way?
3. Pre - cious are all Your thoughts to me, num - ber - less as the sands!
4. Sure - ly Your power will van - quish sin! Sure - ly Your truth shall reign!

and guide me if some wick - ed way would make Your truth un - sought.
In heav - en I am by Your side, in hell You are my stay.
each time I wake I feel my - self still cra - dled in Your hands.
May my life glor - i - fy Your good, - be free of sin and stain.

Ev - ery-thing I would say or do, ev - ery-where I would go,
Dark - ness can have no power to hide, night brings no threat too near;
Tak - ing the wings of morn-ing's rays, dwell-ing in far - thest seas,
Search me, O God, and know my heart, try me and know my thought,

Your love sus - tains my in - most life and heals all sin and woe.
Your pres - ence is my shin - ing light! Your truth dis - pels my fear.
Your hand is e - ven there, to guide, Your right hand, hold - ing me.
and guide me if some wick - ed way would make Your truth un - sought.

from Psalm 139
Adrienne M. Tindall, 1981

OLD 137th CMD
adapted from Anglo-Genevan Psalter, 1556

1. Search me, O God, and know my heart, try me and know my thought,
2. Where could I ev - er hide from You? Where could I flee a - way?
3. Pre - cious are all Your thoughts to me, num - ber - less as the sands!
4. Sure - ly Your power will van - quish sin! Sure - ly Your truth shall reign!

and guide me if some wick - ed way would make Your truth un - sought.
In heav - en I am by Your side, in hell You are my stay.
Each time I wake I find my - self still cra - dled in Your hands.
May my life glor - i - fy Your good, — be free of sin and stain.

Ev - ery-thing I would say or do, ev - ery - where I would go, Your
Dark - ness can have no power to hide, night brings no threat too near; Your
Tak - ing the wings of morn - ing's rays, dwell - ing in far - thest seas, Your
Search me, O God, and know my heart, try me and know my thought, and

love sus-tains my in - most life and heals all sin and woe.
pres - ence is my shin - ing light! Your truth dis - pels my fear.
hand is e - ven there, to guide, Your right hand, hold - ing me.
guide me if some wick - ed way would make Your truth un - sought.

from Psalm 147
Adrienne M. Tindall, 1981

LAC DU FLAMBEAU 19.18.
Erik Routley, 1981

1. Let praise to God fill the mu-sic of earth, let the
   beaut-y of thanks be our song! Our hearts o-ver-flow with the
   bless-ings He gives to His peo-ple all _____ day long.

2. His un-der-stand-ing is in-fin-ite! Lis- -ten, Je-
   ru-sa-lem! Hear, and o-bey. Com- -mand-ments are thun-dered in
   swift ca-denced ech-oes, His peo-ple will _____ not stray.

3. Hap-py am I! for the God who was A- -bra-ham's,
   I-saac's and Ja-cob's is mine! His love is e-ter-nal; and
   all of His chil-dren are blessed in His _____ de-sign.

4. God counts the stars, and He calls them by name,
   snow and ice, frost and cold show His power.
   He covers the heavens with clouds, He sends rains
   which will bring the fields to flower.

5. God takes His pleasure in all who revere Him,
   and place all their hope in His care.
   He heals broken hearts, and He binds up all wounds;
   He will hear the meekest prayer.

6. Lives are transformed, for disciples are stirred
   and the good news is preached, is proclaimed!
   The lame walk with leaping, the blinded see plainly,
   all healed in Jesus' name.

7. Happy am I! for the God who was Peter's
   and Paul's and Christ Jesus' is mine!
   His love is eternal, and all of His children
   are blessed in His design.

A Song of Bethlehem, Christmas Day

Gertrude E. Velguth, st. 1, alt.
Kathleen O'Connor, st. 2, alt.

AIRIKAR SMD
Tune: Adrienne M. Tindall, 1981
Harmonization: Erik Routley, 1981

1. A vil - lage, hum - ble, still, the guid-ing star a - bove; a
2. The shep-herds brought their faith, the wise-men of - fered gold and

shep-herd watch-ing on a hill; the moth - er heart of love; the
cost - ly frank-in - cense and myrrh; each brought his gift of old. What

child of truth and grace, a world to pac - i - fy; an
shall we give to - day? Wealth of the things of earth? Or

an - gel song of joy - ous praise, and God to glor - i - fy!
hearts at - tuned to an - gel songs — and give our own new birth!

It could be Bethlehem

Max Dunaway, 1970, alt.

DUNAWAY 10.10.10.10.
Adrienne M. Tindall, 1980

1. It could be Beth - le - hem, up - on ___ a hill, with
2. And there could be to - night, as there ___ was then, a
3. It could have been that star that shines ___ a - bove which
4. And there could be in us a ho - ly birth of

qui - et shep - herds watch - ing o - ver sheep, _____ for
mul - ti - tude ___ of an - gels sing - ing praise _____ to
shone up - on ___ the man - ger babe that night. _____ And
Christ - li - ness ___ here in this pres - ent place _____ to

in this cit - y now ___ we list - en still, _____ and
God, and prom - is - ing ___ sweet peace to men, _____ if
it could lead as sure - ly to his love, _____ if
bring a - gain up - on ___ this trou - bled earth _____ the

in ___ our ways a Christ - - mas vig - il keep.
we ___ would seek the Christ _____ in all our ways.
we ___ let rays of truth _____ make our lives bright.
glad ___ na - tiv - i - ty _____ of truth and grace.

What is this lovely fragrance?
Translation Adrienne M. Tindall, 1980

QUELLE EST CETTE ODEUR AGRÈABLE? 99.98.99.
Harmonization Adrienne M. Tindall, 1980

1. What is this love-ly fra - grance, shep-herds, which gent-ly en-folds our
2. What burst-ing light has come through dark-ness, to daz-zle our eyes with
3. Fear noth-ing, faith-ful peo - ple, o - pen your hearts to the an - gel
4. Sav - ior of God, your birth in Beth-le - hem's man-ger ex - alts this
5. God of all power, may You be glor-i - fied! Hearts o - ver-flow with

hearts this night? Sweet-er than all the flowers of spring - time,
liv - ing hues? E - ven the day - star's ra - diant or - bit
of the Lord. He tells us all the news of bless - ing:
ho - ly night. Noth-ing shall hin - der our a - dor - ing,
thanks and praise. Let end - less peace em - brace all peo - ple.

as they ex - hale u - nique de - light! What is this love - ly
has not a ra - diance so pro - fuse! What burst-ing light has
good - ness for all ful - fills God's Word. Fear noth-ing, faith - ful
wit - ness-ing our Re - deem - er's light. Sav - ior of God, your
Let grace a - bound in all life's ways. God of all power, may

fra - grance, shep-herds, which gent-ly en - folds our hearts this night?
come through dark-ness, to daz - zle our eyes with liv - ing hues?
peo - ple, o - pen your hearts to the an - gel of the Lord.
birth in Beth-le - hem's man-ger ex - alts this ho - ly night.
You be glor-i - fied! Hearts o - ver-flow with thanks and praise.

based on Matt. 5: 14-16
Adrienne M. Tindall, 1980

GLENCAYNIG 76.86.
Adrienne M. Tindall, 1980

1. Let your light so shine each day that they who see its glow will glor - i - fy the God of love for proofs your works will show.
2. Tow - 'ring cit - ies are not hid, but shine forth through the night. A can - dle on a can - dle - stick will fill the house with light.
3. Love's great teach - er held his light so all the world could see. O, grant that I may live my life so light will shine through me.

4. Let my motives, steps, and goals
be faithful to Your Son,
and let me see with eyes that look
with love on everyone.

5. Through a life of loving works,
impelled by selfless prayer,
we each can let our light show forth
God's glory everywhere.

The Servant
Max Dunaway, 1970

SERVITOR 11.11.11.11.
Adrienne M. Tindall, 1981

1. The great-est man that walked this earth was ser - vant; _____ He
2. May man-kind heed this glor - ious call for ser - vant; _____ Not

knew the high - est, deep - est worth as ser - vant. _____ Who
un - to one but un - to all a ser - vant. _____ May

bet - ter knows how work is blest than ser - vant? _____ To
we know the hu - mil - i - ty of ser - vant, _____ for -

whom be - longs the sweet-est rest? The ser - vant. _____
sake all else, dear Lord, and be Thy ser - vant. _____

Thank You!
Adrienne M. Tindall, 1980

JENNEL 65.77.7446.65.
Tune: Adrienne M. Tindall, 1980
Harmonization: Erik Routley, 1980

1. Thank You, Fa - ther - Moth - er, thank You, on - ly God.
2. Thank You, Fa - ther - Moth - er, thank You, on - ly God.
3. Thank You, Fa - ther - Moth - er, thank You, on - ly God.

Thank You for the gift of life, power to live and move and be!
Thank You for Your gra - cious Son, for the Christ, Im - man - u - el.
Thank You for the Ho - ly Ghost, for the prom - ised Com - fort-er.

Thank You for cre - a - ting all, or - dain - ing all, sus -
Thank You for his heal - ing all, es - teem - ing all, re -
Thank You for em - bra - cing all, for reach - ing all, and

tain - ing all with Your own heaven -ly power!
deem - ing all with Your own heaven -ly love!
teach - ing all with Your own heaven -ly law!

Thank You, Fa - ther - Moth - er, thank You, on - ly God!
Thank You, Fa - ther - Moth - er, thank You, on - ly God.
Thank You, Fa - ther - Moth - er, thank You, on - ly God.

O God, I Grieve
Adrienne M. Tindall, 1980

HIGHLY DEVOTIONAL 76.76.44.6.86.
Adrienne M. Tindall, 1980

1. O God, I grieve with-in me for wrongs, for err-ing ways. I need Your law to guide me — the in-fluence of Your grace. Help me be free of faults I see, but more than this I pray: help me cast out the faults that hide from my own search-ing eye.

2. O God, I am not sin-ning in wild-ly e-vil ways! The world might say I'm win-ning a right to vir-tue's praise. But if I know that as I go I al-ways seek to bless, the glor-y's Yours! Help me cast out thoughts of self-right-eous-ness.

3. O God, my on-ly Sav-ior is Je-sus Christ, Your Son. He prom-is-es this fa-vor: Truth frees us from all wrong. I will not fear! Your love is here to gov-ern me each day. Faults purged through gra-cious words and deeds: for this, O Lord, I pray.

God's Power and Love

Adrienne M. Tindall, 1979

MEAD'S BRIER 87.87.66.12.

Adrienne M. Tindall, 1979

1. From the depths of o-cean tren-ches to the heights of out-er
2. Tak-ing wings of bril-liant morn-ings, find-ing far-thest shores of
3. In the life of our Re-deem-er, in the heal-ing proofs he
4. In the Christ-li-ness of mer-cy, in a life that's no-bly

space, I will wit-ness God's all-pow-er hold-ing
seas, — e-ven vales of death-ly shad-ows will not
gave, in his min-is-try's in-struc-tion and re-
grand, in each act of lov-ing-kind-ness, I can

strong its stead-y pace. No might but His sus-
hide His love from me! His ev-er-pres-ent
demp-tion from the grave, the Fa-ther's love is
see what God has planned. His ev-er-wise con-

tains, His law for-ev-er reigns; no oth-er
care is with me ev-ery-where, His pow-er
proved, the sting of death re-moved; the law of
trol a-bides while a-ges roll, — the heaven-ly

force, no mor-tal power can take His place!
stead-fast and be-nign e-ter-nal-ly!
God is power to heal, and bless, and save.
king-dom held se-cure-ly in His hand.

370

INDEX

disbeliefs 308
dissonances, preparing 179
Dividing the Substance 263
Divine and Moral Songs 19, 21, 32, 48
Doddridge 85
Dougall, Neil 317
DOWN AMPNEY 93
Doxology 299
Draw nigh to thy Jerusalem, O Lord 320
Draw nigh, O Lord 282
Drummond, Henry 252
DUNAWAY 90, 364
Dunaway, Max 90, 92, 94, 104, 135, 364, 367
Dutch Reformed Church,40 ,55
Dykes, John B. 41

Each day, O Lord, I try to do 167, 173, 335
ECCE AGNUS 102
ecumenical 1
Ecumenical Praise 83, 115, 121, 155, 302
Ecumenical Praise editors, photo iv
Eddy, Mary Baker 161, 224
edit, editing 3, 43, 120, 222, 223, 306, 307
editing, ethics 67, 74
editing, integrity 67, 70 ,74
editing, revising 215
Edwards, Lynn 227
elder brother 139
ELLACOMBE 120, 132
Ellinwood, Dr. 119
emotional bureaucracy 184
Energy 262
ENGELBERG 192, 199
English 1968 - 79
English Catholic 79
English Congregational 1740 - 79
English ecumenical 1930 - 79
English Hymnal 41, 53, 54, 108, 184, 220, 228, 300, 307
English Methodist 1973 - 79
English toffee 27
Englishman 236
Episcopal revision 25, 94, 96, 111, 112, 191, 199, 281
Epistles 262
"Erik" 227
"Erik Routley" 1
error 181, 183, 185
ethic of the Gospel 296

European Catholic 1753 - 79
European Catholic 1797 - 79
Evanston 2, 21
EVANSTON NEW 8, 10, 323
EVERLASTING GATES 334
evils, seven 237
Exodus 20 - 32, 48, 328
excellence 307
exile 230
extender lines 5
eye-rhyme,179

Fairest Lord Jesus 107
fascist 110
Father 252
Father, bless this wedding 162-163, 338
Father, with all our Gospel's power 115
Father-Mother 59
Festival Praise 78, 302
Finlay, Kenneth G. 134
First Church of Christ, Scientist 130
five movements of a full service 298
Flatland 266
Flossmoor 1, 82
For me, kind Jesus, was thy incarnation 273
For the fruits of His creation 78
FOREST GREEN 71, 94, 120, 123, 131
format, poetic 13, 17, 34, 300
formula 262
Fountain, Grigg 112, 116, 119
Franck, J. W. 318
Frisbee 297
From all that dwell below the skies 130
From glory unto glory 193
From the depths of ocean trenches 370
From the depths of rolling oceans 15, 16, 20, 324, 370
From the ends of the earth will I cry to God 188, 344
full music edition 109, 199

Garrett (Evanston IL) 7, 19, 38, 43, 50, 74, 141, 147, 150, 154, 253, 295
Gelineau 72
Genevan 39, 115
Genevan Psalter 228
German Pietist 79
GIA191
Giornovichi, Giovanni 349

Give me, O Lord, the strength that is in Thee 85
Glastonbury 205, 213
GLENCAYNIG 30, 366
GLENFINLAS 120, 134
Gloria 299
Glory to the Father give 83
God, help be be Your perfect child 232, 352
God, I trust myself to Your mercy 255, 343
God looked down from heaven 277, 342
God must build the house 196, 356
God speaks, and all things come to be 239
God's law 241
God's Power and Love 13, 20, 370
God, help me be Your perfect child 226
GOLDEN SEQUENCE 302
Good Christian friends, rejoice 25
Good Samaritan, hymn sequence on 322
Goode, Jack C. 130, 329, 336, 355
Goodspeed 22, 24
Gospel song 49
GRAEFENBERG 79
GRAFTON 149
Grant this to me, Lord: let me live 238
greatest man that walked this earth, The 92, 104, 135, 367
Greatest Thing in the World, The 252
Greek 8th century 79
Green, Fred Pratt 192, 199
Greiter 229
Grieve, Nichol 149
Grindal, Gracia 51, 152, 241

Hadow, William Henry 53, 123, 333
HALIFAX 123
Hancock, Gerre 124
handouts in Routley manuscript, handwriting 309-323
Happy are they who walk 115
harmonization 63
Harvard Dictionary of Music 47, 50
Harwood, Basil 139, 142, 149
"hat", melodic 181, 183, 193
Haydn 301
Head (author) 300
Hear me when I call, O God of righteousness 284
Heavenly God, hear my petition 208, 354
Heilig, heilig, heilig 130
HELMSLEY 56

Help me, God! My need is urgent! 235, 347
Help us to help each other, Lord 130
HIGHLY DEVOTIONAL 68, 69, 369
HINMAN 151
Hitler 236
Holy Ghost 57, 60, 63, 66, 83, 252
Holy, holy, holy 130, 300
Holy Purpose 123
Holy Spirit, see Holy Ghost
homemaking 63, 165
Hope Publishing iv, 1, 241, 248
host 296, 299
How brightly shines the Morning Star 9
How good and how pleasant it is 138, 141, 146, 256, 275, 358
How great Thou art 112, 116, 118
How lovely are Your dwellings, Lord 159, 210, 349
HSA 1, 49, 103
HSA convocation 2, 23, 47, 142, 152, 165, 192
HSA search 38, 46, 51
human being 262
HYFRYDOL 130
hymn choosing 303
hymn - definition 58
hymn festival 77, 130
hymn festivals 304
hymn, great 304
hymn, introducing a 302
hymn, message 300
hymn is "non-biblical" 106
hymn program themes 305
hymn relevance 300
hymn sequence, the Good Samaritan 322
hymn sequence, the Prodigal Son 321
hymn services 304
hymn sing 94, 129
hymn singing 297
hymn sung by congregation 49
Hymn The 43
hymn, time to find 303
hymn vocabulary 297, 302
hymn, worst 281
hymnal, a work of art 109
hymnal - layman's book of theology 152
Hymnal 1940 - 108, 192
hymnal committee 103
hymnal committee, *Congregational Praise* 85
hymnal holder 88, 89

O Lord, don't count my faults 145
O Lord my God, I look to You 105, 113, 340
O Lord of life, to Thee we lift 120
O Lord, our Lord, how excellent is Thy name
   98, 99, 136, 330
O Lord, dear Lord, rebuke me not 285
O Love, our Mother ever near 269
O may we be still and seek Him 130
O praise ye the Lord 78
O quanta qualia 220
offering 298, 299
Old Free Kirk 40
OLD HUNDREDTH 130
OLD 137th - 124, 126, 361
Old Regular Baptists 56, 74
omit, amend hymn stanzas 305
OMNIPOTENCE 13, 16
Once to every man and nation 39, 40
100 Hymns for Today 46, 211
one liners 4
oneness 252, 269
Onward, Christian soldiers 301, 303
opposition 56
order of service 8
organ 185
organ, electronic 118
ORREN 356
OT lesson 106
Our God, our help in ages past 35, 50
Our Lives be Praise 35
Oxford 1
Oxford Book of Carols 28, 184

PADUCAH 35
Palm Sunday Processional 320
Palm Sunday readings and music 319
Panorama 14, 24, 112
Panorama, book 2 - 148
Panorama, book 3 -39, 41, 112, 191
paperback 109
parable of worship 295
paradox 261
paradoxes 267
parallels, 5ths and 8ves 101, 148, 151, 154,
   171, 180, 215
Parker, Alice 152
Parry, C. H. H. 79, 139, 142, 149, 204, 205,
   213
pastor and musician 296
Paul 242, 248

Peeters, Flor 130
Perry, David 219
personal - private 3
pharisaical 118
Pharisee 149, 152, 156, 157, 160
pharisee, christian 160
Pharisees 10, 11, 22
photo, *Ecumenical Praise* editors iv
PICARDY, arr. Routley 315
Pilgrim Hymnal 203, 212
pilgrimage 41
pique 111, 114, 115
Piston, Walter 180
plans for psalm versions 142, 327
poetry and prose 297
pograms 236
polarize 249
polarized 253
POLLSTIN 141, 146, 148, 151, 154, 358
Poole, Joseph 56, 75, 81
"position" 51, 52
possible with God 184
post office 97, 181, 185, 189, 268, 272
Post, Piet 130
Praise God from whom all blessings flow 130
Praise the Lord, ye heavens adore Him 78
Praise to the Lord the Almighty 279
Praise we the Lord, for His mercy endureth
   forever 130
Praise, my soul, the King of heaven 78
prayer book 108
prayer, confessional 73
preachers' pay 242, 248
precision 306
Presbyterian Hymnbook 1955 - 78
Princeton Theological Seminary 1
Prodigal Son, hymn sequence 321
protocol 2, 222, 227
Proulx, Richard 77, 82
Psalm 3 - 242, 243, 248, 249, 329
Psalm 4 - 283, 284
Psalm 6 - 283, 285
Psalm 8 - 97, 98, 100, 101, 106, 107, 117,
   136, 330
Psalm 13 - 269, 271, 273, 331
Psalm 15 - 164, 168, 170, 171, 332
Psalm 16 - 51, 52, 93, 101, 103, 110, 123,
   127, 128, 149, 333
Psalm 26 - 167, 169, 171, 173, 178, 335
Psalm 32 - 183